GLOBAL CRISIS REPORTING

Journalism in the Global Age

ISSUES in CULTURAL and MEDIA STUDIES

Series editor: Stuart Allan

Published titles

News Culture, 2nd edition
Stuart Allan

Modernity and Postmodern Culture,
2nd Edition
Jim McGuigan

Television, Globalization and
Cultural Identities
Chris Barker

Ethnic Minorities and the Media:
Changing Cultural Boundaries
Edited by Simon Cottle

Cinema and Cultural Modernity
Gill Branston

Compassion, Morality and the Media
Keith Tester

Masculinities and Culture
John Beynon

Cultures of Popular Music
Andy Bennett

Media, Risk and Science
Stuart Allan

Violence and the Media
Cynthia Carter and C. Kay Weaver

Moral Panics and the Media
Chas Critcher

Cities and Urban Cultures
Deborah Stevenson

Cultural Citizenship:
Cosmopolitan Questions
Nick Stevenson

Culture on Display: The Production of
Contemporary Visitability
Bella Dicks

Critical Readings: Media
and Gender
Edited by Cynthia Carter and
Linda Steiner

Critical Readings: Media
and Audiences
Edited by Virginia Nightingale and
Karen Ross

Media and Audiences
Karen Ross and Virginia Nightingale

Critical Readings: Sport, Culture and
the Media
Edited by David Rowe

Sport, Culture and the Media,
2nd edition
David Rowe

Rethinking Cultural Policy
Jim McGuigan

GLOBAL CRISIS REPORTING

Journalism in the Global Age

Simon Cottle

McGraw Hill

Open University Press

Open University Press
McGraw-Hill Education
McGraw-Hill House
Shoppenhangers Road
Maidenhead
Berkshire
England
SL6 2QL

email: enquiries@openup.co.uk
world wide web: www.openup.co.uk

and Two Penn Plaza, New York, NY 10121–2289, USA

First published 2009

A catalogue record of this book is available from the British Library

ISBN-13: 978 0335 22138 7 (pb)   978 0335 22139 4 (hb)

Library of Congress Cataloging-in-Publication Data
CIP data applied for

Typeset by RefineCatch Limited, Bungay, Suffolk
Printed in the UK by Bell and Bain Ltd, Glasgow

The **McGraw·Hill** Companies

CONTENTS

ACKNOWLEDGEMENTS

As always, this book is dedicated to the usual mob: Ella, Theo, Sam and Lucy. With special mention, this time, of Theo whose pervading soundtrack of music and multimedia creativity kept me company across the late night hours of writing (though sadly absent from the hours of daylight). Mugdha Rai once again has offered invaluable and generous support helping to administer this project to fruition. Stuart Allan, series editor, has provided sterling editorial input and Emma Gilliam an incisive journalist's reading of the draft manuscript. I would also like to formally acknowledge the help of the Australian Research Council for funding the research project 'Television Journalism and Deliberative Democracy: A Comparative International Study of Communicative Architecture and Democratic Deepening' (DP0449505) which informed some of the ideas developed in this study, and Melbourne University and the Faculty of Arts for their assistance in the production of this book which first took shape when I was based at Melbourne. The School of Journalism, Media and Cultural Studies at Cardiff University has subsequently proved to be a congenial academic environment for completing the manuscript and my MA students on MCT494 Global Crisis Reporting have helped to sharpen ideas and their pedagogical structuration now embedded in the pages that follow.

Chapter 2 is a revised and extended version of 'Journalism and Globalization' first published in Karin Wahl-Jorgensen & Thomas Hanitzsch (Eds) *Handbook of Journalism Studies,* Lawrence Erlbaum (2008); and part of Chapter 8 includes a revised summary of 'Global Humanitarianism and the Changing Aid-Media Field: "Everyone was Dying for Footage"' first published in 2007 in *Journalism Studies,* 8(6): 862–878. This article was originally written with David Nolan and I am grateful to him for his permission to reuse some of this material here. I acknowledge and thank all of the above.

Given the global scale and human urgency of many of the issues and crises raised across *Global Crisis Reporting: Journalism in the Global Age*, I am acutely aware of the book's failure to deal with any of them in the depth and detail that they deserve.

This book has barely begun to scratch the surface of how global crises are spawned by and shape our global age, and how they register in the world's news media. The contemporary field of global media and journalism studies more generally, it has to be said, remains theoretically underdeveloped in this critical regard and woefully neglectful of some of the most important global issues of our time. This book provides at most a possible preliminary mapping of a field that has yet to be properly staked out and developed. There is no avoiding the responsibility for the book and its limitations however, and these remain mine and mine alone.

Simon Cottle, Cardiff 2008

Image 1.1: 'The Earth today stands in imminent peril . . .' *The Independent*, 19 June 2007 (© The Independent 2007/Steve Connor)

Image 1.2: 'Death on Camera' *The Mail on Sunday*, 31 December 2006 (© The Mail on Sunday 2006, Photo: AP/Iraqi TV, HO)

Image 1.3: Tenerife, Spain – Arrival of African Immigrants, 1 August 2006 (© AP/ Arturo Rodriguez 2006), also Saddam Hussein Photo in Image 1.2 and Hurricane Katrina Photo in Image 3.6

Image 1.4: 'Why This is No Time for Compassion Fatigue' *The Independent*, 12 October 2005 (© The Independent 2005)

Image 3.1: 'After the Devastation the Grief' *The Guardian*, 28 December 2004 (© Guardian News & Media Ltd 2004, Photo: Arko Datta/Reuters/Picture Media)

Image 3.2: 'We're in for the Long Haul' *The Courier-Mail*, 7 January 2005 (© The Courier-Mail 2005)

Image 3.3: 'The Reluctant Angel of Pantong' *The Courier-Mail*, 7 January 2005 (© The Courier-Mail 2005)

Image 3.4: 'Our Day of Mourning' *Sunday Telegraph*, 16 January 2005 (© News Limited 2005)

Image 3.5: 'They are Not Alone . . .' *Sydney Morning Herald*, 15–16 January 2005 (© The Sydney Morning Herald 2005, Photo: Tamara Dean/Fairfaxphotos)

Image 3.6: 'Criticism of Bush mounts as more than 10,000 feared dead' *The Guardian*, 3 September 2005 (© Guardian News & Media Ltd 2005, Photo: AP/Eric Gay), for photo see AP licence with Image 1.3

Image 3.7: 'Third World Despair? No, Downtown USA' *The Age*, 3 September 2005 (© Courtesy of The Age 2005)

Image 3.8: 'America Stripped Bare' *The Age*, 4 September 2005 (© Courtesy of The Age 2005)

Image 3.9: 'Bush with Fish' *Anonymous* (Source: *www.bushbusiness.com*)

Image 3.10: 'Bush with Guitar' *Anonymous* (Source: *www.q-dog.co.uk*)

SERIES EDITOR'S FOREWORD

Images of global crisis are a routine, everyday feature of our news media. From the morning newspaper's depiction of the tragedies of war in Iraq, to online news reports of the HIV/AIDS pandemic in Southern Africa, to the evening television newscast's coverage of global warming and the melting Arctic ice cap, these images have a profound impact on our perceptions of the human condition. 'Being a spectator of calamities taking place in another country is a quintessential modern experience,' the late Susan Sontag observed, 'the cumulative offering by more than a century and a half's worth of those professional, specialized tourists known as journalists.' This flow of information from distant places amounts to a torrent, featuring conflict, violence and suffering at a seemingly ever-increasing rate – to which the response, Sontag adds, 'is compassion, or indignation, or titillation, or approval, as each misery heaves into view.' For the journalist, confronted with the challenge of bearing witness to horrors, threats and risks on our behalf, the effort to document their human consequences is simultaneously one of interpretation, of assigning apposite meaning and relevance. The representation of disturbing events, in other words, is partly constitutive of their reality, which makes this process of mediation acutely political. Important questions thus arise regarding the exercise of communicative power and influence, in particular the pivotal role of the news media in identifying, defining and framing certain situations as crises of global significance demanding concerted action.

Global crises, Simon Cottle suggests in *Global Crisis Reporting: Journalism in the Global Age*, symbolize the 'dark side of our globalized planet.' In seeking to illuminate the hidden contours of this terrain, he examines an array of different crises – including environmental disasters, the 'global war on terror,' world poverty, and human rights violations, amongst many others – and how they have been reported by the news media. For Cottle, how we collectively recognise and respond to the threats posed to humanity depends, in large measure, on how they are defined and deliberated, constructed and contested by journalists and their sources. Accordingly, he sets out in this book to explore the complex factors shaping how these threats are conveyed – and why others, in sharp contrast, barely register at all across the global mediascape. Throughout the discussion, Cottle interweaves the findings of original research with a careful assessment of pertinent scholarship in the fields of media, communications and journalism studies. He proceeds to show us how the assumptions underpinning current debates can be reconsidered, not least with respect to the capacity of the news media to sustain globalizing forms of awareness. It is in this capacity, he believes, that the prospect of enhanced forms of solidarity, cosmopolitanism and even global citizenship promises to become a lived reality. Thus Cottle's assessment of the forces opposing such efforts, while richly perceptive about the difficulties that lie ahead, advances a cautiously optimistic conception of how a socially responsible news media can effect social change in progressive ways.

The *Issues in Cultural and Media Studies* series aims to facilitate a diverse range of critical investigations into pressing questions considered to be central to current thinking and research. In light of the remarkable speed at which the conceptual agendas of cultural and media studies are changing, the series is committed to contributing to what is an ongoing process of re-evaluation and critique. Each of the books is intended to provide a lively, innovative and comprehensive introduction to a specific topical issue from a fresh perspective. The reader is offered a thorough grounding in the most salient debates indicative of the book's subject, as well as important insights into how new modes of enquiry may be established for future explorations. Taken as a whole, then, the series is designed to cover the core components of cultural and media studies courses in an imaginatively distinctive and engaging manner.

Stuart Allan

GLOBAL CRISIS? WHAT CRISIS?

1

We live in the global age. We live in a world that has become radically interconnected, interdependent and communicated in the flows of information and culture – including, importantly, news journalism. Global crises, from climate change to the global war on terror, from world poverty to humanitarian disasters, represent the dark side of a globalized planet and, increasingly, prompt awareness of our 'civilizational community of fate' (Beck 2006: 13). How we collectively recognize and respond to these different threats to humanity depends in large measure on how they become defined and deliberated, constructed and contested in the contemporary news media. *Global Crisis Reporting: Journalism in the Global Age* sets out to explore how, why, and with what impacts some of these most pressing problems are conveyed and constituted in today's news media – and why possible others barely register at all.

For many of us, the parameters of existence and imagined horizons now extend beyond neighbourhoods and nations, cities and countries, encouraging a sense of the world as a singular, shared, space. This is true not only in that we increasingly have diverse connections with different people, places and destinations *in* the world, but also we have a consciousness *of* the world, as a *whole*. That is, as a bounded, holistic and finite place. This sense of globality, both impinging and imagined, is constructed through various means but increasingly has become visualized in today's global news media. It is not always a comforting image. The globally peripatetic gaze of CNN International, BBC World or Al Jazeera, for example, includes features about cultural differences and the lives of distant others but these are routinely overshadowed by lead stories of conflict, crisis and catastrophe. It is these images and narratives that also cascade through the different national news media, competing for our attention and variously summoning our concern.

The contemporary world confronts catastrophic threats as well as unrealized opportunities to safeguard the lives and life chances of all those who inhabit the planet.

In fact, historically, conditions have never been so propitious for improving the collective well-being of humankind. The world's collective resources, technological know-how, emergent structures of international governance and the continuing march of democracy could all be put to work in overcoming many of the world's most dire problems. And yet, global threats continue to stalk the earth with devastating impacts on vast swathes of the world's population.

Global crises, by definition, encompass or move across geographical terrains and political territories (they are no respecters of nation states or national borders). As they do so they demand wider recognition and concerted, cooperative responses. They include, but are not confined to, climate change and other human-induced ecological threats; the so-called 'war on terror' and new forms of militarism and warfare; world poverty, inequalities of international trade and financial meltdowns; looming energy crises, food insecurity and water shortages; as well as forced migrations and fast moving pandemics. Major disasters and extreme weather events, and worldwide struggles against human rights abuses, also contribute to today's global crises, variously summoning our compassion and support. The world, it seems, has never confronted so many truly global threats and crises and this speaks to the interconnected and interdependent nature of our globalized planet.

Global Crisis Reporting: Journalism in the Global Age sets out to better understand the media's role in the circulation and communication of these global challenges to humanity as well as the conflicts and contentions that surround them. Concerned as we are with crises that transcend national borders, whether in terms of impact or intervention, this book seeks to move beyond narrow national frameworks and nationally focused methodologies. In today's globalizing world, where crises can be transnational in scope and impact, involve supranational levels of governance and become communicated in real time via global media, so national frames of reference and earlier research preoccupations are being superseded. The study of global crisis reporting, necessarily, needs to be situated and theorized in the context of journalism practised in the global age. As we shall explore, contemporary news media occupy a key position in the public definition and elaboration of global crises and are often far more than just conduits for their wider public recognition. In exercising their symbolic and communicative power, the media today can variously exert pressure and influence on processes of public understanding and political response or, equally, serve to dissimulate and distance the nature of the threats that confront us and dampen down pressures for change. In such ways, global crises become variously *constituted within* the news media as much as *communicated by* them. But this is to jump ahead a little.

First, it may be useful to look at eight illustrations before bringing some analytical clarity and theoretical perspectives to bear on global crises as an object of study and as a prelude to exploring in greater depth their complex interrelationship with the news media. We will elaborate further on most of them in the chapters that follow. But for now, simply consider these seemingly disparate moments of global crises in their own terms and with an eye on their evident media inflection and dependency.

Global crises: eight moments

One: the planet imperilled. It's official

The Intergovernmental Panel on Climate Change (IPCC), a panel of world scientists established by the United Nations to assess the impact of human activity on climate change, published its Fourth Assessment Report (a series of four published reports) in 2007 based on peer-reviewed scientific studies from around the world. The first, most important report released in February clearly stated: 'Global atmospheric concentration of carbon dioxide, methane and nitrous oxide have increased markedly as a result of human activities since 1750 and now far exceed pre-industrial values' (IPCC 2007: 2). It went on: 'The global increases in carbon dioxide concentration are due primarily to fossil fuel use and land-use change, while those of methane and nitrous oxide are primarily due to agriculture' (IPCC 2007: 2). Based on an overwhelming consensus of the world's scientists, the report concluded: 'Warming of the climate system is unequivocal, as is now evident from observations of increases in global average air and ocean temperatures, widespread melting of snow and ice and rising global average sea level' (IPCC 2007: 5).

This unequivocal statement and intervention by the world's scientists about anthropogenic or human-induced climate change and its devastating consequences received prominent exposure across the world's news media. For many it seemed to be a wakeup call. Newspaper front pages from around the world proclaimed, for example: 'Worse than we thought: report warns of 4C rise by 2100, floods and food and water shortages likely' (*The Guardian*), 'World wakes to calamity', 'UN issues global warming alert: burning fuel to blame' (*Sydney Morning Herald*), 'Deal with warming, don't debate it, scientists warn' (*Los Angeles Times*), 'Grim warning of climate change' (*China Daily*).

The environmental debate about global warming had seemingly entered a new phase. What many had warned about for years was now front-page news; climate change, previously contested by a small but influential group of sceptics, had become a legitimate public and political concern. Sceptics would no longer be given such an easy ride in the media as calls for international and global responses became more urgent. Media images of melting glaciers and icecaps, drying lakes, vast swathes of the Amazon rainforest laid bare and the effects of drought and encroaching desertification on people and endangered species around the world, as well as pictures of extreme weather events including cyclones, floods and fires (all of which now appeared not quite so 'natural') became more common. Some sections of the news media have frequently sought to visualize climate change through images of the Earth taken from outer space, thus emphasizing the planetary scale of the threat that now confronts us all (see Image 1.1). As this powerful front page rhetorically and imagistically spells out: 'The Earth today stands in imminent peril and nothing short of a planetary rescue will save it from the environmental cataclysm of dangerous climate change. Those are not the words of

(Ireland, €1) 70p
Tuesday 19 June 2007
www.independent.co.uk
NUMBER 6/150

Today
.motoring
16-page supplement inside

The ultimate supergroup
Andy Gill tells the extraordinary story of The Traveling Wilburys IN EXTRA

EXCLUSIVE
BY STEVE CONNOR, SCIENCE EDITOR

The Earth today stands in imminent peril and nothing short of a planetary rescue will save it from the environmental cataclysm of dangerous climate change. Those are not the words of eco-warriors but the considered opinion of a group of eminent scientists writing in a peer-reviewed scientific journal.

CONTINUED ON PAGE 2

Image 1.1 'The Earth today stands in imminent peril . . .' *The Independent*, 19 June 2007 (© The Independent 2007/Steve Connor) eco-warriors but the considered opinion of a group of eminent scientists writing in a peer-reviewed scientific journal.'

Two: a visible death in the 'global war on terror'

Saddam Hussein, the former Iraqi dictator, was executed by hanging on 30 December 2006 after being convicted of crimes against humanity by an Iraqi special tribunal. His execution inevitably attracted worldwide interest. By name and by deed the 'global war on terror' unleashed by the US and its allies in the aftermath of 11 September 2001 has proved to be of truly global consequence and is destined to reverberate for generations to come. The invasion of Iraq in 2003, we now know, was based on implausible claims about Iraq's support for the Al-Qaida terrorist network, incorrect claims about stock-piled weapons of mass destruction and justified claims about human rights violations. Within the wider maelstrom of war and violence that followed the US and coalition invasions, the manner of Saddam's death also held unique global significance. Saddam Hussein's final steps to the gallows at Camp Justice, a former military intelligence centre where suspected opponents of his regime had previously been tortured and killed, was filmed by the Iraqi authorities. An unauthorized use of a videophone by one of those present, however, also recorded the entire execution, both visually and aud-ibly, and this was quickly uploaded to the internet and then circulated by the world's news media (see Image 1.2).

Human rights campaigners and many others were dismayed, both by the execution and the loss of human dignity that the recording represented. Saddam's audible final shouts, 'Allah is great. The Muslim Ummah will be victorious and Palestine is Arab', will also have disappointed many within the US coalition and outside it given this calculated exhortation to continuing religious conflict in the Middle East – and beyond. And the Iraqi Prime Minister, Nuri al-Maliki, was also, no doubt, dismayed because not only did the unauthorized recording capture Saddam Hussein's final words and the moment of his execution but it also recorded the preceding audible taunts of his executioners. They are clearly heard shouting, 'Muqtada! Muqtada! Muqtada!' – a reference to Muqtada al-Sadr, a prominent Shi'a cleric and the son of Grand Ayatollah Muhammed al-Sadr who was probably killed by Saddam Hussein's agents in 1999. Not only that, but a Shi'a version of an Islamic prayer was also heard to be recited by one of the assembled witnesses as Saddam Hussein faced the gallows, again an apparent insult against Saddam Hussein, as he was a Sunni Muslim.

In the context of bloody violence and the power vacuum left by the removal of the Saddam regime, the release of the unofficial recording was inflammatory. It appeared to confirm that the new Iraqi authorities were less than impartial and acting in sectarian ways – a dire impression for a government that claimed to represent national unity. This was not the first time and neither is it likely to be the last of how

Image 1.2 'Death on Camera' *The Mail on Sunday*, 31 December 2006 (© The Mail on Sunday 2006, Photo: AP/Iraqi TV, HO)

new communication technologies have had far reaching consequences in the global war on terror, rendering visible that which many would prefer to remain out of sight – and out of mind.

Three: migrants and colliding worlds

Unprecedented numbers of people are now on the move around the world at any point in time. These flows of people include tourists, travellers and emigrants as well as asylum seekers, refugees and economic migrants. In the affluent west, many of us only know of the existence of asylum seekers and refugees through political calls for immigration controls or the alarmist fears voiced in the media about the threats 'they' are said to pose to 'us' and 'our' national way of life. Very occasionally, however, something happens to bring these normally separate worlds into collision – and sharp media relief. One such moment occurred in July 2006 when western tourists sunbathing on a beach in Tenerife came face to face with 88 immigrants, exhausted, dehydrated and near to death after their perilous journey from Africa in a tiny fishing boat. The shocked tourists offered what help they could: helping them to wade through the last metres of water on to the beach, providing drinking water and dry clothes and shading them from the sun as best they could with their beach towels. According to a local police officer: 'It was totally spontaneous. Every immigrant must have had four or five people looking after them. The beach was full of tourists' (*http://www.guardian/co.uk/spain/article/0,,1834349,00*, accessed 3.9.07).

This moment of colliding worlds was captured by photojournalists and became disseminated by television, newspapers reports and internet news outlets around the world (see Image 1.3).

Momentarily, exceptionally, this event opened a window on the colliding worlds inhabited by people who experience diametrically opposite life chances. Perhaps it provided the means for a deeper understanding of the plight of those vast numbers of people who normally remain invisible and who risk their lives, and sometimes lose them, in perilous journeys to escape the world's divides.

Four: pandemics on planes

It is not only people who are now on the move in unprecedented numbers around the globe. The publication of a recent World Heath Organization (WHO) report, *A Safer Future: Global Public Health Security* (WHO 2007), describes how passenger flights, currently numbering more than 2 billion a year, serve to effectively incubate and globalize diseases at speed around the planet, rendering them almost impossible to contain. According to Margaret Chan, Director General of the WHO, a combination of

Image 1.3 Tenerife, Spain – Arrival of African Immigrants, 1 August 2006 (© AP/ Arturo Rodriguez 2006)

population growth, incursion into previously uninhabited areas, rapid urbanization, intensive farming practices, environmental degradation and the misuse of antimicrobials has disrupted the equilibrium of the microbial world and led to the emergence of at least one new disease every year (WHO 2007: 2). The director general continues:

> These threats have become a much larger menace in a world characterized by high mobility, economic interdependence and electronic interconnectedness. Traditional defences at national borders cannot protect against the invasion of a disease or vector. Real time news allows panic to spread with equal ease. Shocks to health reverberate as shocks to economies and business . . . well beyond the affected site. Vulnerability is universal. (WHO 2007: 2)

Clearly diseases do not recognize national borders. An influenza pandemic, it is estimated, would affect more than 1.5 billion people, or 25% of the world's population. The possible deliberate release of deadly biogenetic organisms by transnational terrorist networks or rogue states, also pose new global threats. Better health security, argues the report, 'calls for global solidarity' and 'international public health security is both a collective aspiration and a mutual responsibility' (WHO 2007: 3).

Five: world disasters, world compassion

According to the International Federation of the Red Cross and Red Crescent Societies, the total number of people affected by natural disasters has tripled over the past decade to 2 billion people, with an average of 211 million people affected each year (Glenn and Gordon 2007: 3). A particularly bad year for disasters was 2005, as *The Independent* in the UK explained under its front-page headline, 'This is no time for compassion fatigue' (see Image 1.4).

The Independent explained its front-page headline as follows:

> This will be remembered as the year in which nature made clear its indifference to the fate of mankind. First came the tsunami, which wiped out 225,000 lives on Boxing Day morning. In Niger, the West was slow to wake up to the famine engulfing the African country. Then came Hurricane Katrina which transformed a vibrant American city into a fetid, uninhabitable swamp. Now comes the Kashmir earthquake. (*The Independent*, 14.10.05: 1)

Disasters, whether 'natural' or created by humankind, and the distinction between the two is now less clear than in the past, can become signalled as global issues through the media spotlight or rendered invisible and forgotten by lack of media attention. Today new portable communication technologies, satellite linkups and 24/7 real-time reporting capabilities should help to render forgotten disasters or media black holes a thing of the past; the fact that they do not always do so begs questions that demand answers. But the news media do not always turn a blind eye to the plight of others. As the impassioned 'This is no time for compassion fatigue' headline and front page in Image 1.4 suggests, the news media can also on occasion adopt a stance of moral champion aimed at mobilizing sympathies for humanitarian relief (and appropriating the concepts and terms of academics and aid agencies as they do so). Perhaps in such ways the media can encourage audiences to broaden their moral compass beyond their immediate family, friends or national frontiers to recognize the human plight and suffering of people in far away, distant, places. Perhaps too they can encourage a sense of the world's 'overlapping communities of fate' (Held 2004a: x), of how life chances and survival become interconnected in a globalizing planet and how different communities of fate interpenetrate and overlap.

Six: poverty and people power

In 2007 the United Nation's published interim reports documenting the progress that its member states had made over the last 7 years in achieving its millennium development goals (MDGs) set in 2000 (UN 2007a, b). These eight MDGs, targeted for delivery by 2015, set out to:

(Ireland €1) 65p
Wednesday 12 October 2005
www.independent.co.uk
NUMBER 5,924

THE INDEPENDENT

NEWSPAPER OF THE YEAR

Today
property
32-page supplement

TWIGGY: THIS YEAR'S MODEL
THE ORIGINAL SUPERMODEL SPARKS AN M&S REVIVAL Pages 16&17

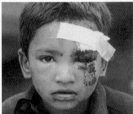

Why this is no time for compassion fatigue

This will be remembered as the year in which nature made clear its indifference to the fate of mankind. First came the tsunami, which wiped out 225,000 lives on Boxing Day morning. In Niger, the West was slow to wake up to the famine engulfing that African country. Then came Hurricane Katrina, which transformed a vibrant American city into a fetid, uninhabitable swamp. Now comes the Kashmir earthquake.

On Saturday morning, a quake measuring 7.6 on the Richter scale hit a mountainous region where Pakistan, India and Afghanistan meet. Men and women were crushed in their homes and workplaces as their roofs fell in. Children were killed as their schools collapsed around them. Whole villages were reduced to rubble in moments.

The death toll has been estimated at up to 40,000. Up to half of those who have died are children. There is a talk of a whole generation wiped out.

This was a disaster that took place half a world away from Britain, but its effects have been felt close to home. Thousands of British subjects have family ties in the region. With communications out, many do not know whether their relatives are alive.

We have witnessed heart-rending images of people being pulled from their destroyed homes. Perhaps most disturbing have been the personal testimonies: the reports of children's voices calling out from the rubble; the pitiful

THE INDEPENDENT

accounts of people scrabbling around the ruins of their homes to free relatives, calling in vain for aid.

A vast number of children have been orphaned. Up to 4 million people are homeless. We must also recognise that when disasters afflict less affluent countries, their governments lack the resources to respond as effectively as they might. The world must

respond to the appeal of the United Nations, which has called for $272m (£156m) in aid, and pool its resources to help.

And we, as prosperous citizens of the Western world, have a responsibility to donate too. That is why *The Independent* is launching an appeal today on behalf of the victims, through the Disasters Emergency Committee, an umbrella body bringing

together a dozen of Britain's best-known charities, including Oxfam and Save the Children.

This is an immediate and positive way for readers to help. Hundreds of thousands are in desperate need of food, shelter, clothing, sanitation and medicine. Unless the survivors receive them speedily, disease will swell the death toll. The aid agencies need funds to prevent this happening, and to rebuild lives.

An over-used phrase this year has been "compassion fatigue". Some have suggested the British public's willingness to donate to emergency relief funds is dwindling. We are confident that this is not the case. You have shown that your willingness to give is dictated not by personal whim but by the scale of the emergency. You showed this during our Darfur appeal last summer. You showed it during the Christmas appeal for Africa, and in the tsunami appeal. We hope you will summon up that same spirit of compassion once more, and use our coupon to donate.

REPORTS, PAGE 2

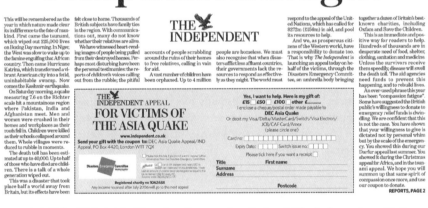

THE INDEPENDENT APPEAL
FOR VICTIMS OF THE ASIA QUAKE
www.independent.co.uk
Send your gift with the coupon **to:** DEC Asia Quake Appeal/IND Appeal, PO Box 4420, London W1T 7QX

Disasters Emergency Committee

Please tick the box if you do not want to receive further information from the Disasters Emergency Committee

Gift aid it and I am a UK taxpayer and want DEC to reclaim tax I have paid on this and any donations I have made in the last six years (or equal to the tax we reclaim (28p for every £1).

Registered charity no 1062638
Any income received after July 2006 will go to the next appeal

Yes, I want to help. Here is my gift of:
£15 £50 £100 other £..........
I enclose a cheque/postal order made payable to
DEC Asia Quake
Or debit my Visa/Delta/MasterCard/Switch/Visa Electron/
JCB/CAF Card/Amex
(please circle one)

Card no:

Expiry Date: Switch issue no:
Please tick here if you want a receipt

Title   First name
Surname
Address
                    Postcode

Image 1.4 'Why This is No Time for Compassion Fatigue' *The Independent*, 12 October 2005 (© The Independent 2005)

1 eradicate extreme poverty and hunger
2 achieve universal primary education
3 promote gender equality and empowerment
4 reduce child mortality
5 improve maternal health
6 combat HIV/AIDS, malaria and other diseases
7 ensure environmental sustainability
8 develop a global partnership for development. (United Nations 2007a)

In 2007, the midway point between the adoption of the MDGs and their target date, Ban Ki-moon, Secretary General of the United Nations reported that 'there have been some gains and that success is still possible in most parts of the world' but, he continued, 'there is a clear need for political leaders to take urgent and concerted action, or many millions of people will not realize the basic promise of the MDGs in their lives' (UN 2007a: 3). The UN's regional update for Africa was explicit: 'Although there have been major gains in several areas and the Goals remain achievable in most African nations, even the best governed countries on the continent have not been able to make sufficient progress in reducing extreme poverty in its many forms' (UN 2007b: 1). The UN's interim reports on the progress of the MDGs and their likely prospects of being met by 2015 barely registered in the world's media, their importance for the multitudes of the world's poor and under-nourished notwithstanding.

This muted media response is in stark contrast to the intensive media coverage that helped to galvanize the Live 8 concerts 2 years earlier in 2005. This spectacular, mega-media event based on 10 staged concerts broadcast around the world and a lineup of the world's leading bands and superstars including Madonna, U2 and Paul McCartney had sought to draw attention to the continuing extremes of poverty in Africa, mobilize popular concern in Europe and America and put pressure on the G8 governments, meeting later that month at the world economic summit. An estimated 3 billion around the world watched the concerts on television, 1.5 million attended the concerts and more than 30 million signed up to the Live 8 web petition. A raft of governmental commitments were pledged 6 days later by the G8 leaders, including extra aid for Africa plus measures on debt relief, international trade and health. For a time at least, and courtesy of global communication systems, it seemed that people power and the mobilization of social justice issues had registered within the corridors of power.

Seven: bearing witness and human rights

In late 2007 Witness, the human rights organization founded by musician and activist Peter Gabriel with the logo 'See it, Film it, Change it' and which 'uses video and online technologies to open the eyes of the world human rights violations', developed a new platform called 'The Hub'. In a press release on its website, this is described as 'an online destination where concerned citizens, activists, journalists, researchers and advocates worldwide will be able to upload human rights related media from handheld devices or personal computers, and create or join communities and calls to action around the abuses they witness' (*http://www.witness.org/*). Over the 15 years of its existence, Witness has worked with thousands of human rights defenders in over 70 countries providing video equipment, training and support so that human rights abuses are brought to the attention of key decision makers, concerned citizens and the media. It lists, for example, the work of its activists and the video films documenting human rights in Burma that helped to put the issue of the persecution of rural villagers on the UN Security Council's agenda for the first time. The publicizing of appalling human rights abuses found in Burma and elsewhere is not confined, however, to activists' websites.

In July 2007 a cross-party committee of British MPs returned from a fact-finding mission to Burma, which was reported widely in the British media. An article by one of the group, John Bercow, Conservative MP, was reproduced in full by a leading UK newspaper. It began:

> Burma suffers a political, human rights and humanitarian situation as grim as any in the world today. The country is run by an utterly illegitimate government that spends 50 percent of its budget on the military and less than $1 (50p) per head on the health and education of its own citizens. The thugs and imposters who rule the roost practice some of the most egregious human rights abuses known to mankind. Rape as a weapon of war, extra-judicial killings, water torture, mass displacement, compulsory relocation, forced labour, incarceration of political prisoners, religious and ethnic persecution, and the daily destruction of rural villages are all part of the story of savagery that has disfigured Burma. (*The Independent*, 26.7.07: 2)

Human rights, as illustrated earlier, are abused in diverse, often systematic and terrible ways in the world today. But human rights are also on the march around the globe and are sometimes powerfully championed through today's different communication media – whether by creative uses of new digital and online technologies or forms of crafted journalism in the conventional mass media. As I was writing this, news media were reporting on mass demonstrations led by Burma's Buddhist monks in September 2007 who were challenging the country's military junta for the first time in 19 years of bloody repression.

Also in the news at the time of writing are the continuing humanitarian emergency and human rights abuses in Darfur, Sudan, and the trial of Charles Taylor, former president of Liberia. Taylor faces an international court in The Hague where he stands accused of war crimes during the diamond-fuelled conflict in neighbouring Sierra Leone. Specifically, he is charged with a raft of offences in violation of the Geneva conventions, crimes against humanity and international humanitarian law. These include being complicit with the Revolutionary United Front's (RPF) deliberate campaign in Sierra Leone against civilians involving systematic mutilation such as the chopping off of arms or hands, and the abduction of women and girls as sex slaves and men and boys as soldiers. Gross violations of human rights continue to cast a bloody stain on the world, but human rights are also at the forefront of pro-democracy movements and struggles for social justice around the globe – and the news media, variously, now report on both.

Eight: financial meltdowns and overlapping communities of fate

One last fragment. In the middle of August 2007 the world's financial markets experienced a sudden and unexpected crisis that threatened to turn into a 'financial meltdown'. Within the space of a few hours billions of dollars were written off share values owned by individuals and institutions such as pension funds and insurance companies. Bank failures threatened in the US and beyond and huge hedge fund losses and an ensuing 'credit crunch' prompted unprecedented injections of billions of dollars by central banks in the US, Europe and Asia to help restore liquidity and confidence in the world's failing financial markets. BBC Online News reported the crisis and sought to bring some clarity to this confused situation. It deployed a question and answer format that began thus:

> Stock markets around the world have been falling sharply on fears of a credit crunch that could affect the financial sector. What is causing the fall and how will it affect the ordinary individual?

It then proceeded to explain:

What are the markets worried about?
The underlying fear relates to the collapse of the so-called sub-prime mortgage market in the US.

In the past five years, extraordinarily low interest rates in the US have led banks and other financial institutions to lend substantial sums of money to people with poor or no credit histories.

The idea was that, even if they eventually couldn't pay, the banks could recoup any losses by repossessing and reselling the houses – and in any case, house price rises would cushion the blow.

In the most extreme cases, mortgage brokers were handing out what came to be known as 'Ninja' loans, to people with no income and no job or assets.

Often the loans were 'no-doc', where the borrower did not have to provide proof of how much they earned. Recent research suggests that in many if not most of these, borrowers (or their brokers) lied about their income.

But now as interest rates have risen, so have repossessions. The US housing market has collapsed and the banks find themselves saddled with a lot of bad debts.

However, it is not just a problem for US banks.

Globalisation has meant that much of this mortgage debt has been sliced up into small pieces, repackaged as 'collaterised mortgage obligations' and sold on to financial institutions and individual investors around the world.

And now, no one, including the central banks, is certain how much of these bad debts financial institutions or individuals are holding.

The BBC News Q&A concluded by relating these developments to its online readers thus:

What does it mean to you?
Many individuals own stocks and shares – about half of all US households, and around a quarter of those in the UK.

If the stock market falls continue, they may feel less wealthy – and be less likely to buy goods and services, slowing the economy.

In addition, many pension funds own shares which make up part of their portfolio used to pay people's occupational pensions.

If shares fall, they may have less money to pay future pensions, and employee contributions may have to rise. (*http://news.bbc.co.uk/go/pr/fr-/1/hi/business/ 6939899.stm*) (accessed 10.9.07)

This latest threatened financial meltdown was brought under control temporarily by injections of funds by central banks around the world and serves to illustrate something of the precariousness (and essential amorality) of complexly structured and interdependent global financial markets. These normally invisible global flows of finances are poorly understood by most people but can prove disastrous nonetheless for millions who become caught up in their consequences. In this instance, crucially, some of the world's poor were more centrally involved than usual through the provision of high-credit, high-risk mortgages that banks were prepared to back and a system of property repossessions. The BBC's analysis, as we have heard, operates largely within the parameters and presuppositions of the world of business, markets and finances and addresses its readers likewise, as interested observers and potentially affected consumers. This helpful *pedagogy for consumers* – it is certainly not 'pedagogy of the oppressed' (Freire 1985) – fails to explore, however, the human reality of 'sub-prime' mortgage holders whose collective predicament, in this case at least, seems to have ratcheted up through the financial systems with tumultuous global impacts. Once again, distinct but in fact overlapping communities of fate have collided, momentarily rendering visible the inequities of contemporary interdependent lives.

Global crises defined

Each of the global crisis moments we have just examined helps to provide a glimpse into some of the different kinds of crisis unfolding in the world today – crises that exemplify the interconnected dark side of our globalizing world and its overlapping communities of fate. How these crises are communicated around the globe is, as we have seen, often integral to their public standing as 'global crises'. Global crises today include the following:

- climate change and ecological risks which now threaten the world's ecosystems and all life as we know it
- increasing major disasters and humanitarian emergencies that summon global calls for compassion, donations and active support from individuals, non-governmental organizations (NGOs) and governments around the world
- new forms of war including the so-called 'global war on terror', asymmetric warfare and transnational terror networks as well as 'new wars' and 'hidden wars' causing mass civilian casualties
- so-called 'military humanism' and humanitarian interventions conducted in the name of protecting human rights and/or international security
- continuing global threats from a new generation of weapons of mass destruction (WMD) and a possible resurgence of 'cold war' style politics and pre-emptive strikes
- world poverty and related health issues whose worldwide indices (measured, for example, in the United Nation's millennium development goals targeted for 2015 delivery), continue to point to the massive inequalities and injustices in the distribution and consumption of the world's available resources
- new and increasingly transnational pandemics – SARS, AIDS, influenza H5N1, drug-resistant salmonella – and the serious challenges these pose to governments and the necessity for international systems of cooperation, planned prevention campaigns and global responses
- the rise in world population and the increased flows of 'forced migrants' including asylum seekers and political and environmental refugees encountering new racisms and policies of border control and exclusion
- systematic and deliberate abuse of human rights around the world and the continuing struggles of NGOs and others to bolster international frameworks of human rights law and to bring to justice all those who violate them, including former heads of state
- global financial markets and world trade that produce periodic financial/market crises, ever increasing production and exploitation of the world's resources – contributing to the depletion of fossil fuel energy supplies and exacerbation of food insecurity, water shortages and conflicts.

This list is not exhaustive by any means and others may wish to add to it or possibly redefine some of the identified crises in ways that better reflect their political outlooks and analysis of the state of the world, its determinants and dynamics (see for example, Held 2004a; Boyd-Barrett 2005; Energy Watch Group 2007; Glenn and Gordon 2007; IISS 2007; Lull 2007; UNEP 2007; Seitz 2008). There is, in fact, no shortage of 'global crises' or potential sponsors committed to defining them as such in the public eye. And this, in part, is the point. Global crises require sponsors or 'claims makers' to conceptualize and articulate them in the media if they are to become legitimate public concerns and sites of wider political mobilization and action. But even so, the ontology of contemporary global disasters both precedes and threatens to exceed social constructionist accounts confined to practices of language, claims making and media discourse – important as these undoubtedly are. Such is the scale and destructive force of many global crises today that some intervene within the world as a force unto themselves, exerting 'agency' through their threatened materiality of impacts and commanding news attention worldwide. As we shall explore, critical realism (*crisis realism*) and social constructionist epistemologies *both* need to come into play when approaching the mediating and constitutive role of news media in global crises. Whatever one's preferred epistemological position and disciplinary allegiance, most informed commentators can probably concede, nonetheless, that the global crises indicated here comprise some of the most profound threats and challenges confronting the world today.

We also need to recognize, however, that many global crises are not self-contained or discrete phenomena but interpenetrate and/or mutate into related crises and exacerbate yet others. In other words, the mutability and complexity of real-world crises is rarely captured by neat typologies and distinct categories and, indeed, many humanitarian professionals refer to 'complex emergencies'. For example, climate change and extreme weather events can exacerbate competition for land, water and food, creating conditions for civil strife and political instability. Increasingly they are seen as issues of national and international security (IISS 2007). Climate change can also lead to the incubation of deadly diseases and produce environmental refugees and forced migrations. It has been predicted, for example, that by 2080 climate change will lead to 1.1–3.2 billion people experiencing water scarcity, 200–600 million suffering hunger, and 2.7 million a year subject to coastal flooding, leading to 250 million permanently displaced people (IPCC cited in Vidal 2007).

A combination of factors is also thought to have contributed to the global food crisis of 2008. These include: world population growth, increased demand for (grain-intensive) meat production in developing economies such as China and India, poor harvests exacerbated by climate change in others, the production of biofuels displacing food production in the south to support climate change policies in the north and rising energy costs. Together these contributed to rising world food prices and a global food crisis – a crisis that impacts hardest on the world's poor.

The global war on terror and transnational terrorism, for its part, has produced systematic and indiscriminate killing of civilians and human rights abuses. This, in turn, has undermined economic capacity and caused increased poverty and food shortages as well as deliberate environmental damage and the threatened releases of deadly biogenetic organisms. Some major disasters not only lead to pandemics, poverty and population movements, however, but can also create political and economic opportunities to both literally and politically 'capitalize' on the 'disaster shock' of catastrophic events (Klein 2007).

It is important, therefore, to keep this multidimensional, mutually interpenetrating and mutating character of global crises in mind if we are to avoid disciplinary tunnel vision or fragmenting perspectives. Here, then, we need to move beyond our opening illustrations of global crises and begin to think a little more theoretically and analytically about the nature of global crises and why and how today's media play such a crucial role in their wider definition, elaboration and forms of response.

So what distinguishes some conflicts and threats as 'global crises'? Most are not confined to a particular national context or a unique set of circumstances but register wider, often endemic, states of affairs in the world. Their scale and severity of impacts, both actual and potentially, as well as their engendered international forms of response, also help to define them as 'global crises'. Even so, these characteristics alone are not sufficient to guarantee them wider recognition and standing as 'global crises'. For this, they depend on prominent exposure and elaboration in the media – such is the centrality of media systems today within processes of problem definition, awareness, legitimation and mobilization. To put it boldly, for a global crisis to exist, it must generally be seen to exist and by a great number of people – not all of whom will be directly involved. A global crisis, therefore, requires widespread media exposure. The scale of death and destruction or the widespread and endemic nature of certain crises is no guarantee that a calamity or conflict will register prominently, if at all, in the global media, much less that it will be defined therein as a global crisis. We know that 'hidden wars' and 'forgotten disasters' still abound in the world today and, because of their media invisibility, can command neither global recognition nor wider political response.

If they are to register as issues of global importance, concern and possible action, global crises depend on their signalling and elaboration within the media, and news media particularly. This is no longer such a simple proposition. Today's complex journalism ecology comprises different western, regional and national news formations (commercial, public service, state-controlled), news flows from the west to the rest, the local to global, as well as various regional contraflows and oppositional counterflows and alternative cross-over journalism productions (see Figure 1.1). Traditional mainstream press and broadcasting are also now surrounded and interpenetrated by the increasingly ubiquitous presence of the internet with its enhanced connectivity, interactivity and invigoration of new forms of citizen and online journalism. These established and dominant centres of journalism have also established themselves online. For the most part, however, they decline to surrender their traditional editorial control, agenda-setting functions or capacity to authorize who enters the news domain and how and when – new models of journalism found elsewhere on the net notwithstanding.

For crises to register as global crises today, they must do so through this more complex news media ecology. It is still probably fair to say, however, that most

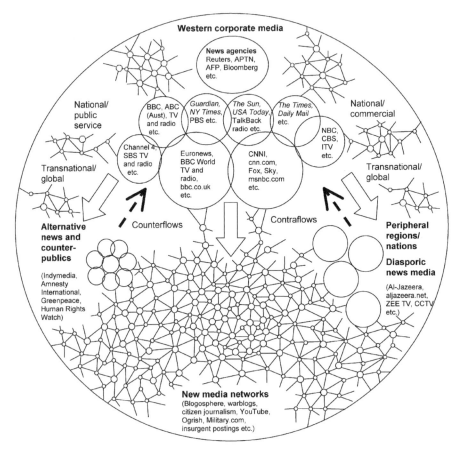

Figure 1.1 Global news ecology

continue to depend principally on the world's corporate news media and news agencies if they are to become widely communicated and regarded as global crises, even though they may have had a presence in the wider media ecology and its circulating communication flows for sometime before this. It is in the established mainstream news media, principally, that global crises are visualized and dramatized, symbolized and narrativized and publicly elaborated – and for many of us it is here too that they are first encountered, possibly 'felt' and 'known'.

Martin Shaw has also argued for the constitutive role of media in global crises. In *Civil Society and Media in Global Crises* (Shaw 1996), a study based on the 1991 Gulf War and ensuing humanitarian crisis of the Kurds, he summarizes his position, as follows:

> I have argued that in the post-Cold War era, global crises may be constituted even where the interests of major powers are not involved in a direct or obvious way, if

there is a world-wide *perception* of large-scale violations of life and globally legitimate principles. I also argued that the existence of a global crisis can be confirmed by the occurrence of, or significant pressure for, internationally legitimate *intervention* (humanitarian, political or military) to resolve the crisis. I indicated that media coverage has much to do with the constitution of global crises in these senses. (Shaw 1996: 156)

Shaw's position is instructive but can be qualified nonetheless. It possibly remains too indebted to an informing international relations perspective and a delimited *political* conception of crises. As we have heard, global crises today can, in fact, assume diverse forms not all of which revolve around political crises or political calls for intervention. Some global crises, such as major 'natural disasters' or the threat of pandemics, for example, even though signalled prominently in the media, do not necessarily involve 'perceptions of large-scale violations of life and globally legitimate principles'. Calls for intervention, moreover, may only be voiced at certain points in an unfolding global crisis, not at others, or sometimes not at all. Global crises, then, come in different guises and are more diverse in range and dynamic in nature than Shaw's definition extrapolated from his analysis of the first Gulf War and related humanitarian crisis, tend to suggest. But these are qualifying points only. His approach remains broadly productive in positioning the media centre stage in terms of their role in the public constitution of global crisis. To what extent it is also permissible to argue, as Shaw does, that television news can compel governments into humanitarian intervention is another matter and this will be returned to later on (see Chapter 7).

More than a decade on since Shaw's book, and with seemingly very different global crises now in view, we need to go deeper theoretically into their nature and constitution – and this is so in at least two major respects. If the media, and news media specifically, are so central to the constitution of global crises then clearly we need to get a better theoretical fix on their nature, dynamics and determinants – especially when theorized and discussed in the field of global journalism studies (this forms the subject of Chapter 2). But we also need to better situate and theorize global crises in the context of a globalizing world, discussed next.

Global crisis in context

As intimated by the global crisis moments and discussion already, global crises are not usefully conceptualized and approached as geographically confined events without wider context or antecedents. Certainly it makes no sense to see them as destructive aberrations that strike without warning, like acts of god to make people suffer. Neither, for the most part, can they be adequately understood as the dreadful remnants of an earlier premodern era that has somehow escaped the civilizing forces of modernity. In a global world that has become radically interconnected and interdependent, global crises are part of that same world – both spawned and shaped by it. From climate change to the global war on terror, from forced migrations to world pandemics, from financial meltdowns to world poverty, these different global crises, as we have heard, are deeply enmeshed within today's global world. They are expressive of it. Put more dialectically, global crises are both *constituted by* and *constituting of* a negatively inflected and enveloping globality. Global crises, then, must be theorized in relation to our global age since it is in this context that they are determined and defined. The ideas of major social theorists on globalization help to indicate how this is so (Harvey 1989; Giddens 1990; Robertson 1992; Albrow 1996; Bauman 1998; Beck 1999; Waters 2001; Held and McGrew 2003; Held 2004b; Ritzer, 2007).

Anthony Giddens' oft quoted definition of globalization doesn't refer specifically to global crises, although his formulation clearly holds considerable relevance in terms of its spatio-temporal understanding of the intensification of worldwide social relations:

> Globalization refers essentially to that stretching process, in so far as the modes of connection between different social contexts or regions become networked across the earth's surface as a whole.
>
> Globalization can thus be defined as the intensification of worldwide social relations which link distant localities in such a way that local happenings are shaped by events occurring many miles away and vice versa. This is a dialectical process because such local happenings may move in an obverse direction from the very distanciated relations that shape them. Local transformation is as much part of globalization as the lateral extension of social connections across time and space. (Giddens 1990: 64)

Giddens' conceptualization of 'time–space distanciation', 'disembedding' and 'reflexivity' are all apposite in the context of global crises and each has clear bearing, for example, on the global crisis moments described earlier. Time–space distanciation with its reference to the 'stretching' of social relations, 'disembedding' and associated ideas of 'action at a distance,' and 'reflexivity' with its signalling of the increased propensity of individuals and institutions to consciously monitor and respond to rapidly altering circumstances (including flows of world communication) (Giddens 1990, 1994, 2002, 2005) *all* potentially speak to global crises and their mediation worldwide.

Disappointingly, however, Giddens doesn't go on to develop their relevance in respect of particular global crises or the gross inequalities endemic to a globalizing world that generate them. He does, though, point to the role of globalization in the creation of new 'fundamentalisms' that become pitted against 'cosmopolitan tolerance' on the battleground of the 21st century (2002: 4) and argues for the media's indispensable involvement in the forward march of democracy: 'In a world based upon active communication,' he suggests, 'hard power – power that comes only from the top down – loses its edge' as authoritarian regimes become undermined by their 'loss of information monopoly' in today's 'intrinsically open framework of global communications' (Giddens 2002: 72–73). But, apart from these generalizing statements, we hear little about the role of today's global communications in respect of particular global crises and how both are endemic to the global age.

David Harvey's depiction of a globalizing world that has both accelerated and shrunk through processes of 'time–space compression' (Harvey 1989) also points to the reconfiguration of social relations based on new forms of electronic communication. Similarly, more recent statements by David Held and Anthony McGrew who regard globalization as 'the widening, intensifying, speeding up, and growing impact of world-wide interconnectedness' (Held and McGrew 2003: 4) also point to the changing infrastructure of global communications as one of its 'deep drivers' (Held 2004a: 11). In these and other notable statements about globalization, global communication systems and accelerating communication flows are invariably acknowledged as central to processes of globalization though questions of global crises – the dark side of globalization – and their mediation in and through the news media remain largely unexamined and untheorized.

In this last respect, Martin Albrow's *The Global Age* (1996) represents an important departure. His disquisition on the changed nature of our times and its perceived rupture with modernity theoretically posits at least some global crises as fundamental to the increasingly interdependent and globally reflexive nature of the global age:

> Fundamentally the Global Age involves the supplementing of modernity with globality and this means an overall change in the basis of action and social organization for individuals and groups. There are at least five major ways in which globality has taken us beyond the assumptions of modernity. They include the global environmental consequences of aggregate human activities; the loss of security where weaponry has global destructiveness; the globality of communication systems; the rise of a global economy; and the reflexivity of globalization where people and groups of all kinds refer to the globe as the frame for their beliefs. (Albrow 1996: 4)

Albrow's philosophical–historical treatise on the nature of the global age encourages us, then, to approach 'global crises' along with other, more positive expressions of globalism, as both constituted by and constituting of an era in which global interdependency, crises, communications, awareness and reflexivity all signal an important departure from the past – including the assumptions of the social sciences that have too long taken the nation state as its natural frame of reference and understanding. Zygmunt Bauman (2007) is even more explicit, challenging the political capacity of nation states to deal with today's global 'metaproblems' which he sees as deeply rooted in a 'negatively globalized planet'. He elaborates as follows:

> On a negatively globalized planet, all the most fundamental problems – the metaproblems conditioning the tackling of all other problems – are *global*, and being global they admit of no local solutions; there are not, and cannot be local solutions to globally originated and globally invigorated problems. The reunion of

power and politics may be achieved, if at all, at the planetary level. As Benjamin R. Barber poignantly put it, 'no American child may feel safe in its bed if in Karachi or Baghdad children don't feel safe in theirs. Europeans won't boast long of their freedoms if people in other parts of the world remain deprived and humiliated.' . . . The future of democracy and freedom may be made secure on a planetary scale – or not at all. (Bauman 2007: 25–26)

Here, at last, global crises begin to come into theoretical view as the dark side of globalization or in Bauman's terms as *'globally originated and globally invigorated problems'* in a *'negatively globalized planet'*.

It is the social theorist Ulrich Beck, more than any other, however, who puts global crises at the very core of his theorization of the global age. His work on 'global risk society' and its relationship to an emergent 'cosmopolitan outlook' (Beck 1999, 2006) speaks directly to many of today's global crises and his ideas demand, therefore, further consideration and elaboration. Beck states his fundamental position, theoretically positing global crises at the heart of 'global risk society', as follows:

> Some time in the not-too-distant past a qualitative transformation in the perception of social order took place. The latter was no longer perceived primarily in terms of conflict over the production and distribution of 'goods'; rather it is the production and distribution of 'bads' that contradict the steering role claimed by the established institutions of the nation-state. This category shift in self-perception precipitated an interdependency crisis in the way modern societies organized their institutions and functions, a crisis which found quite diverse expressions: climate change ('risk of ultraviolet radiation'), global poverty, transnational terrorism, the BSE crisis, AIDS etc. I call this interdependency crisis 'world risk society'. It also precipitates a crisis in the social sciences and political theory, which follow Marx and Weber in constructing modern societies as capitalistic and rational. The truly epoch-making difference consists in the expansion of culturally produced, interdependent insecurities and dangers, and the resulting dominance of the public perception of risk as staged by the mass media. In world risk society what is at stake at all levels is accordingly the compulsive pretense of control over the uncontrollable, whether in politics, law, science, the economy or everyday life. (Beck 2006: 22)

Beck's thesis of risk society (1992) and, later, world risk society (1999) has received considerable academic scrutiny as well as wider public interest, which is perhaps not surprising given its seeming ability to address the rising awareness of ecological crises and the felt anxieties of living 'on top of the volcano' in the 'risk society'. He characterizes today's society as a period of 'second modernity'. Unlike the first modernity of industrialized capitalism and the manufacture of goods, the period of second modernity is characterized by the global production and distribution of 'manufactured uncertainties' or potentially catastrophic risks. These evade the capacity of scientists and experts, administrators and politicians, to calibrate, predict and control them. It is within this technologically and scientifically advanced, but potentially catastrophic period of second modernity that the media, according to Beck, are theoretically posited with a new central importance in the communication and symbolization of risks. For example, he states:

> The risk society can be grasped theoretically, empirically and politically only if one starts from the premise that it is also a knowledge, media and information society at the same time – or, often enough as well, a society of non-knowledge and disinformation. (Beck 2000: xiv)

His ideas of world risk society and their relevance for the study of environment and ecology in the media have been discussed elsewhere (Cottle 1998, 2006a: 120–142; Allan et al. 2000; Mythen 2004). But what is interesting about his more recent work in the context of global crisis reporting is the extension of ideas of risk to a much wider field of conflicts and crises. Beck discerns at least three different axes of crises in world risk society which he terms, respectively, *ecological*, *economic* and *terrorist* 'interdependency crises' (Beck 2006: 22).

Perhaps this extension of his earlier theoretical focus on the circulation of environmental *bads* in contrast to commercial *goods* around the world ('poverty is hierarchic, smog is democratic') concedes ground to his former critics, many of whom were disquieted by his seeming marginalization of inequalities of class in his account of risk society as well as his relative neglect of its underlying, capitalist, political economy. Perhaps it simply incorporates the obviousness of real-world events and developments since 9/11, the war on terror and the ascendancy of neoliberal ideas in the operations of world markets. Be that as it may, his latest theoretical treatise (Beck 2005, 2006) seeks to advance both a political economy of the global age and, importantly, a 'cosmopolitan vision' based on the discerned dynamics of crisis endemic to the contemporary world.

Beck, more than most other major theorists of globalization, points to the endemic nature of world crises within these processes, but is not content to see them only in terms of global society's dark side, its nightmares become real; he also sees them as the potential harbinger of progressive change. Today's global threats and potentially catastrophic global crises, he argues, may yet unleash radical impulses in a new 'civilizational community of fate' (2006: 13), forging an emancipatory cosmopolitan outlook when confronting, as we all must, the dangers and threats of the contemporary world:

> What, then, does the cosmopolitan outlook signify? It does not herald the first rays of universal brotherly love among peoples, or the dawn of the world republic, or a free-floating global outlook, or compulsory xenophilia. Nor is cosmopolitanism a kind of supplement that is supposed to replace nationalism and provincialism, for the very good reason that the ideas of human rights and democracy need a national base. Rather, the cosmopolitan outlook means that, in

a world of global crises and dangers produced by civilization, the old differentiations between internal and external, national and international, us and them,
lose their validity and a new cosmopolitan realism becomes essential to survival.
(Beck 2006: 13–14)

Beck's theoretical intervention within the normally idealist discourses of cosmopolitanism is founded, epistemologically, on a position that could be termed '*crisis
realism*'. That is, a standpoint that seeks to explicate the dynamics and determinants
of underlying processes of global interdependency and which intrude into the world
forcing collaborative forms of response and growing recognition of our shared 'civilizational community of fate'. This theoretical standpoint seeks to conceptually appre-
hend and respond to those real-world incursions from ecological, economic and
terrorist crises – contemporary interdependency crises – that can only be grappled with
beyond the level of single nation states. His thesis, then, provides a powerful theoretical
backdrop for thinking about different global crises and their interdependencies as well
as their potential to support a new cosmopolitanism, a world outlook that tentatively
struggles to move beyond bounded cultural parochialisms, methodological national-
isms and the delimited political horizons of a world organized in terms of nation
states.

Beck occasionally alludes to the significance of the media in staging public perceptions of risk, as we have heard, but his ambitious theoretical sweep rarely pauses to
ponder the mechanisms and meanings, determinants and dynamics of the contemporary media or exactly how they channel and construct the public elaboration of particular global crises. And this, it has to be said, is a silence that is shared across most major
theorists of globalization and global society. While most certainly acknowledge the
'globality of communication systems' (Albrow 1996: 4), the 'consolidation of global
media system' (Robertson 1992: 27) and see 'media and communications, and their role
in promoting global interdependencies, as the most dynamic force' (Giddens 2005: 68;
see also Giddens 1990: 77), for the most part they do not empirically examine the
processes and practices, formations and flows of today's global media ecology or how
they shape and enter the communication of different global crises.

Here, then, we need to attend empirically and in detail to processes of '*social construction*' in the mediation of global crises without jettisoning Beck's critical realism,
or '*crisis realism*,' that theorizes the endemic and intervening nature of global interdependency crises within real-world processes today. Global crises are an integral and
inextricable part of the global age, its dark side, but, as we have heard, too often they
become theoretically occluded in relatively abstract claims about the nature of globalization. The news media, it has also been suggested here, are complexly implicated in
the circulation, construction and challenges of global crises which, crucially, cannot
register fully as 'global crises' at all without wide media exposure and elaboration.
This too remains theoretically under-developed in contemporary social theoretical
debates about globalization and demands thorough examination.

Plan of the book

Global Crisis Reporting sets out to examine these complexities and critical dependencies in the communication of some of the most humanly pressing global crises of our age. These include: major disasters (Chapter 3), climate change and ecology (Chapter 4), forced migrations and human rights (Chapter 5) and new wars and the global war on terror (Chapter 6). We also examine debates about media-induced compassion fatigue in the context of news reports of human suffering and its claimed opposite, the 'CNN effect', in galvanizing governments into humanitarian interventions (Chapter 7) and the changing field of humanitarian aid and news media interactions (Chapter 8). But first, Chapter 2 sets out to redress the underdeveloped discussion of global journalism in contemporary social theoretical approaches to globalization and does so by considering major positions and debates in the field of global journalism studies. Informed by these perspectives as well as by the positions of social theory considered earlier, we will then be in a stronger position to examine different global crises and their complex interrelationships and dependencies with the news media in the chapters that follow.

This book develops on the previous one, *Mediatized Conflict: Developments in Media and Conflict Studies* (Cottle 2006a), which examined, with the help of some of the best media and communications research and scholarship, new theoretical departures and research trajectories in the contemporary field of media and conflict study. At the very end of that book it was suggested that the unprecedented perils as well as democratizing potential that inhere within processes of globalization demand sustained attention by media scholars – and that this will only become more so in the years to come (Cottle 2006a: 193). *Global Crisis Reporting: Journalism in the Global Age* is a modest attempt to begin to respond to this challenge in respect of how the news media signal and communicate some of the most pressing conflicts and crises in the world today. It is also based on a mix of original research and the research of others who have sought to engage with some of these most pressing global issues. By this means it seeks to throw some light on the dark side of global society as well as the media's capacity to sustain forms of global awareness, global citizenship and even, perhaps, an emergent global cosmopolitan outlook.

② | JOURNALISM IN THE GLOBAL AGE

The world we live in today is changing rapidly, in no small part because worldwide television, communication satellites, high-speed transmission of news and data, and other computer and electronic hardware and software (including the Internet) have transformed the ways that nations and people communicate with one another. The fact that a news event can be transmitted almost instantaneously to newsrooms and onto television and computer screens (and into cellphones) around the world can be important as the event itself. . . . Long-distance mass communication has become a rudimentary central nervous system for our fragile, shrinking, and increasingly interdependent, yet fractious, world. (Hachten and Scotton 2007: xiv).

Major contemporary social theorists acknowledge, as we have heard, the integral, fundamental even, role played by media communication in processes of globalization. Influential ideas of 'time–space distanciation' (Giddens 1990) and general statements about globalization as the 'widening, intensifying, speeding up, and growing impact of world-wide interconnectedness' (Held and McGrew 2003), for example, recognize the constitutive role of media communications within these defining characteristics of globalization. But they have yet to address the media's role within globalization's dark side and address how media feature within and frame particular global crises.

Influential theorists of the 'information society' and 'global complexity' seemingly suffer from a similar theoretical blindspot. Manuel Castells *magnum opus* on the 'network society' places communications infrastructures and the advent of computing decisively at the core of his theorization of powered global geometry or the global 'space of flows' (Castells 1996) but does not pursue how exactly this impacts different global conflicts and crises. John Urry's thesis of 'global complexity' (Urry 2003), to take just one more, observes how 'emergent systems of information and communication are the bases for increased reflexivity' and argues this helps create a world of fluids in which 'the "structure" of "societies" has progressively less purchase' (p.139). But he notes only in passing that 'collective global disasters are the key to forming', what he terms, 'cosmopolitan global fluids' or the capacity to live simultaneously in both the global and the local, the distant and the proximate, the universal and the particular (pp.135–137).

Social theorists who have attended to the '*metaproblems*' of a '*negatively globalized planet*' (Bauman 2007) and positioned '*interdependency crises*' at the centre of the theorization of '*world risk society*' (Beck 1999, 2006), then, have certainly helped to move beyond the theoretical myopia of most globalization theorists who fail to see and theorize how conflicts, catastrophes and crises are endemic to an inegalitarian globalizing world (Chapter 1). The ideas of Ulrich Beck in particular provide a backdrop of relevance to this study but here also the discussion of the media and news media specifically remains theoretically underdeveloped and empirically unexplored. Before we begin to examine with the help of recent research studies the mediation of different global crises, therefore, we also need to get a better fix of the world of journalism and its academic theorization in global context.

The field of media and communications study has been interested in globalizing communication flows for some time, although it is generally fair to say it has been slow to incorporate the ideas of more recent contemporary social theorists. Concerns about transnational media corporations, the dominance of western-led news agencies, foreign news values and news flows and their contribution to producing homogenized world media and culture have, for example, received critical discussion for some time (Galtung and Ruge 1965; MacBride 1980). More recently, regional media formations, emergent contraflows and the cacophony of views and voices emanating from the web have been theorized as the more contradictory and uneven expressions of globalization. Much still hangs, evidently, on what exactly is understood by 'globalization' (Ritzer 2007) and the parts played by journalism within this.

To get a better fix on this, the current chapter sets out to review the contemporary field of journalism studies when approached through the competing paradigms and theoretical perspectives of international communications and media globalization. The field of international and global news study has long proved contentious, which is understandable given the essentially contested terrain of international relations, geopolitical power and opposing interests and ideological outlooks that both shape and become struggled over in the formations and flows of global news. This chapter provides a map of the major theoretical approaches and debates now structuring the research field and considers their respective contributions for understanding global crisis reporting in a global age, discussed across subsequent chapters.

International communications and media globalization

In broad terms, two overarching research paradigms, one long established in international communications research, the other still emerging in the wider field of media and globalization studies, currently set the parameters for much of the work undertaken in the field of global journalism studies. Each has its own disciplinary antecedents, leading exponents, distinctive ontologies and epistemologies and characteristic research agendas (see Figure 2.1).

Studies within the 'global dominance' paradigm generally work within and update the critical tradition of political economy while those conducted under the 'global public sphere' paradigm represent a more diffuse grouping of recent disciplinary infusions from cultural studies, anthropology and approaches to the global 'network society'. At their respective cores are deep seated differences of theoretical orientation towards international and global communications as well as questions about the mechanisms and meanings of power. Whereas studies conducted under the 'global dominance' paradigm generally approach questions of power in terms of the structures and interests of geopolitical dominance and market determinations rooted in political economy, those coalescing under the 'global public sphere' paradigm tend to pursue the emergence of world cosmopolitan citizenship and a global public sphere theorized in terms of transnational cultural flows, fluids, mobilities and networks (see Figure 1.1). Global dominance theorists are paradigmatically inclined to investigate the operations

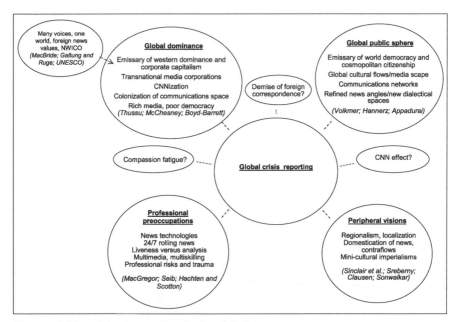

Figure 2.1 Theorizing journalism in the global age

of markets and corporate interests in the structural conditioning of today's cultural industries. Global public sphere theorists, for their part, are disposed to explore the flows of cultural meanings and discourses of identities that circulate around the globe. These essentially different theoretical orientations to global media formations and communication flows have shaped the study of global news.

News media as emissaries of global dominance

Under the global dominance paradigm, researchers generally observe news and journalism through a lens of geopolitical economy that sees transnational media corporations and western-dominated global news agencies positioned by history and market ascendancy to capitalize on contemporary internationalizing market processes (Boyd-Barrett and Rantanen 1998; McChesney 1999; Thussu 2003). In an era of economic liberalization marked by deregulation, privatization and transnational corporate expansion, fuelled in part by the market exploitation of digitalization and new communications delivery technologies (Murdock 1990), processes of media corporate concentration and conglomeration have become exacerbated (McChesney 1999). It is in this context that transnational corporations and regional formations of capital seek to 'colonize communications space' (Boyd-Barrett 1998). From this contemporary political economy perspective the earlier cultural imperialism thesis underlined by the 1974 UNESCO report on international media flows (Nordenstreng and Varis 1974), essentially still holds firm (Schiller 2005) and this is so notwithstanding developed critiques across the years (see Tomlinson 1991, 1999; Sreberny 2000; Mackay 2004).

Continuing in this critical tradition, Daya Thussu (2003) has argued that a 'CNNization' of television news is taking place with leading US and western networks such as CNN and the BBC effectively setting the agenda in the global news market where smaller, regional players monitor their content and adopt their models of production. Rather than contributing to a diversified 'global public sphere', then, new regional news channels represent a universalization of 'US-style' journalism and an increasing homogenization of news structures and content around the world (Thussu 2003). In the context of global war reporting for example, this leads to a form of war reporting described as 'virtual war, live TV and bloodless deaths' – at once democratically impoverishing and ideological:

> There are major implications of infotainment for public-opinion formation and its manipulation, not just within the West but indeed globally, given the extent to which US/UK news organizations can influence news agendas worldwide. . . . Such is the power of US-inspired television that even non-Western networks tend to follow the news agendas set by the West. This is particularly the case during times of conflict. Many regularly and routinely showed the cockpit videos of 'successful' precision bombings, procured through the Pentagon and broadcast

satellite pictures of combat areas acquired through US spy satellites. They seemed to reproduce the war language and the imagery of the Pentagon: the coverage of the 'war on terrorism' in Afghanistan by Star News – India's best known 24 hour news channel – is a case in point. Given that Star News is part of Rupert Murdoch's global media empire, it used live coverage of the war from its sister 24/7 network Fox News, relaying, sometimes in their entirety, Pentagon briefings, as well as jingoistic studio discussions and US government press conferences. (Thussu 2003: 127)

Thussu's critique of the US-dominated global news media is grounded principally in a political economy analysis of the role of market forces, privatized and conglomerate media industries and their production of infotainment in pursuit of viewers, ratings and advertising revenues – determinants that drive these media empires to reach out around the globe to pursue their corporate interests – interests that largely coincide with those of the political centre of US society.

In such ways, these theorists of global news dominance are *sceptical* about the validity of ideas of the 'global' and globalizing news formations and news flows which, more accurately, reflect the relentless capitalist expansion and worldwide 'westernization' (or, for some, 'Americanization') of culture and commerce. Here discourses of globalization are likely to be rejected as little more than an ideological smokescreen concealing the continuing geopolitical realities of western power, corporate interests and neoliberal economics. From this critical vantage point, 'corporate transnationalism' not 'globalism' best describes the 'swelling global flows of the cultural industries' (Schiller 2005), global media are perceived as the new 'missionaries of corporate capitalism' (Herman and McChesney 1997), and western 'rich media' are destined to produce 'poor democracy' around the world (McChesney 1999). In the context of global crisis reporting, this battery of critical arguments and analyses grounded in political economy compels us to consider how the corporate structuration of media formations and world markets will impact on the selection and communication of different global crises.

News media as emissaries of the global public sphere

Global public sphere theorists, for their part, challenge the pessimistic accounts of the geopolitical economists above. Building on Marshall McLuhan's notion of a 'global village' (1964) and refashioning Habermas' well-known concept of the public sphere (1989), Ingrid Volkmer, for example, argues that world satellite news channels are engendering the emergence of a mediated 'global public sphere' (1999, 2003) and thereby laying foundations of cosmopolitan citizenship (Volkmer 2003: 15). CNN, she argues, 'invented a new form of international reporting, which extended the narrow, "national" journalistic concept by including new political contexts and enlarging the political horizon beyond a single-nation-state' (Volkmer 2002: 245). News angles are thus seen to have become 'refined' and CNN is said to have played 'an important role in the global public sphere by reconfiguring journalistic styles and formats' (2002: 245). The complex communications cross-traffic and counterflows around the world today underpins the network society and this helps to constitute 'a new concept of (world) citizenship' (Volkmer 2003: 15). Much is made, for example, of CNNI's 'World Report', a distinctive programme in which journalists from around the world can broadcast their own stories and story angles on CNNI's platform:

> The national 'gatekeeper' role is still exercised by national media outlets today. However, it is increasingly directly paralleled and influenced by the inflow of new transnational news media, reaching not media systems but worldwide 'lifeworlds.' . . . In this advanced and complex stage of the current globalization process, the 'lifeworld universe' seems to become a new space of opposing and contradicting supra- and sub-national, polarized worldviews. . . . These dialectical spaces, which we have not begun to understand, increasingly impact on public participation, notions of political identity and 'citizenship', the agenda of political journalism as well as the formatting of 'news' within the global public sphere. (Volkmer 2003: 15)

Volkmer's emphasis on the news media's contribution to a global cross-traffic of images and ideas and therefore as an important constituent in the development of a global public sphere is surely important and encourages a deeper appreciation of how news can display cultural differences as well as communicate conflicts around the world. The anthropologist Ulf Hannerz similarly observes in a study of contemporary foreign correspondents how a 'conspicuous part of reporting . . . is not devoted to hard news and unique events but to a continuous thematization of difference itself' (Hannerz 2004: 112). Here in-depth news features and the subjunctive style of news writing contribute, he suggests, to 'thick cosmopolitanism' or feelings of being at home within a culturally heterogeneous world. The work of Volkmer, Hannerz and others invites us, therefore, to re-examine the cultural flows of global news and dis-cover to what extent cultural disjunctures and differences are valorized in today's global 'mediascape' (Appadurai 1996), and how global media contribute to a new 'global ecumene' (Hannerz 2004) or sense of global belonging and world citizenship.

For these *globalists*, the contemporary international configuration of news delivery represents real changes in the global news landscape; processes that exemplify the spatial–temporal transformations that are thought to lie at the heart of globalization rather than western market concentration and corporate control. In the context of global crisis reporting these general ideas sensitized to the cultural display of others and the media's enactment of a global public sphere encourages us to consider to what extent and how global crises reporting may embed notions of global citizenship, an ethics of care and politics of collective response.

Peripheral visions and professional preoccupations

The contemporary field of international and global journalism studies also hosts a number of 'peripheral visions' and 'professional preoccupations' that serve to qualify, whether theoretically or on more pragmatic grounds, the generalizing tendencies and global claims of these two overshadowing paradigms.

Peripheral visions

A number of disparate studies collectively termed here 'peripheral visions' (Sinclair et al. 2002) are now beginning to qualify the overarching claims of western media dominance and they also exhibit a more theoretically circumspect or cautious stance towards claims of an emergent global public sphere – whether advanced in the field of news and journalism study or media globalization studies more widely. Included here are studies of new regional media formations and regional media production (Sreberny 2000; Chalaby 2002; Sinclair et al. 2002; Sonwalkar 2004a), contraflows from new regional players (El-Nawaway and Iskander 2003; Azran 2004), discerned 'mini-cultural imperialisms' enacted by former colonies and new regional powers (Sonwalkar 2001, 2004a), the national 'domestication' of news exchange materials and news reports of global events (Cohen et al. 1996; Clausen 2003), and studies of world news audiences (Jensen 2000). Together these open up a host of new dynamics and complexities in the study of global communication formations and news flows.

This more complex, variegated and regionalist perspective, sensitive to the specificities and dynamics of production and flows both within as well as across the international communications environment, qualifies western-led and western-centric accounts of contemporary journalism. Processes of news 'domestication', both in respect of global news exchange materials and their cultural inflection by national broadcasters (Cohen et al. 1996) and processes of national construction of major global events such as the UN's world conference on women (Clausen 2003), for example, point to the constitutive role of culture, not simply commerce, in processes of news mediation and manufacture. Studies of world news audiences also suggest 'varied local cultures manifest themselves in the interpretation of foreign as well as domestic news' and 'culture shines through' in processes of audience news reception (Jensen 2000: 190). These studies seemingly dent, then, presumptions about the western news media's capacity to export ideological frames and impose meanings on local cultures and, in this respect, news remains 'a potential resource for action in a specific time and place' (Jensen 2000: 190).

Prasun Sonwalkar (2001, 2004a) also encourages a less western-centric understanding of today's news media. Post-colonial societies exhibit their own powered geometry in terms of media formations and markets and cannot adequately be theorized through a prism of 'west to the rest' communications:

> In large multicultural settings such as India, for the first time, local cultures and politics are being presented and represented within the country and to the rest of the world in ways that not only enhance local democratisation, a sense of nationalism and regional cohesion, but also a greater awareness and integration with global cultures and global politics ... the proliferation of television since the mid-1980s has further enhanced India's cultural appeal in the region and created commercial opportunities to reach out to the 25 million strong South Asia diaspora across the globe ... at the regional level, Indian cultural industries have the makings of 'little cultural imperialism'. (Sonwalkar 2004a: 112–113)

These disparate studies of contemporary global journalism, each in their own way, contribute to a more multifaceted, less western-led and deterministic theorization and in these respects entertain a more *transformationalist* (Held 2004b) view of the nature of contemporary news organizations, journalist practices, news output and processes of news reception around the globe. None, however, has sought to ignore the market conditioning of political economy or fails to acknowledge something of the democratizing impulses that register in the contraflows and regional dynamics of contemporary media formations. These peripheral visions are nonetheless less inclined on grounds of global complexity, to simply accept totalizing theoretical claims of either western global dominance or global public sphere theorists. In the context of global crisis reporting they also begin to suggest a more complex set of communicative transactions between media organizations, news producers, news sources and news audiences and point to the necessity for engaged empirical studies.

Professional preoccupations and practices

Also informing the academic field of journalism and globalization studies are professional journalist discourses about the changing nature of news production and practices. Here concerns are frequently raised about how new technologies of production and delivery are impacting journalists practices and their professional standing. These professional preoccupations often tend toward the technologically determinist and are generally atheoretical in their conceptualization, contextualization and explanation of changing news processes and performance. Their concerns are normatively framed and frequently point to the changing technologies and infrastructure that are thought to facilitate or restrict the practices and performance of journalists working in international and global contexts. As William Hachten and James Scotton lament in their book, *The World News Prism: Global Information in a Satellite Age*, and following their more mesmerized view of the technological driven change in world news communications that opened this chapter:

> Yet there can be disconcerting side effects. The accelerating speed and efficiency of news media transmission have often created severe strains on the standards and ethics of responsible journalism. The same system can and does report much trivia, sensation, and misinformation. . . . news now breaks 24 hours a day, around the clock, instead of at a more leisurely pace that prevailed before the rise of twenty-four hour cable television news and interactive news on the Internet. As fierce competitors such as MSNBC, the Fox Channel, and CNN with their talk shows have proliferated on cable and online, some news organizations have relaxed their rules on checking and verifying sources. There is a growing sense that getting it first is more important than getting it right. One result is journalism that is sometimes shaky, inaccurate or worse, and with it has come a serious loss of public trust in news media. (Hachten and Scotton 2007: xiv)

These and other professional preoccupations centre on journalism's normative concerns with changing news technologies. They principally comprise the following:

1 the industry's fetish for 'live' 24/7 news facilitated by cable and satellite delivery systems around the globe, and its detrimental impacts on professional standards of journalist reporting
2 the potential of the internet and new online forms of news to undermine, respectively, traditional news forms, the use of accredited sources and established journalist norms of impartiality, detachment and balance
3 the role of mobile telephony and camcorders in the rise of citizen journalism, freelance (often at-risk) war correspondents and underpaid and casualized video journalists
4 the impact of new electronic systems of news production in reconfiguring newsrooms and facilitating multimedia news production and multiskilled (or 'deskilled') journalism.

Changes in news technology, then, are often taken by those in the news industry to be at the heart of processes of professional change, although, as we heard earlier, social theorists are less inclined to interpret such changes solely in terms of technology. Academics have pursued some of them further in ethnographic and systematic studies (for a review see Cottle 2003a, 2007). 'Breaking news' as well as 'live two-ways' and 'hotel stand-ups' are professionally often said to be a poor substitute for in-depth reportage delivered by knowledgeable correspondents based in the field (MacGregor 1997; Seib 2004). Interestingly, a study of BBC World and other 24/7 UK channels put to the test the industry's claim to be providing live, breaking news and systematically documented how, in fact, significant 'breaking news' (that is, up-to-the-moment news and live reporting as the story happens) is something of a rarity on these channels – granting credence to professional concerns over the sacrifice of in-depth news analysis for superficial, content-thin, immediacy (Lewis et al. 2005).

An ethnographic study of the introduction of new production technologies and multiskilling at the BBC has also demonstrated how technological developments in multimedia news production and delivery do not, in and of themselves, dictate corporate policy much less determine how they are incorporated and shaped in professional practice (Cottle 1999; see also Marjoribanks 2000). The introduction of electronic news production systems, video-journalists and increased internet facilities, for example, were all found to be part of the Corporation's management strategy within an increasingly globalized and competitive news environment to reduce costs and maximize efficiency gains as were the introduction of multiskilled, multimedia working practices. It was in this context that professional status, traditional hierarchies, career opportunities and traditional medium demarcations all become unsettled (Cottle 1999: 38–39).

Studies such as these can help to go behind professional and normative concerns about new technologies to reveal something of the complex mediations 'at work'. In the context of global crisis reporting, new technologies, changing journalist practices and new forms of news similarly all need to be explored in context and not presumed to be likely panaceas for former reporting deficiencies (see Livingston and Van Belle 2005). New technologies may nonetheless prove to be powerful allies in improving world communications and supporting global crises awareness. For example, the role of new communication technologies including videophones in raising world attention about humanitarian disasters, internet communications in their subsequent relief coordination, and dedicated websites in providing journalists and others with background information and up-to-the-moment briefings all need to be taken seriously and explored further (Chapter 8). New communication technologies may also, of course, as our illustration of Saddam Hussein's death suggested earlier (Chapter 1), be used less benignly and even as possible weapons in information wars and asymmetric warfare – and this too needs to be explored empirically and theorized in respect of different global crises.

Professional and normative concerns also feature in major debates of considerable relevance to global crisis reporting: the recent demise of foreign correspondence, so-called 'compassion fatigue' and its obverse the 'CNN effect'. The last two debates are discussed in some detail later in the book (Chapter 7), but here it is useful to consider the debate about the demise or changing nature of foreign correspondence in a globalizing journalist context.

The demise of foreign correspondence?

The debate surrounding the demise of foreign correspondence is positioned between the explanatory logic of political economy and global dominance on the one side and new forms of global interconnectedness and claims of an emergent global public sphere on the other (see Figure 2.1). It reflects, in other words, the distinctive 'takes' of surrounding theoretical positions and perspectives and, as we shall encounter across different chapters, these same positions of theory in the field of journalism study surface across different debates and studies of global crisis reporting.

Amidst wider claims of 'dumbing down' in the journalism field are specific concerns about the shrinkage of foreign news both in the press and on TV (Utley 1997; Pew Centre 2002). Garrick Utley, for example, charted the shrinkage of foreign news (specifically, foreign bureau reports, foreign policy coverage and overseas news) over an 8-year period and across the three main US networks, ABC, CBS and NBC, finding that foreign news had generally reduced by half across this period (Utley 1997: 6). More recently, research conducted by the Pew Centre has pointed to the US audience', need for more informed understanding of the world following the attacks of 9/11 (Pew Centre 2002). Systematic studies of international issues in the news and general factual programming in the UK have also documented a decline in the public representation of serious issues over recent decades (DFID 2000; Stone 2000; Dover and Barnett 2004). Foreign coverage in factual programming, for example, is now much more likely to be concerned with wildlife and travel than development, the environment and human rights (Stone 2000). The decline in international journalism documented by Utley and others clearly goes to the heart of concerns about an informed citizenry and its capacity for understanding today's global world, its interdependencies, inequalities and crises.

In this context, so-called 'parachute journalism' is often taken as a poor substitute for correspondents based in countries overseas with their on-the-ground knowledge and source contacts built up over time (Pedelty 1995). Whether political economy explanations accent the 'economic' (based on market imperatives and the economic costs of supporting correspondents overseas) or the 'political' (in terms of the influence of geo-political interests and outlooks inhibiting 'foreign news' reports from politically remote places), these arguments are paradigmatically disposed to see such developments in terms of 'business as usual'. When approached through an optic of globalization seen as intensified interconnectedness and cultural flows, however, a less pessimistic account comes into view:

> But do these perceived declines accurately measure the quantity and quality of foreign reporting that actually exists? We think not. The alarm, we propose, is based on an anachronistic and static model of what foreign correspondence is and who foreign correspondents are. (Hamilton and Jenner 2004: 303)

In a world of increasingly porous borders, Hamilton and Jenner argue, the lines between foreign and domestic news have become blurred, just as they have in the world of commerce, health, culture and the environment. In this interconnected and interpenetrating context, they maintain that 'local reporters can find sources for foreign news among those they interact with daily' (Hamilton and Jenner 2004: 306) and 'the new media landscape that undermines the old news flow structures allows foreign events to be covered in entirely new ways' (p.313). On these grounds, they question the use of numbers of traditional foreign correspondents and even the numbers of 'overseas news stories' as the appropriate yardstick for measuring 'foreign news'.

Clearly they have a point. What does constitute 'foreign' in a globalized world where the former 'outside' is now found on the 'inside' and vice versa? In other words, the mutual interpenetration of cultures and lives, business activities and social relations, commerce and environment does indeed destabilize rigid categories of us and them, inside and outside, either/or. While this may increasingly be so in respect of shared practices and cultural affinities, the territoriality of the world and its state system nonetheless continues to condition and segregate the globe in important respects and here, for example, human rights abuses, forgotten disasters and hidden wars may not be so readily accessed or rendered understandable without journalists on the ground – although to what extent local journalists could provide a similar or better service is, of course, a further consideration to bear in mind (Pedelty 1995).

This debate about foreign correspondence, clearly, has direct relevance for an understanding of global crisis reporting and can only benefit from detailed empirical study in respect of different cases. We shall revisit this issue in some of the substantive chapter discussions that follow.

Emergent new(s) trajectories in the research field

The foregoing has mapped in broad outline the principal paradigms and some of the major theoretical perspectives structuring the field of international and global journalism studies and these, no doubt, will continue to have relevance for understanding the nature and forms of global crisis reporting in the foreseeable future. Before we conclude this part of the discussion however, we can also note some further themes and emergent trajectories of relevance. These concern, first, the representational complexities of news mediation. This includes attending to the imagistic, deliberative and sometimes ritualized forms and expressions of news as well as the political dynamics and contingencies of unfolding crises and how these play out in the media over time, sometimes challenging elite-driven and deterministic models of media performance. Second, we address two recent theoretical statements in the field which discern increased global complexity (and enhanced political opportunities) in the contemporary world of communications and which are theorized, respectively, in terms of 'culture-on-demand' (Lull 2007) and 'cultural chaos' (McNair 2006). Engaged discussion with both these helps to throw into relief what's at stake in contemporary positions of media theory when pitched in terms of a globalizing world and, by extension, in respect of global crisis reporting.

Mediating global crises

Studies conducted under the guiding global dominance and global public sphere paradigms generally pay little attention to how conflicting views and voices are enacted in and through the different communicative forms of journalism and the different opportunities that these receive to make their case and get their message across. Generalizing statements about the emergence of a democratizing 'global public sphere' or its claimed denial by the corporate media's manufacturing of 'poor democracy', for example, require further investigation in respect of particular conflicts and issues and how these are mediated in practice. How global crisis reporting serves to reproduce the voices of the powerful or variously gives vent to the range of views and contention that surround, shape and inform crises clearly constitutes an important, though often overlooked, dimension of the media's role in global crisis reporting. We need, then, to attend much more closely to the communicative forms and differentiated nature of news reporting and how these provide different opportunities for the public elaboration, deliberation and visualization of crises (Cottle and Rai 2006).

The forms of journalism and news reporting arguably take on added significance in late modern societies where traditional beliefs, political institutions and scientific and other authorities and corporations feel compelled to pursue their aims, defend their claims and seek wider legitimacy on the media stage. New social movements, transnational activists and diverse interest groups also now seek out the media in pursuit of wider recognition and public support and they do so in a period of diminishing deference to authorities and a global profusion of migrating ideas, beliefs and values (Giddens 1990, 1994; Castells 1997; Beck 1999). It is in this mediated sphere of vying interests and contention that claims and counter-claims, argument and debate, reason and rhetoric circulate (Benhabib 2002). These constitute an accessible and widespread resource for processes of mediated deliberation, from the local to the global. Lest we should simplistically presume this deliberative resource is something akin to a polite academic seminar, John Dryzek usefully reminds us that in today's globalizing context deliberative democracy is not best conceived, as 'genteel conversation', but is rather a series of embattled fields of contention, insurgency and reflexivity that are local to transnational in scope (Dryzek 2000, 2006). These fields of contention can become focused in respect of different global crises and variously enacted in the media.

We also need to consider the contribution that images as well as ideas, rhetoric as well as reason, affect as well as analysis can play in the public enactment and elaboration of global crises. Spectacular images, dramatic narratives and experiential accounts and emotive testimonies can all lend affective as well as informational force to the media's construction and circulation of global crises. How these become professionally crafted within the structures and appeals of different forms of global crisis reporting demands serious consideration and this will also inform the chapter discussions that follow. In the context of debates about so-called 'compassion fatigue' (Tester 1994; Moeller 1999; Chouliaraki 2006) and its opposite, the 'CNN effect' (Robinson

2002; Gilboa 2005), for example, closer engagement with the range of news forms and their inscribed appeals promises to take us beyond the stalemate of relatively abstract debate (see Chapter 7).

Global crises are also subject to contending political forces and dynamics that unfold across space and time (Wolfsfeld 1997). Too often these dynamics and contingencies of outcome, the *stuff* of politics in action, are marginalized within *a priori* expectations of some variants of media theory. In the context of global crisis reporting, there are now good empirical grounds on which to develop a more dynamic understanding of some of these processual complexities. Recent studies of war reporting (and peace reporting), for example, have become increasingly attuned to the changing nature of reporting through time and in relation to shifts of political and public opinion (Hallin 1986; Wolfsfeld 1997, 2004; Entman 2004; Tumber and Palmer 2004; Murray et al. 2008). In so doing they either implicitly or explicitly challenge relatively static and deterministic accounts of media power including, for example, the propaganda model elaborated in Herman and Chomsky's *Manufacturing Consent* (1988).

The study of global media events and mediatized rituals also challenges entrenched theoretical views about media power, its locations and determinations (Cottle 2006b; Alexander et al. 2006) and points to further complexities that cannot be adequately fathomed through an information-based or 'transmission model' of communications (Carey 1989). Some global crises, as we shall see, exhibit ritualized dimensions and expressions and these can sometimes open up productive spaces for social reflexivity, political critique and even dissent within civil and wider societies (Cottle 2006b). The media's performative use of resonate symbols, dramatic scenes, personalized narratives and embedding of emotions and public performances can sometimes confront the strategic power of institutions and vested interests and may even lend moral gravitas to the claims of victims and challenger groups within society. Mediated disasters, whether Hurricane Katrina or the Asian tsunami for example, can threaten to turn into politically disruptive globalized media events and the nature of their unfolding media coverage could not always be predicted in advance (discussed in Chapter 3).

How these, and other, major media events become circulated and consumed, contested and challenged in the global flows and forms of journalism and with what impact on political elites and the formations of publics around the world, therefore, are questions of considerable relevance for the study of global crises reporting.

Theorizing contingency and complexity

Imagistic, deliberative and sometimes ritualized forms of journalism's reporting as well as the unpredictable outcomes of political contention played out on the ground (and, increasingly, in and through today's complex global news ecology) all point to a situation of complexity and, possibly, more political opportunities than has been generally recognized and theorized within the field of media and communications – until recently.

James Lull's *Culture-on-Demand: Communication in a Crisis World* (Lull 2007) argues that a combination of powerful globalizing forces – most related to the advance of new communication technologies – have created new conditions for global dialogue and enhanced cultural understanding across the world's divides. These propitious conditions, he suggests, include today's unprecedented access to different cultural forms, global connectivity, temporal and spatial flexibility, creativity and hybridity, immediacy of experience, digitization of communication and cultural forms, and an expanded range of personal communication options (Lull 2007: 84). Together these help to create a highly individualized 'cultural pull', in contrast to a top-down or corporate 'cultural push', and this, argues Lull, bodes well for the development of a more human and less adversarial or conflictual world of communication and cultural understanding. Lull identifies the existence of religious, national and market fundamentalisms as the principal crisis in world communication that 'militate against the cosmopolitan promise of the Communication Age' (p.187) but, ultimately, this does not dent his optimistic view of global communications in the 21st century:

> In the search for whatever common bonds of humanity we might call upon to bring us together more and achieve greater social justice, a broad commitment to promoting greater cultural understanding will be essential. The pen ultimately may not be stronger than the sword when push comes to shove in geopolitical struggles, but cultural transparency, expanded awareness, global public opinion, and the counter-hegemonic force of symbolic power in general have become influences that no nation, religion, culture or high-profile leader, no matter how dominant or confident, can ignore. . . . The open spaces of global communication promise not unity, but opportunity for meaningful dialogue and the nurturance of the global public sphere. (Lull 2007: 168–169)

Lull's ideas clearly demonstrate an affinity with the global public sphere theorists referenced earlier, although his concern with fundamentalist beliefs and practices, and the crisis of world communication that they pose, possibly grounds his claims for enhanced forms of media deliberation and dialogue more firmly in present conflicts. Theorized at the level of culture, however, his thesis tends to underestimate the continuing structuration of media and the output of media industries in terms of political economy arguments of global dominance, peripheral visions of regional media formations and dynamics, as well as professional media practices and news production. And it also has little to say about the range of global threats now confronting humanity, their unequal impacts and forms of mediation.

Brian McNair's *Cultural Chaos: Journalism, News and Power in a Globalized World* (McNair 2006) also sets out to examine the changing world of global journalism but this is now theorized in terms of radical indeterminacy, rather than 'culture-on-demand'. His importation of chaos theory into the field of journalism scholarship (explicitly prefigured in the work of Appadurai 10 years earlier) (see Appadurai 1996: 46), reads as a frontal assault on what he terms as the dominant 'control paradigm' (exemplified, for example, by Herman and Chomsky's *Manufacturing Consent* and their propaganda model). Specifically, he challenges three fundamental premises: (1) 'the reproduction of capitalist societies requires ideological control', (2) 'the media are a key ideological apparatus in the control of ruling elites' and (3) the 'media are effective in generating variants of false consciousness, not least in times of war and global conflict' (McNair 2006: 34). Contrary to the control paradigm and its under-pinning premises, McNair counterposes a model of multi-causality, contingencies, feedback loops and unpredictability:

A *chaos model*, on the other hand, approaches features of content such as plurality of opinion and dissent not as aberrations but as the manifestations of external environmental factors working on the journalistic production process; the unplanned outcomes of a combination of many factors and forces, acting independently of one another. . . . From this perspective news is not manufactured (neither, therefore, is consent), nor is it 'constructed'. Nor does it just happen. It *emerges* from the interacting elements of the communication environment which prevails in a given space. (McNair 2006: 48–49)

In the context of global crisis reporting specifically, McNair's model suggests therefore:

[W]hile the desire for control of the news agenda, and for definitional power in the journalistic construction of meaning, are powerful and ever-present, not least in time of war and perceived global crisis, the capacity of elite groups to wield it is effectively more limited than it has been since the emergence of the first news media in the sixteenth century. (McNair 2006: 4)

McNair's thesis reads as a provocative challenge to those who continue to see journalism as a powerful tool that is routinely bent by the dictates and discourses of the powerful. In the context of this study with its concern with global crisis reporting, his theorizing also suggests that matters of representation may be less closed and controlled than previously assumed. His characterization of the 'control paradigm', however, runs the risk of perpetuating its own reductionism in that it tends to carica-ture a field that is far more theoretically differentiated and a little more sophisticated than suggested. As we have already heard in the context of global journalism studies, this field cannot accurately be reduced to a simple paradigmatic binary of 'control' versus McNair's 'cultural chaos' but, in fact, provides a range of theoretical, political and epistemological approaches and perspectives (see also Cottle 2006a: 13–32).

The generalizing claims of radical indeterminacy, couched in the terms of chaos theory, where news *emerges* from a system of interacting elements within a shared communications environment, rather than being manufactured or constructed, also tends to suggest a weightless equivalence of interacting elements within a depoliticized communications environment. This flies in the face of countless studies documenting how cultures and contexts of news production and surroundings fields of source contention are far more powered and unequally weighted than this rather benign view of the journalism field tends to suggest. And nor can we afford to theoretically eclipse the continuing reality of market determinations and other systemic imperatives routinely conditioning the selection and shaping of news stories from afar.

In the context of global crisis reporting, as suggested by the preceding discussion, we need to be more sharply attuned to the continuing systems of constraint and corporate imperatives as well as the dynamic play of strategic interests and operations of power and how all become infused in the practices and performance of media production and output. We need, in other words, to investigate complexity, causality and contingency in engaged studies situated in specific empirical contexts. Or, in more traditional sociological parlance, we need to attend to both structures and agency and their mutual interpenetration and conditioning within the field of global journalism. To do so, however, we need to do more than proclaim a new theoretical paradigm; we need to engage empirically and analytically as well as theoretically and conceptually with the complexity of different global crises and their processes of news mediation. Brian McNair's thesis, nonetheless, provides a valuable point of reference. It encourages us to reconsider established theoretical premises and presumptions and to engage with the world of contemporary journalism in a more open-minded way, sensitized to the possibility that complexities and contingencies, as well as market determinations and strategic dynamics of power, are all likely to be at work and that representational outcomes cannot always be theoretically predicted in advance.

The positions of social and media theory, discussed earlier, prove useful if we are to engage in an informed and analytically focused way with the complexities of global crisis reporting. Wherever possible, however, these same positions of theory need to be put to empirical test and refined, revised or possibly rejected on the basis of their analytical and explanatory purchase on the contemporary media field, including global crisis reporting. Before we can conclude that global journalism is best theorized, for example, as a medium of embryonic global dialogue and cultural understanding brought about by generalized processes of 'cultural pull' or represents the outcome of 'cultural chaos', a radical indeterminism of 'emergence' rather than causality and predictable mechanisms of power, we really need to get down to cases and explore the complexities involved.

The chapters that follow, which are based on discussion of different global crises and the findings of a wide range of research studies, aim to provide a more closely engaged and empirically encompassing understanding of global crisis reporting. Together they help to reveal something of the multiple complexities, causalities and multidimensionality of global crisis reporting today and how different crises are variously constructed, communicated and contested in and through the world's news media.

3

(UN)NATURAL DISASTERS: THE CALCULUS OF DEATH AND THE RITUALIZATION OF CATASTROPHE

Climatic disasters are on the increase as the Earth warms up – in line with scientific observations and computer simulations that model future climate. 2007 has been a year of climatic crises, especially floods, often of an unprecedented nature. They included Africa's worst floods in three decades, unprecedented flooding in Mexico, massive floods in South Asia and heat waves and forest fires in Europe, Australia, and California. By mid November the United Nations had launched 15 'flash appeals', the greatest ever number in one year. All but one were in response to climatic disasters.

At the same time as climate hazards are growing in number, more people are being affected by them because of poverty, powerlessness, population growth, and the movement and displacement of people to marginal areas. The total number of natural disasters has quadrupled in the last two decades – most of them floods, cyclones, and storms. Over the same period the number of people affected by disasters has increased from around 174 million to an average of over 250 million a year. Small- and medium-scale disasters are occurring more frequently than the kind of large-scale disasters that hit the headlines. (Oxfam 2007)

So-called 'natural disasters' in the context of anthropogenic climate change are increasingly known to be *un*natural phenomena, the product of what Ulrich Beck calls the 'manufactured uncertainties' of global risk society (Beck 1999). That is, they are the unintended consequences of late modernity, with its rapacious pursuit of economic growth and production of unintended environmental risks. We shall examine the media's changing relationship to the global crisis of climate change in the following chapter. But extreme weather events and the human disasters they cause can also be considered *un*natural in the more socially proximate sense that the term 'natural disaster' is really a misnomer for the ways in which extreme weather events and other hazards are collectively anticipated, prepared for and responded to. In this sense, 'disasters' represent the failures to deal with hazards and are therefore contingent on the social structures and relations that mediate them and the available resources directed at their prevention, mitigation and response. John Holmes, United Nations Under-Secretary-General for Humanitarian Affairs and Emergency Relief Coordinator, and Markku Niskala, Secretary General of the International Federation of the Red Cross and Red Crescent Societies, usefully elaborate:

> Risk reduction aims to reduce the odds of disastrous consequences by doing everything possible before the event to protect life, limit damage and strengthen a vulnerable community's ability to survive and to bounce back quickly. The solution may lie in simple things like educating children on what to do in emergencies or planting trees on unstable hillsides to prevent landslides. The more complex include early warning systems, earthquake-safe construction, and responsible urban planning.
>
> The point here is that there is no such thing as a natural disaster. Floods, hurricanes, cyclones, typhoons, heat waves, droughts, even non-climate-related events like earthquakes, are natural hazards. They become disasters only when they exceed a community's ability to cope.
>
> Natural hazards and the disasters they trigger hit all countries and communities, rich and poor, but it is the poor people who usually live in the most exposed and dangerous places and whose lives will be most seriously disrupted by calamity. They become poorer, deprivation deepens. (Holmes and Niskala 2007: 2; see also UNEP, APELL 2007; (http://www.unep.fr/pc/apell/disasters/lists/nat_diaster.htm)

As these opening observations suggest, so-called 'natural disasters' are, in fact, complexly dependent on and are increasingly seen as determined by the human world and in these senses can often be taken as *un*natural (we shall deal specifically with climate change in Chapter 4). Disasters, in this context, are profoundly socially produced phenomena and this is no less so in terms of their social construction within the news media. As Jonathan Benthall (1993) observed in *Disasters, Relief and the Media*:

> [T]he coverage of disasters by the press and media is so selective and arbitrary that, in an important sense, they 'create' a disaster when they decide to recognize it. To be more precise, they give institutional endorsement or attention to bad events which otherwise have a reality restricted to a local circle of victims. Such endorsement is a prerequisite for the marshalling of external relief and reconstructive effort. The endorsement is not decided by some mysterious Moloch but by quite small numbers of professional editors and reporters, whose decisions on whether or not to apply the 'hallmark' of recognition can have far-reaching chains of consequences, both positive and negative. (Benthall 1993: 11–12)

This first substantive chapter about global crisis reporting begins by examining recent patterns of western news disaster coverage, mapping its salient contours and silences and observing the disproportionate coverage that some disasters receive, no matter the scale of loss of life and human suffering involved. This raises profound questions about western news predilections and news agendas and the operation of a professional 'calculus of death' or the routine professional judgments made about the differing newsworthiness of death, destruction and human suffering around the world. We shall explore this further with the help of academic studies that have analyzed the role of geopolitical interests, national cultural outlooks and 'foreign news values' involved.

The second part of the chapter then moves to explore more qualitatively some of the representational complexities and political dynamics that also characterize major mediated disasters. Specifically, we consider the powerfully ritualized forms of some disaster reporting and how these embed and communicate public emotions of grief and empathy, invite public performances and variously invoke a sense of moral solidarity, imagined community and nationhood. In such ways, some disasters are not simply being relayed and reported or 'mediated', they are in fact being publicly enacted and media propelled, that is, 'mediatized' (Cottle 2006b). With the help of further examples, the chapter then explores how some disasters play out differently, unfolding across time and space and providing opportunities for discursive contention and even, on occasion, political dissent. The discussion illustrates how mediated disasters can, in fact, open up opportunities for political challenge and opposition on the national and international media stage and are, therefore, far more contingent and politically unpredictable than studies wedded to static notions of 'news values' or even the operation of geopolitical interests may allow. Today's international communication flows and complex global news ecology (see Figure 1.1) are found to play an increasingly important part in reconfiguring disaster communications as well as the social relations of communicative power embedded within them.

Geopolitics and the calculus of death

To begin, we first need to get some empirical purchase on how the news media cover disasters. A recent study, *Western Media Coverage of Humanitarian Disasters* (CARMA 2006) helps here, providing basic findings that generally endorse those from earlier research (Galtung and Ruge 1965; Harrison and Palmer 1986; Benthall 1993; Philo 1993; Minear et al. 1996; Rotberg and Weiss 1996; Allen and Seaton 1999; Moeller 1999; Bacon and Nash 2000, 2002; IFRCRCS 2005; Seaton 2005a, b). Based on a systematic analysis of press reporting in Europe, the US and Australia, including 64 daily and weekly publications and a sample of 1967 articles, the CARMA study compares the reporting of six recent major disasters. These comprise the Pakistan Kashmir earthquake (8 October 2005), Hurricane Stanley in Guatemala (1 October 2005), Hurricane Katrina (23 August 2005), the Indian Ocean tsunami

(26 December 2004), the earthquake in Bam, Iran (26 December 2003), and the humanitarian crisis in Darfur, Sudan (February 2003–2005). The period of analysis ranged from 2 days prior to the disaster to 10 weeks following with the exception of Darfur which, because of extremely low news coverage and an indistinct beginning, was sampled between 2003 and 2005 or 150 weeks. The CARMA report proves disquieting reading.

Of the six humanitarian disasters analysed, Hurricane Katrina and Hurricane Stanley caused the fewest deaths (circa 1300) and Katrina had one of the lowest population displacement figures and yet Katrina received far more media coverage than any other disaster, representing 50% of the entire sample. When Hurricane Stanley hit Guatemala a few weeks later, in contrast to Katrina, it hardly registered at all in the news media sample and quickly disappeared from news attention after initial news reports. The Kashmir earthquake attracted similar media interest to the earthquake in Bam though causing 3.5 times as many deaths (90,000). The tsunami had twice the coverage of Darfur (notwithstanding the extended sample frame of the latter) though both generated a similar death toll (circa 180,000). A principal finding of the CARMA report, then, is that 'there appears to be no link between the scale of a disaster and media interest in the story' (p.6).

The report also argues that 'economics is a better guide to press interest than human suffering' (p.6). Seventeen per cent of articles relating to Katrina, for example, were found to concentrate on economic issues. The tsunami also seemingly attracted news attention in part due to its economic impact on the global tourist industry and the involvement of foreign nationals. The countries whose press coverage is analysed in the CARMA report only accounted for 0.5% (903) of the total number of confirmed tsunami fatalities (174,542) and yet no less than 40% of all coverage on people impacted by the disasters focused on these western victims. Even more closely correlated to press interest than perceived economic interests is geopolitics however, which the report suggests determines the timing, level of interest and story angle of disaster reporting. The report concludes: 'Western self-interest is the pre-condition for significant coverage of a humanitarian crisis' (p.5).

These findings from the CARMA report, based on a systematic and comparative analysis of press coverage, generally reinforce findings from earlier studies and point to the continuing patterns of salience and silence that characterize western disaster reporting. An Australian study that includes discussion of television coverage as well as radio and press, documents further patterns and insights. *News/Worthy*, a study by Wendy Bacon and Chris Nash (2002) is based on a systematic analysis of news output, selected cases studies of emergency reporting as well as more qualitative examination of NGO interactions with the news media. Among its principal summary findings are the following:

- The news media tend to focus on a few stories at any one time. Tightly focused, intensive coverage is the norm rather than the exception.

- Television concentrates even more intensively on a small number of stories than does radio or print. Saturation coverage of the biggest stories is becoming the norm, squeezing out coverage of other major stories.
- Disaster stories are more prominent on television than in print and on radio, which reflects the television news preference for dramatic images.
- The concentrated news agenda means that very few stories are covered at any one time. Some geographical patterns revealed in this study partly reflect the big stories of the time which in turn reflect contemporary global conflict and disasters. However, some parts of the world are consistently covered less than others. Editors noted there was a 'cultural adjustment' made in the coverage of disasters that favoured the United States and Europe.
- Only a few major disasters receive any more than a passing mention in the media.
- Even when a major disaster is covered, the role of human causes such as dam construction, poor farming practices, pollution, underlying poverty and lack of resources are only occasionally mentioned, let alone examined in depth. (Bacon and Nash 2002: 9–16)

Similar findings have generally been documented across a number of different studies (Harrison and Palmer 1986; Philo 1993; Minear et al. 1996; Rotberg and Weiss 1996; Bacon and Nash 2002; IFRCRCS 2005). They should cause pause for thought. A terrible 'calculus of death' has seemingly become institutionalized and normalized in the professional judgments, practices and news values of the western media, a calculus based on crude body counts and thresholds as well as proximities of geography, culture and economics (Galtung and Ruge 1981; Benthall 1993; Allen and Seaton 1999; Moeller 1999; Seaton 2005b). This 'calculus of death' surfaces in journalist accounts of professional news practices and thinking as well as patterns of news coverage.

Susan Moeller in her book *Compassion Fatigue: How the Media Sell Disease, Famine, War and Death* (1999), for example, records how US journalists provide various 'equations' for determining which crises to cover and which to ignore. Offered in tongue-in-cheek ways they nonetheless point to an underlying professional outlook, that can indeed be termed 'the professional calculus of death'. Consider:

At the *Boston Globe*, 'it was a figure of about 2.43 and divide the number of bodies from the miles to the Boston Common. I can't remember if it was the numerator or the denominator but if it was over 2.43 it was a page one story,' joked former foreign correspondent Tom Palmer. You also have to put the GNP of the country into the formula. 'For example, if it's Japan, that cuts the mileage in half.' More simply, said Ted Koppel, 'The closer to home that a crisis strikes, the more likely it is to get attention.' . . . 'Is it a place Americans know about? Travel to? Have relatives in? Have business in? Is the military going there? You are not going to get on page one with something about Bangladesh nearly as much as you do with something about some country where your readers have some kind of connection.' (Moeller 1999: 21)

Nick Pollard, head of Sky News when the Asian tsunami hit on Boxing Day 2004, offers further reflections on the professional thinking and dilemmas informing such journalistic judgments in his published 'diary of a disaster' (Pollard 2005). His account is interesting because it reveals something of the sensitivity and reflexivity exhibited by some journalists toward the 'calculus of death' in the very moment that it becomes enacted.

> Even on that Boxing Day morning an issue is emerging that needs serious thought and sensitive handling – the balance between Western and local casualties. Probably because of its highly developed tourist industry, the most detailed early accounts of the story emerge from the coast of Thailand bear Phuket, a magnet for British and Western tourists, particularly in the middle of Europe's winter. There are obviously going to be British deaths, maybe dozens or even hundreds of them. That would be a big story in itself, but how should we balance that against the likelihood, the certainty in fact, of how far, far more local people perishing? We'll find ourselves returning to this issue again and again in the next few days. (Pollard 2005: 8)

Disaster relief agencies such as the International Federation of the Red Cross and Red Crescent Societies also observe how 'editors routinely sort stories with the crude question: "How many dead?"' and note that disasters 'that are baffling get less attention' and disasters 'that are unusual yet explicable and cause a significant amount of death, injury or destruction in accessible places' and which 'the audience is believed to care about get covered' (IFRCRCS 2005: 128). These professional comments, endorsing the news media's normally unstated 'calculus of death', lend support to claims made in an influential academic study over forty years ago. A study of 'foreign news values' by Joanne Galtung and Marie Ruge (1965) has proved to have continuing explanatory relevance in the field of international news study and helps to account for the professional calculus of death and influence of geopolitical outlooks in disaster reporting (Galtung and Ruge 1965, reprinted in Cohen and Young 1981; Tumber 1999).

Based on an analysis of the Norwegian press coverage of crises in the Congo (1960), Cuba (1960) and Cyprus (1964), Galtung and Ruge identified a number of news selection criteria that seemed to account for the inclusion of certain foreign news stories and not others insofar as these satisfied the conditions of:

1) Frequency	7) Continuity
2) Threshold	8) Composition
3) Unambiguity	9) Reference to elite nations
4) Meaningfulness	10) Reference to elite people
5) Consonance	11) Reference to persons
6) Unexpectedness	12) Reference to something negative

(Galtung and Ruge 1965)

The inclusion of foreign news stories based on these professional judgments about news values appears to help explain the selection, salience and silences of disaster reporting around the world. The 'negativity' of disasters and their sudden occurrence as 'events' rather than say longer term processes of recovery or development coincides with the known predisposition of news encapsulated in such clichés as 'bad news is good news' and 'if it bleeds it leads', and also the production cycles of news. The 'unexpectedness' of disasters especially when punching through the news 'threshold' of scale and numbers also means that bigger disasters are generally speaking more newsworthy though this, as we have already heard, can also be qualified by the news media's geopolitical orientation and its interest in 'elite nations' and 'elite people'. And disaster stories are also selected and conditioned by their perceived 'consonance', 'meaningfulness', 'unambiguity' and 'continuity' with pre-existent news interests and surrounding cultural values and interests. Finally, the 'composition' or routine patterns of different types of news story as well as their inclusion of 'person'-based or human interest stories can also condition when and how disasters get covered.

Joanne Galtung and Marie Ruge's early study, then, continues to help explain 'how events become news' and also underscores the importance of journalism seen as a process of social construction. This said, their list of news criteria can also have the unintended consequence of concealing, as well as revealing, important factors and dynamics at work in the reporting of global crises. It is not clear, for example, to what extent their proposed list of news criteria actually selects possible news stories or rather becomes infused in their representation through processes of journalistic treatment once selected. There may, in practice, be much more going on behind the scenes that can account for processes of news selection especially when conducted in an extensively networked and commercialized news environment and in interaction with competing news sources (see Chapters 4 and 8). These behind-the-scene processes and practices are not readily apparent or recoverable from simply 'reading' patterns of foreign news coverage, including disaster stories. The assumption that news is 'event' driven in conformity to the daily frequency of news output also possibly speaks to an earlier period of journalism and may be less relevant in world where 24/7 news provision and ongoing news narratives not simply news events characterize much of today's news output. Some forms of news journalism are also evidently capable of producing background features and in-depth analyses or may even be driving the news agenda, rather than simply selecting and responding to major events. Tony Harcup and Deirdre O'Neill (2001) further suggest that Galtung and Ruge's 'reference to elite nations' should now be subsumed under a much wider category of 'relevance to readers' given that tourist destinations, not necessarily elite nations, now have added news value for many readers and 'reference to elite people' could also now more plausibly be refined and disaggregated into elite organizations and institutions as well as celebrities (Harcup and O'Neill 2001: 277–278).

Much has changed, evidently, in the world of news reporting since Galtung and Ruge's first proposed their list of foreign news values and helped to focus attention on the social construction of news and our mental image of important world events, including foreign disaster reporting. There are further levels of complexity and contingency which now also need to be taken into account and theorized – discussed next.

The ritualization of catastrophe and the politics of despair

The preceding discussion has documented some of the general research findings that have mapped the basic parameters of disaster coverage, its geopolitical contours and informing calculus of death. As suggested, however, this is not the complete story by any means. The world of journalism, as well as the nature of global crises, is fast changing and researchers are becoming increasingly aware of further levels of complexity. One of these is the different ways in which news reports of disasters play out as scenarios over time:

> All told, the media attention span is limited to about one week after the first sensation, no matter if there is a short quake or a long-ranging flood. After the initial sensation, the second day marks the climax of media commotion. Camera teams have had the time to fly in and put their cameras into position. In subsequent days, the interest abates step by step. Images repeat themselves and no longer raise the same attention. (Media Tenor Journal 2006: 26–27)

Based on an analysis of US and German TV news coverage this particular study documents how the coverage of the Pakistan earthquake in 2005 and the US reporting on the Central European floods in 2002 conformed to this typical weekly news cycle (Media Tenor Journal 2006: 26). However, it also observes how some news disasters depart from this general scenario, generating a number of coverage peaks and building to further media climaxes after the flurry of initial media interest. The German television news coverage of the Elbe River floods in 2002, for example, climaxed with considerably more stories on both the third and fifth day than the first two days of reporting with further peaks on day eight and ten. Interestingly, this major flood in the heart of Europe barely registered in the US TV news networks. The German TV coverage of Hurricane Katrina, in contrast, following an initial delayed reaction, quickly gathered momentum and then produced four or five discernible peaks over a 5-week period, broadly mirroring the extensive US coverage across the same period.

Explaining these different scenarios of disaster coverage, the report states: 'Mega-disasters, which pass a certain attention threshold of around 30 news stories per day have repercussions on the political and societal debate, and in turn the debate itself becomes a focus of coverage' (Media Tenor Journal 2006: 26). Here we may want to query the exact relationship between the news media and the wider political debate and ask whether or under what conditions the news media may follow or lead political debate (see Chapter 7). And so too do we need to go behind the seeming magical threshold of 'around 30 news stories per day' that points to wider political repercussions and ask what generates this political response. We can nonetheless acknowledge that some disasters stories certainly appear to gain increased political animus through time. In such moments, as we shall hear, heavily mediated disasters can become politicized and may even tip over into full-blown mediatized political scandals.

Before we investigate the politically disruptive capacity of some mediated disasters, however, we can first observe how some disasters are subject to heavily ritualized forms of communication. Here disasters are presented not only extensively but also *intensively* and inscribed with emotion and appeals to a sense of imagined community in response to the tragedy and trauma of the disaster (Cottle 2006b; Pantti and Wahl-Jorgensen 2007; Riegert and Olsson 2007). On such occasions considerably more is being communicated, then, than the latest body counts, the facts of destruction or even the analysis of what went wrong. In such moments journalism is not simply functioning as a 'transmission model' relaying information, rational accounts and dispassionate analysis but is communicating expressively and in the way of a 'ritual model', affirming collective bonds of support and moral solidarity, inviting appropriate public performances and appealing to a sense of shared community (Carey 1989) – as illustrated next.

The South Asian tsunami: rituals of solidarity and the 'Cruel Sea'

The South Asian tsunami of December 2004 was caused by an underground earthquake in the Indian Ocean off the coast of Aceh on the northern Indonesian island of Sumatra. The devastating waves led to massive destruction and an estimated loss of over 200,000 lives across coastal regions of Indonesia, Thailand, Burma, India, Sri Lanka, Maldives, Somalia and Seychelles. The sheer scale of the devastation and multiple countries and regions affected positioned it as a major humanitarian crisis and it became reported, as we have already heard, through the geopolitical outlooks and informing professional calculus of death of the western news media. But *how* exactly it was reported and represented demands further exploration.

The world's press, as may have been anticipated from the preceding discussion, initially focused on the death and destruction caused by the tsunami, and noticeably fixated on the ever rising death toll, as these typical frontpage headlines suggest:

Deathwave. Death Toll 9,500 and counting. India 3,200' (*The Indian Express*, 27.12.04)

Wave of Destruction. World's Biggest Earthquake for Forty Years Devastates Asia. Wall of Water 10 Meters High Inundates Popular Tourist Resort. Toll passes 7,500 with Sri Lanka, India and Indonesia the Worst Hit (*South China Morning Post*, 27.12.04)

Toll Tops 24,000 as Disease Fears Grow (*The Age*, 28.12.04)

Toll in Undersea Earthquake Passes 26,000. A Third of the Dead are said to be Children (*The New York Times*, 28.12.07)

After the Destruction, The Grief. Tsunami Death Toll Climbs to 25,000, 30,000 Missing on Remote Indian Islands, Disease Fears as Huge Relief Effort Launched' (*The Guardian*, 28.12.04)

In the calculations of death, however, newspapers also sought to provide background and analysis of what exactly had happened, many providing elaborate maps charting the course of the destructive waves and their devastating impact on different islands and coastal communities. Prominent among this coverage was a concerted effort to relay first-person accounts, bearing witness and providing graphic testimonies of the death and destruction caused by the tsunami. News articles under first-person headlines such as the following were common: 'How paradise turned to hell' (*The Age* 27.12.04), 'Suddenly we heard this loud rumbling noise' (*The Guardian* 27.12.07) and 'I was being swept out to sea, I felt afraid, powerless' (*The Indian Express*, 27.12.04).

According to Mervi Pantti and Karin Wahl-Jorgensen (2007) the 'discourse of horror' that accompanies initial disaster reports is about 'bearing witness and giving testimony to the carnage' (Pantti and Wahl-Jorgensen 2007: 13) and they quote John Langer who comments: 'Victims become more authentically sympathetic and worthy of our "reflex of tears" when an ordinary person located in the real world, rather than someone from the potentially manipulative world of professional newsmakers, can guarantee the details of misfortune' (John Langer cited in Pantti and Wahl-Jorgensen 2007: 13) (see Image 3.1).

As time moved on, national newspapers also reported on their government's relief responses. *The Age*, in Australia, for example, produced headlines such as: 'Federal aid up by $35m "with more to come" ' (*The Age* 30.12.05) and 'Canberra steps up help for Indonesia' (*The Age*, 31.12.07). But it was the involvement of their own nationals, predominantly tourists killed and missing, which preoccupied the press in countries such as Australia. 'Fears rise for thousands of missing tourists' (*The Age*, 28.12.07), 'A jet ski in the lobby, a shark in the pool' (*The Age* 28.12.07), 'For a ruptured family, the net recovers a toddler believed lost in the waves', 'Holiday trip turns into horror ride' (*The Age*, 30.12.07), 'Waiting and hoping for a phone call that never comes' (*The Age*, 31.12.07). We hear in such headlines not simply news interest in involved nationals *en masse*, but the deliberate attempt to provide personalized stories and emotive accounts encouraging identification and empathy with the plight and suffering of *their* national victims. Everyday, taken-for-granted, objects and technologies – phones, computers, the net and even a jet ski incongruously found in a swimming pool (alongside a shark) – can all help to relay added poignancy and gravitas in the aftermath of disaster, the visible signs of ordinary lives shattered and/or the desperate attempts to reconstitute normality and relocate lost loved ones.

Such news reporting, then, generally conforms to geopolitical outlooks and the

Image 3.1 'After the Devastation the Grief' *The Guardian*, 28 December 2004 (© Guardian News & Media Ltd 2004, Photo: Arko Datta/Reuters/Picture Media)

professional calculus of death already discussed but, as we can also detect in these headlines, the press is also making a concerted effort to invoke something of the perceived human reality of these same events and their aftermath. It does so through the deliberate embedding of personal experiences and accounts of the tragedy of lives cut short and families wrenched apart by the destructive force of nature (see Image 3.1). Catastrophe produces death, destruction and disruption and generates a profound sense of dislocation. It is a moment outside of normal time and space and becomes marked in the media through intensive and extensive forms of news reportage – a liminal period that ritualistically contains possibilities of emergence and the reassertion of social 'structure' and 'communitas' (Turner 1982). Mediated disasters, as we have heard, are often reported in terms of established news scenarios.

After the initial disaster and aftermath reports, reporters soon began to emphasize the bonds of community and solidarity born of adversity as well as sympathetic responses from distant countries and communities (see Image 3.2). In such ways newspapers provided a moral infusion into the wasted human landscape, seeking out and celebrating the selfless and heroic acts of survivors and rescuers as well as publicizing collective forms of solidarity embodied in institutional relief efforts, charity donations and the symbolic actions of elites. Collectively such stories recolonized space and place momentarily lost to the amoral (immoral) forces of nature anthropomorphized in the media in terms of 'The Cruel Sea' (*International Express*, 4–10.1.05), 'Deadly sea, brutal and indiscriminate' (28.12.04) and 'Nature's fury' (*The Courier Mail*, 7.1.05).

This public valorization of moral community found expression through a succession of newspaper articles and features with headlines and captions such as: 'Britain unites to help victims', '£1 Million Raised in One Hour After Tidal Wave disaster', 'Generous Britons pledge to help victims' (*International Express*, 4–10.1.05); 'Friendship blossoms in the rubble, Indonesia, Australia closer' (*The Sydney Morning Herald*, 5.1.05), 'Aid forges closer links', 'Generosity worldwide amazes UN' and 'We're in for the long haul, Howard tells Indonesians' (*The Courier Mail*, 7.1.05).

In the aftermath of catastrophic disasters politicians and other elites invariably go on 'media parade', symbolically positioning themselves among the carnage and devastation, conducting walkabouts and meeting survivors and commending emergency services and relief workers on their professionalism and heroic efforts – all in front of news cameras. The Australian Prime Minister, John Howard, meeting the Indonesian president and pledging his country's support, is one such example of symbolic solidarity (see Image 3.2).

In such moments, elites are obligated to publicly demonstrate their personal concern as well as active agency in 'taking charge' and restoring normality. Such symbolic images, then, encode relations of social hierarchy and power at the same time as they proclaim to represent collective solidarity and community compassion. Ordinary people, as we have heard, are also afforded enhanced news presence in mediated disasters and these are often allocated moral roles in the news media's preferred *personae dramatis* and scripts of mediated disasters (see Image 3.3). An article headlined,

← 6 thecouriermail.com.au The Courier-Mail Friday, January 7, 2005→

 Nature's fury

We're in for the long haul, Howard tells Indonesians

I HAVE just personally conveyed to President Yudhoyono the condolences and genuine sympathy of the Australian people to the people of Indonesia for the appalling loss of life and terrible suffering from the disastrous impact of this great natural disaster.

No country has suffered more than Indonesia. The loss of life will probably never be accurately calculated, and I have personally conveyed to him on behalf of the Government and the people of Australia how much we had sprung to our hearts for what had occurred to his people.

I'm able to announce what is a historic step in relations between Australia and Indonesia in the wake of this terrible natural disaster which has inflicted such suffering and destruction on the people of Indonesia.

I can announce an Australian-Indonesian Partnership for the Reconstruction and Development.

It will involve the largest single aid package in Australia's history – $1 billion will be made available in an aid package to involve the reconstruction and development of Indonesia. It will be made up of $500 million in grants and $500 million in concessional loans.

The grants will be used for more short-term restorative projects,

This is an edited transcript of the press conference at which Prime Minister John Howard announced $1 billion in aid for tsunami victims

the longer-term development projects.

The program will be administered by a joint commission which will be overseen by President Yudhoyono and myself.

Our foreign ministers – and in each case no economic minister – will ensure that the program proceeds smoothly. There will be a joint secretariat which will comprise people from both countries.

It will, in every respect, be a partnership between Australia and Indonesia.

I think it is very important in the wake of all of the aid that is flowing into this country to remember that we are guests in Indonesia, that we are here to help the Government and the people of Indonesia. The ultimate responsibility for co-ordinating the provision of that aid naturally rests with the Government of Indonesia. But, insofar as the Australian aid program is concerned, it will be a joint commission.

We have, in fact – with the ready acquiescence and approval of the Indonesian Government – entered into an arrangement where there will be Australian officials seconded to the Indonesian co-ordinating agency for this disaster.

In every way, we'll be working together as partners and friends to bring about the wise and valuable utilisation of this very significant commitment.

I want to make it clear that this $1 billion is in addition to existing Australian aid to Indonesia.

It is completely over and above what we now provide, and that will bring the proportion of aid over the next five years to something in the order of $1.8 billion and, of course, it is in addition to the resources that have already been announced by the Government, the commitment of $60 million and all the air force, all the ADF and other assistance that the Government is already providing.

This is a human tragedy on a scale that none of us in our lifetime have seen and it does require a response above the ordinary.

I am very proud of the fact that Australia was the first on the scene among foreign countries helping Indonesia and that it is something that is deeply appreciated by the Indonesian President.

The response of the Australian people to this tragedy has been remarkable and it demonstrated that Australia has a good heart and the people of Australia will always respond to a deserving cause in a very generous fashion and they've certainly done that.

I believe that the decision that I've announced tonight, which I will report to the conference tomorrow, will have the overwhelming support of the Australian people.

We see Indonesia's need, respond to that need, but we respond to it in a way that respects the sovereignty of Indonesia and also respects the need for our two countries to work in partnership.

The meeting I had this evening with President Yudhoyono had all the elements of two leaders wanting to work together as friends and partners in a time of challenge and distress for one of us.

So I'm very pleased to announce this decision as it will place relations between our two countries on an even firmer footing.

GRATITUDE … Indonesian President Susilo Bambang Yudhoyono embraces Australian Prime Minister John Howard in Jakarta

Generosity worldwide amazes UN

Leyla Linton

AUSTRALIA was singled out for its "phenomenal contribution" by the United Nations yesterday, with the world body reporting that worldwide donations for tsunami victims were arriving faster than they could be recorded.

"We are recording pledges of between three and four billion dollars ($3.9 million to $5.2 billion), which shows that indeed the world is coming together in a manner we have never ever seen before," UN humanitarian chief Jan Egeland said.

He described the pledges made by Australia of $1 billion and Germany of $US674 million as "phenomenal" and thanked all the donors.

"Be with us in the long term," Mr Egeland said.

Super powers the poorest, his staff had to ask donors to repeat their offers to make sure they heard correctly the number of zeros.

"Germany and Australia, if I can believe the pledging news, will alone give more than a billion dollars. This is just incredible. It comes on top of the $US3.5 billion we had confirmed as of yesterday.

"We are just not able to record all the generous offers. They are coming in so often and they are so big."

Mr Egeland said aid pledges last year were unimpressive, with a total of $US8.9 billion committed for the countries where the UN operates.

"This year is different," he said.

"This is the year of compassion and, from now on, it should be like this."

He repeated his criticism that usually rich nations did not give enough to help those in need.

"There are the old rich nations and they are all giving too little on average. I appeal to all rich nations to step up to the plate," he said.

"They should be giving more of their riches."

He warned that unless countries made sure their pledges did not take away from money earmarked for other humanitarian emergencies, there was a danger the year would start with "unparalleled generosity" and finish with "stinginess".

"Humanitarian crises such as in Sudan, as it is in Sri Lanka or Thailand," Mr Egeland said.

Asked to explain why the response to the tsunami crisis had been so great, he said there were "many

reasons" but highlighted the media coverage of the disaster. "It's what we see a lot per TV screens which is the driving force," he said.

He also said the involvement of nationals from many donor countries in the disaster might have contributed to the high levels of giving. "In some countries, it meant a lot that they have lost their own citizens."

Moreover, donors in the region were motivated to help their neighbours, he said.

The pledges had been so generous that the aid appeal by UN Secretary-General Kofi Annan in Jakarta would be "comfortably met" than the pledges received so far, Mr Egeland said.

The relief effort in the Indian Ocean region would go down in the history books as the "most effective" ever, he said.

Donor nations vying to be the most generous

CANBERRA has pledged the most; Washington didn't give enough in the beginning. And China outdid arch rival Taiwan by promising eighty more.

The geopolitics of humanitarian aid and financial pledges in response to the December 26 tsunami are being analysed as closely as the shifting tectonic plates beneath the Indian Ocean that set it off.

And, as in a bidding war at Sotheby's, nations are upping the ante of their generosity.

Germany trumped Japan on Thursday, promising $671.1 million to Tokyo's $643.30 million.

As hour later, Australia topped that by pledging $1 billion.

Ngaire Woods, who teaches politics and international relations at University College in Oxford, said countries might be sizing up their pledges to ensure that the tsunami

relief effort remained multilateral in nature, not dominated by only one nation.

"The crisis presents opportunities to countries and governments to consolidate their grip in the region," she said.

Analysts said a successful relief effort in Indonesia could help boost Washington's sagging image among Muslims and set the stage for a resumption of military ties between the two countries.

Aid agency Oxfam yesterday praised Australia's contribution to the relief effort.

Oxfam policy director James Ensor, who is in Jakarta, said Australia had set a fine example for other nations and "there are some important aspects to this announcement other rich countries should follow".

— Reuters, AFP

'Reluctant Angel of Patong dives into hell' (*The Courier-Mail*, 7.1.05), for example, commends and discursively constructs the selfless actions of a young Australian woman who returned to the scenes of devastation to help. She becomes, as we can see, publicly sacralized as a 'reluctant angel', a signification reinforced through her voluntary entry into 'hell'. As Pantti and Wahl-Jorgensen observe: 'The shift of focus from the sufferers to the heroes allows the rhetorical shift from despair to hope and national pride' (Pantti and Wahl-Jorgensen 2007: 14) (see Image 3.3).

As time passes, further opportunities also present themselves for the ritualization of catastrophe through public ceremonies of remembrance – both religious and secular. For many people these religious and civic rituals are principally enacted within and through the news sphere: 'Let us pray: a nation stops to remember' (*Sunday Telegraph*, 8.1.05) (see Image 3.4) 'They are not alone: Australia stops in sorrow, in fraternity' (*Sydney Morning Herald*, 8.1.05) (see Image 3.5).

As we can see, and possibly feel, the news media did not hold back in its efforts to craft powerful visual frontpages in international solidarity and with suitable reverence and encoded emotion for such ritual occasions. Images of bereaved children, mothers and wives served to symbolize the victims of the tragedy and became positioned as the focal image around which an imagined nation was summoned as a moral community united in sympathy and grief. It is worth commenting on, for example, the unusually aestheticized not to say angelic portrait of the mother and child *survivor* in the *Sydney Morning Herald* in Image 3.5 – a seemingly choreographed image in contrast to earlier 'raw' newspaper photographs of mangled bodies and people in distress. In contrast to these earlier 'victim' scenes, the depicted image offers a dignified even reverential view of the 'survivor' as subject, one more fitting to the projected ritual occasion.

In such aesthetic, affective and emotionally laden ways, the tsunami catastrophe became heavily ritualized by the press and was subject to the discourses and sentiments, performances and symbols, rhetoric and ideals of national collectivity and moral community. A more in-depth examination of the tsunami and its news reportage around the world would also no doubt detect important differences between national and regional contexts, reflecting differences of geopolitical outlooks and national cultures. Such an analysis would also find evidence for less than fully harmonious or integrative forms of media coverage. Some points of narrative disruption would include, for example, the British press criticisms levelled at UK Prime Minister, Tony Blair, for staying on holiday when his leadership was seemingly demanded at home; the controversy surrounding some relief agencies, which requested that the public desist from making donations given the unprecedented funds already collected for emergency relief (see Chapter 8); media scares about trafficking and the prostitution of orphaned children; as well as the failure of countries in the tsunami region to install early warning systems.

Dissent and disagreement, then, certainly surfaced in the media's treatment of the tsunami but this at most assumed a minor aspect when set against the generally integrative tenor of the reporting and its ritualization of collective grief and inscriptions of

Image 3.3 'The Reluctant Angel of Pantong' *The Courier-Mail*, 7 January 2005 (© The Courier-Mail 2005)

S^{THE}unday Telegraph

January 16, 2005 $1.60 Including GST

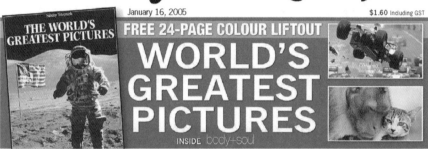

THE WORLD'S GREATEST PICTURES

FREE 24-PAGE COLOUR LIFTOUT

WORLD'S GREATEST PICTURES

INSIDE body+soul

EXCLUSIVE POLL

Beazley preferred to Latham as leader

By TONY VERMEER

LABOR powerbrokers are plotting a leadership change after the latest opinion poll showed Mark Latham's support is crumbling.

Kim Beazley is now the most popular choice to lead the Opposition, well ahead of Mr Latham in a poll conducted exclusively for *The Sunday Telegraph*.

The poll was taken on Friday — after Mr Latham revealed he was suffering a relapse of pancreatitis.

ALP factional chiefs said the party had to deal with the leadership crisis sooner rather than later.

"Latham is finished. It's just a question of who replaces him," a senior ALP powerbroker said.

The poll also revealed a collapse in Labor's vote since the October 9 election, which has party officials deeply concerned.

The Coalition now has a resounding 20-point lead over Labor on a two-party preferred basis — 60 per cent to 40 per cent.

❏ Full story: Page 9

Under fire: Mark Latham with wife Janine

OUR DAY OF MOURNING

LET US PRAY

A nation stops to remember

Homeless: Irvanas, aged 3, at a refugee camp in Aceh

AUSTRALIA will fall silent at 11.59 am today as we unite in mourning for those lost in the Asian tsunami tragedy.

Heads and flags will be lowered exactly three weeks after an earthquake created the devastating tsunamis that killed more than 150,000.

Prime Minister John Howard said the day should also be marked by wearing a sprig of wattle or other native flora.

"Let us all find time today, in our own ways, to mourn the lives lost and changed forever by this disaster," Mr Howard said.

❏ More reports: Pages 4, 5

Image 3.4 'Our Day of Mourning' *Sunday Telegraph*, 16 January 2005 (© News Limited 2005)

Image 3.5 'They are Not Alone . . .' *Sydney Morning Herald*, 15–16 January 2005 (© The Sydney Morning Herald 2005, Photo: Tamara Dean/Fairfaxphotos)

moral community just described. Not all disasters, however, prompt such consensual and integrative forms of ritualized news coverage as we shall hear.

Hurricane Katrina: disaster myths and the ritualization of dissent

When mediated, disasters can also tip over into something far less consensual, becoming political opportunities for political criticism, contention and challenge. On such occasions they can become, in the terms of Jeffrey Alexander and Ronald Jacobs (1998), 'mediatized public crises', or in the terms of Tamar Liebes, 'disaster marathons' (1998) – media phenomena that discernibly move away from the more integrative appeals of ceremonial 'media events' (Dayan and Katz 1992; see also Alexander 2006):

> Celebratory media events of the type discussed by Dayan and Katz tend to narrow the distance between the indicative and the subjunctive, thereby legitimating the powers and authorities outside the civil sphere. Mediatized public crises, on the other hand, tend to increase the distance between the indicative and the subjunctive, thereby giving to civil society its greatest power for social change. (Alexander and Jacobs 1998: 28)

In other words, Alexander and Jacobs are here suggesting that 'mediatized public crises', unlike more celebratory or ceremonial 'media events' of the kind discussed by Dayan and Katz, can throw into sharp relief the distance between how society 'is' and how people think it 'ought to be'. This distance, normally covered over or ignored in the media and wider public discourse, becomes focused in the exceptional moment of a mediatized public crisis, forcing difficult issues onto the public agenda, demanding their recognition and prompting different forms of response. Tamar Liebes also contrasts her understanding of 'disaster marathons' to that of integrative and consensual 'media events', observing how the former can serve to construct a moment of 'time out' opening up new opportunities amidst the commotion and concern – opportunities that the news media and journalists are well positioned to take advantage of:

> In contradistinction to media events, the shared collective space created by disaster time-out, zooming in on victims and their families, is the basis not for dignity and restraint but for the chaotic exploitation of the pain of participants on screen, and for the opportunistic fanning of establishment mismanagement, neglect, corruption, and so on. Whereas the principle of broadcast ceremony is to highlight emotions and solidarity and to bracket analysis, a disaster marathon constitutes a communal public forum where tragedy is the emotional motor which sizzles with conflict, emphasizing anxiety, argument and disagreement. (Liebes 1998: 75–76)

Some disasters, evidently, do not conform to the rituals of national integration and solidarity based on the public elaboration of emotions and consensual values, but become the site for discursive contention and even political dissent. News reporting of Hurricane Katrina was a powerful case in point. An analysis by Kathleen Tierney, Christine Bevc and Erica Kuligowski (2006) documents how the news reporting of Hurricane Katrina perpetuated a number of 'disaster myths' and 'framed' the aftermath of the disaster in politically consequential and damaging ways. The author's summarize their findings and argument as follows:

> [I]nitial media coverage of Katrina's devastating impacts was quickly replaced by reporting that characterized disaster victims as opportunistic looters and violent criminals and that presented individual and group behaviour following the Katrina disaster through the lens of civil unrest. Later, narratives shifted again and began to metaphorically represent the disaster-stricken city of New Orleans as a war zone and to draw parallels between the conditions in that city and urban insurgency in Iraq. These media frames helped guide and justify actions undertaken by military and law enforcement entities that were assigned responsibility of the postdisaster emergency response. The overall effect of media coverage was to further bolster arguments that only the military is capable of effective action during disasters. (Tierney et al. 2006: 60–61)

Based on an analysis of *The New York Times*, *The Washington Post* and the *New Orleans Times-Picayune* this study documents how media reporting perpetuated the 'disaster myth', the idea that under such circumstances survivors panic, social order breaks down and a state of chaos and lawlessness ensues that requires a law-and-order or even a military response. In fact, argue Tierney et al., situations of disaster in the US and elsewhere are known to generate altruistic social behaviours and group bonding as people try to organize and help each other under abnormal and adverse conditions. This, however, was most definitely not the image portrayed by the US press:

> Chaos gripped New Orleans on Wednesday as looters ran wild . . . looters brazenly ripped open gates and ransacked stores for food, clothing, television sets, computers, jewelry, and guns. (*The New York Times*, 1.9.05)

> Things have spiraled so out of control (in New Orleans) that the city's mayor ordered police officers to focus on looters and give up the search and rescue efforts. (*The Washington Post* (1.9.05)

These and many other examples provided by the authors demonstrate the general news framing of the aftermath situation in terms similar to riot reporting. Moreover, a focus on young black males in the context of claims about spiralling violence and chaos not only stereotyped all young blacks and possibly the wider community in similar terms, but also ignored the pro-social behaviours of the survivors and community organizations. Press agency images of young black people up to their chests in water with captions stating they were 'looting' fed into this stereotype of US riot-related behaviours but was distorting in a context where residents were compelled to seek out food and drinking water in the absence of state help. As the authors say, 'the distinction between disasters and urban unrest is an important one' but this did not hinder the news media's sensationalizing rumours, innuendo and unsubstantiated claims including, for example, the widely reported claims of multiple murders, child rape and people dying of gunshot wounds in the Superdome where survivors had taken refuge. Although later found to be groundless these news reports had accepted such claims, say the authors, because they were consistent with the media frame that had characterized New Orleans, to use a press headline of the time, as 'the snakepit of anarchy' (Tierney et al. 2006: 68).

As time moved on, the 'civil unrest' frame gave way to an 'urban war zone' frame which inevitably supported a militarized response. This, in turn, produced a number of profound consequences for how the disaster became responded to. For example, curfews and a suspicious view of survivors' movements around the city inhibited neighbourhood residents helping one another and also led officials to ignore the possibility of working with survivors to deliver assistance. Emergency responses became diverted to law enforcement, jeopardizing the lives of the hurricane survivors. News media images of looting and lawlessness may also have caused organizations outside the region to hesitate before committing resources and help. And the racial divides of US society are also likely to have become further entrenched on the basis of the news media's stereotypical portrayal, a finding supported by public attitude surveys after the worst of the disaster.

On the basis of their detailed analysis and discussion, Tierney and her colleagues propose that: 'Hurricane Katrina may well prove to be the focusing event that moves the nation to place more faith in military solutions for a wider range of social problems than ever before.' If this turns out to be the case, they conclude, 'the media will have helped that process along through its promulgation of myths of lawlessness, disorder, and urban insurgency' (Tierney et al. 2006: 78).

Disasters, evidently, can become political 'focusing events' with repercussions that extend far beyond the immediate scenes of death and destruction. Naomi Klein goes further. In her book, *The Shock Doctrine: The Rise of Disaster Capitalism* (2007) she argues that major disasters are put to work in the service of political elites and corporate interests:

> [T]he coup, the terrorist attack, the market meltdown, the war, the tsunami, the hurricane – puts the entire population into a state of collective shock. . . . Like the terrorized prisoner who gives up the names of comrades and renounces his faith, shocked societies often give up things they would otherwise fiercely protect. [Victims of Hurricane Katrina] were supposed to give up their housing projects and public schools. After the tsunami, the fishing people in Sri Lanka were supposed to give up their valuable beachfront land to hoteliers. Iraqis, if all had gone according to plan, were supposed to be so shocked and awed that they would give up control of their oil reserves, their state companies and their sovereignty to U.S. military bases and green zones. (Klein 2007: 17)

Clearly, Klein conceives of 'disasters', whether natural or manmade, as political opportunities capitalized on by elites who use them to pursue political objectives and corporate interests. The account by Tierney et al. of Hurricane Katrina, as we have heard, lends some support to this argument insofar as the media are found to have played a crucial part in the continuing militarization of US society and future disaster responses. In both these accounts, then, disasters are theorized as intricately enmeshed within the wider fields of politics and political culture: post-9/11 militarism in the case of Tierney et al. and the wider economic and political logic of neoliberal capitalism for Klein.

To what extent and in what ways different disasters can be theorized in the generalized terms of furthering elite political ambitions demands careful, comparative research as does the exact mechanisms that could help to explain the news media's seeming compliance with, and willing propagation of, elite views and interests (a similar set of arguments, for example, that can be applied to moral panic theory; see Cottle 2006a: 56–58). Even so, Tierney et al. and Klein usefully serve to remind us of how 'disasters' take place within particular political–ideological as well as geographical contexts and thereby become infused with surrounding discourses and represented through available cultural and media templates. Some mediated disasters, however, can also provide symbolic and discursive resources for challenge and dissent as well as consensus and political integration.

Tierney et al. emphasize the violent framing of the aftermath of Hurricane Katrina and the residents of New Orleans because frames of 'civil unrest' and 'war zone' were congruent with preceding press frames of urban rioting and the contemporary culture of threat spawned in the aftermath of the events of 9/11. However, this leaves open the possibility that other media frames and discourses were also present in the media presentation of these same events and, of course, there is more to the media than the three 'representative' US newspapers selected by Tierney and her colleagues for analysis (see, for example, Bennett et al. 2007). This can be developed further with the help of a penetrating study of the discourses of emotion found within and across different news disaster stories.

High-profile mediated disasters, according to Pantti and Wahl-Jorgensen (2007) in their study of six UK national disasters, are generally inscribed with four discourses of emotion: horror, grief, empathy and anger:

[T]he coverage of disaster always opens with an account of the horrific aspects of the event – what we here call 'the discourse of horror.' This is followed by the discourse of grief, which focuses on the suffering of victims and the bereaved. Such accounts, in turn, give rise to the discourse of empathy, which constructs imagined communities of shared loss by telling stories of individuals acting empathetically and heroically for the benefit of others. They call on feelings of national and community pride in accounts of heroes who provide hope and optimism by saving victims. Finally, discourses of anger assign blame and call those responsible to account by telling stories of the justified rage of the afflicted. (Pantti and Wahl-Jorgensen 2007: 21)

The first three of these emotional discourses of disaster reporting, as we have heard, map remarkably closely the reporting of the Indian tsunami. In Hurricane Katrina, both the mainstream media in the US and internationally also gave vent to the emotion of anger over time. Criticisms of city officials, failed evacuation plans, inadequate relief efforts and the seeming abandonment of some of the poorest people in American society to their fate as well as the militarized response to the aftermath all became voiced in the news media. The President of the United States, George Bush, also became targeted as the source of blame as Hurricane Katrina exposed the normally invisible inequalities of 'race' and poverty in American society. Hurricane Katrina, then, became an opportunity for political appropriation by different projects and discourses, both nationally and internationally (see Images 3.6 and 3.7).

In this context, the US president was forced to publicly try and offset the mounting criticism of his perceived lacklustre response, inadequate disaster planning and lack of resources made available by his political administration see Image 3.8).

Other state officials such as Michael Brown, head of America's Federal Emergency Management Agency (FEMA) also became singled out for public criticism as claims of incompetence, fanned by the media, circulated and effectively undermined George Bush's initial commendation of state officials for 'doing a great job'.

Hurricane Katrina not only played out in the US press, but also in the world's press and other media (see Figure 1.1). The BBC online news website, for example, positioned itself as a portal for world opinion, exhibiting opinion pieces from America and around the world and providing hyperlinks to some of the world's press. It is instructive to examine just a few of these different voices found in the world's press and reproduced on the BBC's web page (*http://news.bbc.co.uk/1/hi/world/americas/ 4216142.stm*):

> Bush is completely out of his depth in this disaster. Katrina has revealed America's weaknesses: its racial divisions, the poverty of those left behind by its society, and especially its president's lack of leadership. (Phillipe Grangereau in France's *Liberation*)

> The biggest power of the world is rising over poor black corpses. We are witnessing the collapse of the American myth. In terms of the USA's relationship with itself and the world, Hurricane Katrina seems to leave its mark on our century as an extraordinary turning point. (Yildrim Turker in Turkey's *Radikal*)

> Hurricane Katrina has proved that America cannot solve its internal problems and is incapable of facing these kinds of natural disasters, so it cannot bring peace and democracy to other parts of the world. Americans now understand that their rulers are only seeking to fulfill their own hegemonic goals. (editorial in Iran's *Siyasat-e Ruz*)

Image 3.6 'Criticism of Bush mounts as more than 10,000 feared dead' *The Guardian*, 3 September 2005 (© Guardian News & Media Ltd 2005, Photo: AP/Eric Gay)

Image 3.7 'Third World Despair? No, Downtown USA' *The Age*, 3 September 2005 (© Courtesy of The Age 2005)

Image 3.8 'America Stripped Bare' *The Age*, 4 September 2005 (© Courtesy of The Age 2005)

Co-operation to reduce greenhouse gas emissions can no longer be delayed, but there are still countries – including the US – which still do not take the issue seriously. However, faced with global disasters, all countries are in the same boat. The US hurricane disaster is a 'modern revelation', and all countries of the world including the US should be aware of this. (Xing Shu Li in Malaysia's *Sun Chew Jit Poh*)

This tragic incident reminds us that the United States has refused to ratify the Kyoto accords. Let's hope the US can from now on stop ignoring the rest of the world. If you want to run things, you must first lead by example. Arrogance is never a good advisor. (Jean-Pierre Aussant in France's *Figaro*)

Hurricane Katrina will bury itself into the American consciousness in the same way 9/11 or the fall of Saigon did. The storm did not just destroy America's image of itself, but also has the power to bring an end to the Republican era sooner than expected. America is ashamed. (Michael Streck in Germany's *Die Welt*)

Katrina is testing the US. Katrina is also creating an opportunity for world unity. Cuba and North Korea's offer of sympathy and aid to the US could also result in some profound thinking in the US, and the author hopes that it will not miss the opportunity. (Shen Dingli in China's *Dongfang Zaobao*)

As we can see, differences of geopolitical interests and cultural outlooks clearly register in these very different national views from around the world and relayed on the global media stage. The exposure of America's continuing racial divides and depth of poverty for some sullied its projected international image as a 'free democracy'. Countries normally regarded as political pariahs or as economic suppliants by the US government turned the tables and offered their support to the world's mightiest power in its evident failure to respond to its home-grown humanitarian disaster. And yet others took the opportunity to make the connection to climate change and the irony of the US position having not signed up to the Kyoto Treaty. Indeed, such was the mounting criticism played out in the news media that commentators even began to speak of George Bush's 'Katrinagate', likening his situation to the Watergate scandal that brought down Richard Nixon and the critical part played by the news media in his downfall. But, as we have also heard, the part played by some sections of the US media in circulating myths of urban warfare both nationally and internationally undermines a generalized argument about the US media regaining its critical independence and acting as a collective political watchdog. Still, the world's press reporting of Hurricane Katrina undoubtedly provided a diverse range of nationally inflected responses circulated and available via web pages and the so-called blogosphere that infused information, criticisms and much-needed insider accounts into the chaos and confusion of Hurricane Katrina (Allan 2006: 156–165).

In such ways, Hurricane Katrina was extensively and intensively mediated around the globe, reverberating across the wider geopolitical field and becoming infused with diverse discourses and political projects (see Images 3.7, 3.8 and 3.9). An unlikely emotion also became added to Patti and Wahl-Jorgensen's disaster emotions of horror, grief, empathy and anger: humour. When directed satirically, humour can also play its part in the politics of disaster as the following images circulated widely around the world on the internet demonstrate (see Images 3.9 and 3.10).

Such contrived, biting, images possibly spoke for many and their mounting political scepticism toward the presidency of George Bush and his administration's inept handling of the Katrina disaster and, possibly more so, the transparent media public relations efforts to regain the political initiative (see Image 3.8).

*(Un)*natural disasters as global focusing events

In today's global news ecology, the flows of news and commentary traversing continents, countries and cultures can infuse different views and values into the field of disaster communication (see Figure 1.1). Some mediated disasters evidently become 'focusing events' in relation to the surrounding political field, its contending discourses and struggles for change as well as in respect of moments of national integration and/ or the pursuit of political and corporate projects of control. In these diverse and sometimes contested ways, disaster reporting exhibits complexities that have yet to be fully explored and properly theorized. As the studies and findings reviewed indicate, however, a body of research and findings exists that neither supports invariant models

Image 3.9 'Bush with Fish' *Anonymous* (Source: www.bushbusiness.com)

Image 3.10 'Bush with Guitar' *Anonymous* (Source: www.q-dog.co.uk)

of determinism and control or indeterminism and chaos. The earlier discussion has, in fact, identified a number of dimensions and complexities that have proved capable of empirical recovery and theorization.

Mediated global disasters demand increased attention from media researchers in the future, both empirically and theoretically. This is because, as the opening statement to this chapter indicates, major disasters are now on the increase and becoming ever more destructive around the globe, a trend destined to continue for the foreseeable future (see Chapter 4). We therefore need to better understand how the news media variously enter into their constitution and forms of response as well as preparations for future disasters. But we also need to attend to mediated disasters more closely because they speak to our global age and the extent to which disasters and misfortunes in one part of the globe can be recognized and responded to in another (without necessarily becoming solely constituted through national frames of reference and parochial outlooks). In this sense, disasters have become not only 'focusing events' for national power plays and projects but also the wider, transnational and globalized field of humanitarian responses and the extent to which cosmopolitan outlooks can be detected in the discourses and debates that circulate through the global communication flows and interlocking networks of news.

4

ECOLOGY AND CLIMATE CHANGE:
FROM SCIENCE AND SCEPTICS TO
SPECTACLE AND . . .

Worse than we thought: Report warns of 4C rise by 2100 and food and water shortages likely.

The world's scientists yesterday gave their starkest warning yet that a failure to cut greenhouse gas emissions will bring devastating climate change within a few decades.

Average temperatures could increase by as much as 6.4C by the end of the century if emissions continue to rise, with a rise of 4C most likely, according to the final report of an expert panel set up by the UN to study the problem. The forecast is higher than previous estimates, because scientists have discovered that Earth's land and oceans are becoming less able to absorb carbon dioxide.

An average global temperature rise of 4C would wipe out hundreds of species, bring extreme food and water shortages in vulnerable countries and cause catastrophic floods that would displace hundreds of millions of people. Warming would be much more severe towards the poles, which could accelerate melting of the Greenland and West Antarctic ice sheets.

The report, for the Intergovernmental Panel on Climate Change (IPCC), is written by hundreds of scientists across the world and has been approved by every government. It leaves little room for doubt that human activity is to blame. Achim Steiner, executive director of the UN Environment Program, said: 'February 2 2007 may be remembered as the day the question mark was removed from whether people are to blame for climate change.' (*The Guardian*, front page, 3.2.07)

Climate change, above all other global crises, is now contributing to '*the experience of crisis in world society*' and prompts awareness of our 'civilizational community of fate' (Beck 2006: 7). This global outlook and sensibility, however, too often remains confined behind national borders and geopolitical interests. Journalism is not exempt from national parochialisms as we saw in the 'professional calculus of death' routinely enacted by journalists when reporting disasters around the globe (Chapter 3). In respect of ecological crises and climate change, however, there are signs that Beck's 'civilizational community of fate' is now stirring. We see its emergence in UN treatises and government responses to the protocols emanating from Rio (1992), Kyoto (1997) and Bali (2007), in the protests and demands of transnational networks calling for environmental justice and, increasingly, in the expressed environmental concerns of ordinary people. The west also occasionally bears witness to it in the distant 'voices of the side-effects' (Beck 1992), people whose habitats and ways of life are undermined or overwhelmed by processes of climate change. Whether, for example, the population of Tuvalu, a South Pacific atoll 4 metres high, confronting the disappearance of their homeland beneath the waves, the Inuit communities of Canada and Alaska threatened with the loss of their traditional way of life and hunting grounds by melting permafrost or the African farmers of Darfur slaughtered by Arab nomads moving ever further south to avoid encroaching desertification and the loss of pastoral lands.

As the front page news article that opens this chapter reports (just one of many around the world delivering the grave IPCC findings in its Fourth Assessment Report of 2007; see Chapter 1) the world's climate is now fast changing and this, based on a consensus of the world's scientists, is human induced. If IPCC predictions and those of more recent scientific modelling come to pass over the next few decades (and the latter suggest that earlier IPCC predictions underestimated the acceleration, severity and cumulative effects of feedback mechanisms on the world's climate systems) then climate change may yet prove to be the most powerful of drivers summoning into existence Beck's 'civilizational community of fate'. As *The Guardian's* front page report suggests, the IPCC report of 2007 can be regarded as one of the most important milestones in the career of climate change to date. It constitutes a critical moment in its transformation from relatively infrequent and scientifically framed news reports of a few years ago into a prominent, often spectacular, news global crisis.

As we can see from Table 4.1, which maps the frequency of references to 'climate change' and/or 'global warming' across a sample of the world's press, the language of climate change has progressively entered into news discourse across the 10-year period 1997–2007 (albeit with regional differences and patterns of prominence across different newspapers).

Climate change, evidently, is now established on news agendas around much of the world and this looks set to increase in the foreseeable future. Frequency tables though useful cannot tell us about the determinants and dynamics involved in the news *construction* of climate change as a public issue over time or *how* exactly these representations have entered into public understanding and forms of political response. With the help of recent research findings and discussion this chapter sets out to examine how climate change has become progressively signalled in the news media over recent years

Table 4.1 Global warming and the world's press 1997–2007

Country	News outlet	1997	1998	1999	2000	2001	2002	2003	2004	2005	2006	2007	Total
Africa													
Kenya	The Nation	n/a	3	5	0	0	0	2	5	29	53	93	190
South Africa	All Africa	n/a	29(4)	45	26	98	263	132	152	431	670	1996	3842
Uganda	New Vision	1(7)	0	1	3	0	0	2	10	18	31	134	200
Asia													
China	South China Morning Post	45	31	20	34	39	35	36	94	149	302	603	1388
India	The Times of India	31	40	47	115	40	24	32	30	63	53	354	829
Indonesia	The Jakarta Post	24	11	7	13	11	27	21	44	45	97	728	1028
Japan	The International Herald Tribune (Herald Asahi) (S)	70(3)	21	19	0	0	21	20	46	62	54	146	459
Singapore	Straits Times	36	18	26	26	59	19	11	49	52	119	579	994
Thailand	Bangkok Post	23	18	31	49	39	43	23	40	87	91	344	788
Australia and Oceania													
Australia	The Australian	284	113	100	146	140	75	106	244	453	1040	3004	5705
New Zealand	The Press	23	29	25	55	38	75	46	73	152	359	433	1308
Europe													
UK	The Guardian/The Observer	347	264	250	462	585	604	500	1227	2068	2559	4219	13085
France	International Herald Tribune	11	17	20	26	63	37	93	83	59	69	116	594
Republic of Ireland	The Irish Times	116	66	73	154	142	114	93	176	296	391	1019	2640
Russia	The Moscow Times	3	7	4	3	12	5	8	13	9	6	12	82
Scotland	The Herald	137	128	124	182	169	102	71	174	362	342	538	2329
Turkey	Turkish Daily News	1	11	7	18	36	14	22	2	54	56	410	631
Middle East													
Israel	The Jerusalem Post	14	14	14	21	21	16	15	12	17	41	37	222
United Arab Emirates	Gulf News	16(2)	12	6	11	10	12	5	16	53	24	112	277
The Americas													
Canada	The Globe and Mail	255	189	156	213	192	236	132	212	397	682	1337	4001
The United States	The New York Times	242	165	148	309	321	231	214	293	434	705	1276	4338

n/a = not available, ( ) = months only

as a global crisis. As the chapter title suggests, news reporting of climate change has moved through discernible phases and, at the time of writing, looks poised to do so again. These successive phases, broadly, can be characterized in terms of *science*, *sceptics* and *spectacle*.

Climate change and global warming could yet move into a further news phase of *intra*national and *inter*national contention and *spin* as government targets for carbon emission reduction and other schemes of adaptation and mitigation become missed or fudged in the years ahead. Or perhaps it will yet become a story about intensified calls for *ecological solidarity* and *international action* as the impacts of climate change, including increased *un*natural disasters and environmental deterioration affect more and more people on the planet. Recent research into environmental reporting more widely reveals some of the principal determinants and dynamics involved in the news circulation, construction and contention of climate change as a global crisis – possibly the most profound challenge confronting the world today.

Environmental reporting: what's known

The reporting of climate change and other ecological threats takes place within the established parameters and precedents of environmental reporting more generally. Over recent years environmental and risk reporting has received considerable research interest and some of the fundamental drivers of this coverage are now known (Hansen 1993; Anderson 1997; Chapman et al. 1997; Allan et al. 2000; Wilson 2000; Allan 2002; Cottle 2006a: 120–142; Cox 2006: 161–240; Lester 2007). The following, therefore, sets out to provide a brief reprise of some of the principal research findings and positions that help to explain the nature of environmental reporting and which can also help to explain the news media's changing representations of climate change.

As with any potential news story, the operation of deep seated, if often unspoken, news values (Galtung and Ruge 1965; Chibnall 1977; Hall 1981; Lowe and Morrison 1984; Harcup and O'Neill 2001) can predispose journalists to identify some environmental issues and concerns as newsworthy and not others. Different lists of news values abound in the academic literature, but most generally recognize how these orient processes of news selection and representation to the negative, deviant, dramatic and conflictual and, in the case of visual media, to arresting images or spectacular scenes.

The upshot of the operation of general news values in this context, then, is clear. Dramatic environmental events such as environmental disasters are likely to find news coverage but not longer term processes of incremental environmental deterioration or invisible hazards. Dramatic environmental protests, especially those involving conflict or violence, are also likely to attract news cameras but not the more mundane processes of political lobbying or behind-the-scenes bargaining and negotiations by different interests. And environmental issues that can be rendered into simple binary oppositions (protestors versus police; local residents versus property developers; industrial polluters versus defenders of local wildlife) are also likely to shape the news agenda and not the multiple perspectives or detailed arguments of complex disputes. Environmental concerns that are culturally proximate and 'close to home' rather than those which are geographically distanced or 'culturally remote' are also destined to be seen as more newsworthy.

The adequacy of news values as an explanation for the extent and forms of news coverage, as discussed in Chapter 3, however, is at best limited. They can provide a *generalizing* approximation only of the complexities and dynamics involved in environmental news reporting. Other factors and dimensions, research tells us, also need to be taken into account. These include processes of agenda setting, or the signalling of some issues in the news as relatively more or less important than others (McCoombs and Shaw 1972). The model of agenda setting prompts a more contingent, less universalizing or timeless, approach to environmental agendas than news values and can therefore help to map the rise and fall of environmental issues in the news over time, even though the scale or severity of the problems to which they refer remain constant or even progressively worsen across the same period (Hansen 1991, 1993). Ideas of agenda setting also encourage empirical investigation of the changing composition of news agendas and therefore the processes and practices of 'social construction' that have informed their news production.

This, in turn, invites closer examination of *how* news issues are actually represented and not simply where they are positioned in the news agenda. Studies of news 'frames' and 'framing' attend to processes of news selection and salience and how news representations are structured to promote a 'particular problem definition, causal interpretation, moral evaluation and/or treatment recommendation' (Entman 1993: 52). From a slightly wider angle, news frames can also be seen as '*organizing principles* that are socially *shared* and *persistent* over time' and 'that work *symbolically* to meaningfully *structure* the social world' (Reese 2003: 11; see also Gamson and Modigliani 1989; Hannigan 1995; Hansen 2000; Miller and Riechert 2000).

If the study of news frames encourages a more detailed appreciation of how news frames organize the representation of environmental issues in ways that invite particular understandings (and possible actions), the sociological study of news sources, in this context, also invites a more sophisticated appreciation of how contending and competing news sources gain news entry and/or seek to influence environmental news agendas and the representation of particular issues (Anderson 1993; Hansen 2000). Sociological studies of 'source fields', including environmental sources, have generally found them to be structured by competing interests and identities and unequal opportunities to influence the news agenda and processes of news framing, though here communication tactics and other resources – financial, organizational, symbolic and cultural – can all come into the frame and sometimes offset disadvantages of institutional power between, say, environmental protesters and vested corporate interests (Wykes 2000; Anderson 2003; Lester 2006, 2007).

The empirical exploration of news sources and communication strategies can also prompt investigation of processes of agenda building or how environmental interest groups and others can maximize their influence and impact by forming coalitions, for example, to collectively advance their preferred environmental agenda in the news media over time. This can also involve the provision of 'information subsidies' (Gandy 1980) by news sources or the generation of packaged information and, more recently, visual materials of broadcast quality by Greenpeace and others. By such means, protest groups and others aim to get their message across by providing an attractive 'subsidy' to cash-strapped, time-poor, competitive news organizations (Davis 2003). On securing news access, sources may also pursue agenda-shifting tactics as in, for example, the micro-politics of news interviews encounters where the interviewee deliberately questions or ignores the informing premise of the interviewer's questions and seeks to impose a new topic of discussion (Clayman and Heritage 2002).

The study of news agendas and source fields, then, demands that we study patterns and processes of news access, of who get on or in the news and how they are able to advance their preferred point of view (Cottle 2003b). Studies of 'claims makers' and 'claims making' pursue the different opportunities afforded by news personnel to some news entrants to advance their claims and aims, whether government scientists or victims of environmental disasters. This can be combined with inquiry into the structured patterns of news access as well as the different discursive opportunities enabled (or disabled) by different news formats (Cottle 2000a). Studies of so-called 'primary definers' and 'primary definition' (Hall et al. 1978) tend to be more firmly rooted in a preceding theorization of the social structures and operation of hegemonic ideological power and, as such, interested in the privileged opportunity granted by the news media to political, economic and social elites to publicly define and prescribe in relation to public issues. But it too is sensitized to *how* processes of primary definition come to set both the parameters and terms of reference for the public elaboration of conflictual issues.

In this context, Ulrich's Beck's discussion of the 'relations of definition' also holds relevance. This refers to the matrix of ideas, interests, epistemologies and different rationality claims (scientific, social, legal etc.) that compete and contend within the fields of risk and ecological interdependency crises. In the 'second modernity' of world risk society, which Beck sees simultaneously as the 'information and media society' (see Chapter 1), relations of definition take on a new importance in comparison to the relations of production that helped characterize the first modernity of industrial capitalism. Who manages to define the nature of public threats in the media and prescribe courses of action (or inaction) in relation to them, clearly, occupies a commanding strategic position and one of considerable communicative power. In the field of environmental news discourse, this communicative power encompasses more than the recognition and investigation of the 'hierarchy of credibility' (Becker 1967) or news sanctioned patterns of hierarchical access. It also refers to the different epistemological underpinnings to different news stories and forms of speech, the advancement of scientific knowledge, say, or lay knowledge. Whether accessed news voices advance their point of view and arguments in the dispassionate, impersonal and statistically probabilistic claims of scientific rationality or the emotionally felt, communally lived and culturally experienced views and values of social rationality can register quite differently in the news mediated field of environmental discourses and contention (Beck 1992; Wynne 1996; Cottle 2000a).

Here it becomes apparent, then, that research into the media and the environment has to extend its sights beyond media centrism and the exclusive focus on media practices and processes to examine the field of *interactions* between different institutional arenas and how these influence the representations and discourses of environmental news. The 'public arenas model' (Hilgartner and Bosk 1988) remains relevant in this regard, encouraging us to examine how social problems (including environmental issues) compete with others for attention within different public arenas, whether those of politics, science or the media, for example, and how each of these institutional arenas has differing 'carrying capacities' (or available space and time to allocate to different issues), 'principles of selection' (such as 'news values' for example) and specific 'networks of operatives'. This institutional model clearly holds relevance for the fields of environment and risk communications and invites examination of the interactions between the public arenas of media, government and science – to name only the most obvious. It also encourages closer examination of the practices and professional cultures of their 'networks of operatives', including specialist environment correspondents (Peters 1995; Anderson 1997).

It is not only established institutional arenas and their interactions with the news media that inform and shape environmental reporting today, but also protest groups, new social movements and, more recently, transnational activist networks that momentarily come together to form loose coalitions and mobilize both online and in the real world (Norris 2002; Opel and Pompper 2003; Jong et al. 2005; Chesters and Welsh 2006; Castells 2007; Cottle in press). Here researchers have begun to examine the complex networks and communication strategies, tactics and celebrities deployed by increasingly media savvy environmental groups and protestors (Anderson 1997; DeLuca 1999; Allan et al. 2000; Lester 2006, 2007). This work also helps to ground the analysis of environmental coverage within the wider and moving terrain of environmental politics.

Across recent years political parties in western democracies and elsewhere have generally proclaimed their green credentials and this now routinely informs public pronouncements and policy objectives. The incorporation of environmental concerns and agendas into mainstream politics inevitably perhaps distances the ideological divides that characterize the wider field of environment and ecology, including perspectives on 'deep ecology' in contrast to environmentalism and critiques of perpetual economic growth, intensified capitalist production and associated technocratic and instrumental rationalities (Lowe and Morrison 1984; Eder 1996; Lash et al. 1996; Dobson 2007). Mainstream green politics has entered into mainstream news media discourse in recent years though this can also vary considerably across continents, countries and cultures (Linné and Hansen 1990; Chapman et al. 1997).

The deep seated and historically forged 'cultural resonance' of the environment as a cipher for feelings and values about nature also finds expression in and through the news media, although this is unlikely be explicitly advanced as a formed ideology of ecology. We can see it, however, through the news media's conventionalized 'rhetoric of environmental images' (Cottle 2006a: 130–137) and in the image politics of environmental protests (Deluca 1999; Lester 2007). Whether depicted in terms of the *spectacularization* of nature as pristine, timeless and pure, or through symbolic images of nature as despoiled, exploited and *under threat*, the succession of such culturally resonant images in the news media provide an affective and potentially critical charge to environmental discourses and the politics of risk now circulating throughout societies (Cottle 2000a, 2006a: 130–137) – including, as we shall see, via recent news visualization of climate change.

Although this rhetoric of environmental images is potentially universalizing via today's global media, we also know that the meanings and politics of such scenes can be interpreted quite widely when seen through the prism of different cultures, indigenous practices and traditional identities. The predominant discourses on whaling found in the British press, for example, concern the protection of endangered species and the immorality (cruelty) of catching whales or cetaceans in general. In the Japanese press, further discourses come to the fore, however. These include the economic consequences on whaling industries and the cultural impact the ban on whaling has on existing whaling communities (Murata 2007). It seems plausible, then, that images of whaling can be read quite differently by such communities of readers and especially when these same images are 'anchored' (Barthes 1977) in the 'vice' of surrounding headlines, captions and news language.

Audience studies tell us that people make sense of media representations of the environment through multiple and often overlapping interpretative frames whether based on personal outlooks and experiences, political orientation or appeals to reason, evidence and/or affect as well as expectations of media balance and reporting fairness (Corner et al. 1990; Macnaghten and Urry 1998; Buckingham 2000; Lorenzoni et al. 2006; Etkin and Ho 2007). In this sense, much more is going on than information-based processes often assumed in approaches to the public understanding of science. Whether environmental risks are global or local in scope, for many they are experienced 'close to home' or in settings and through identities embedded in local communities and familial relationships (Macnaghten and Urry 1998). It is here that feelings of 'ontological insecurity' (Giddens 1990) in the face of the perceived failure of officialdom to deal with Beck's 'civilization of threats', for example, are often keenly felt. In the face of potentially devastating environmental change, the media have a responsibility to not only illuminate the 'bads' of global risk society but also to democratize them by enfranchising all those who are affected by them to have their say, communicating across geographical frontiers, and the world's cultural and other divides, and participating in how they should be perceived, managed or curtailed in the future (Cottle 2006a: 142). Climate change, in this sense, becomes a crucial test case for media enacted democracy.

Climate change: science and sceptics

Research documents how news coverage of climate change in the 1980s was an occasional story only, deferentially reporting the findings of scientific studies published elsewhere. Over time and as scientists began to calculate the magnitude of the problem and the scale of responses required so climate change became increasingly politicized and the site of contested claims – including denial and scepticism. The science of anthropogenic climate change clearly plays a crucial part in the public understanding of this issue, but climate change is also about much more than science. Climate change constitutes both a threat to and challenge for humanity. It is principally caused by western developed nations but we know its worst effects are and will be experienced by the least developed regions and the poorest, most vulnerable, populations in the world (Oxfam 2007). It demands concerted political action in respect of policies of adaptation and mitigation and responses from individual to institutional and international levels; it will have profound impacts on economies as well as ecosystems (Stern 2007). Climate change, then, is much more than 'science' though we cannot hope to respond to it without understanding something of the science that explains its *causation* and *consequences*. The fact that the technical details and complexities of the science involved can find simplified or sparse treatment in news reporting should not, therefore, be presumed to be the main cause of concern or research focus (Hargreaves et al. 2002: 50).

As the issue has become so prominent on news agendas in recent years it seems probable that public understanding of climate change will have improved somewhat, especially with the help of more pedagogic news features encouraged by the 'rising tide', so to speak, of global warming news reports. A recurring finding about conflict reporting, for example, is that as an issue becomes more salient in terms of news frequency and extent of coverage, so the formats deployed to cover the issue can often become more expansive and even reflexive in their reporting (Hallin 1986; Butler 1995; Cottle 2004). This can include increased use of news features, background analyses and discussion formats in addition to 'thin' news reports (Cottle 2005; Cottle and Rai 2006) and this reflects journalists' attempts to elaborate and explain something of the complexities, whether technical, scientific or political, involved. There are now grounds to suggest that this has happened in recent years following the release of the IPCC reports and general increase of climate change reporting (see later).

The main finding documented by studies of the changing news career of climate change, however, is not to do with the informational deficit or impoverished representation of climate change science but rather the way in which the science itself has been subject to a sustained, vociferous and seemingly effective challenge by small group of global warming sceptics. We shall come to this in a moment, but, first, it is worth pausing on the nature of scientific reporting in the context of climate change and how 'science' has been embedded and defined quite differently in news reports across time and in different news outlets.

An exemplary detailed study by Anabela Carvalho (2007) demonstrates how the standing of scientific knowledge in the reporting of climate change in the British 'quality' press changed across the period 1985–2001. Based on a detailed analysis of the conservative and pro-establishment *The Times*, left-leaning *Guardian* and non-aligned *The Independent* she observes key 'critical discourse moments' in the changing coverage of climate change – including the release of earlier IPCC reports – and how these different newspapers legitimated knowledge claims supportive of their preferred editorial positions. The science of climate change, in this context, became selectively positioned and defined in ways that helped to bolster the ideological outlooks of the newspapers concerned, a tendency that became even more pronounced over time. As the stakes of climate change became higher and the threat to the status quo more evident, so *The Times*, in particular, began to question the credibility of the science involved and gave access to the voices of the sceptics. Carvalho summarizes her findings thus:

> While the press acted jointly as spokespeople for the science establishment in the first few years examined in this article and enhanced its social authority and power, a radically different image started to emerge at the end of the 1980s, when climate change was politicized. Skepticism and contestation of mainstream scientific claims appeared in *The Times* and, to a less extent, in *The Independent*. In contrast with its earlier strategy of certainty-making, *The Times* cast doubts on the greenhouse effect and on human causation of the problem. Discrediting the agents of unwanted knowledge was part of that discursive route. When knowledge claims appeared to constitute a threat to ideological principles and arrangements in the political, social and economic realms, *The Times* did not hesitate to harm the reputation of an institution like the IPCC. In 'critical discourse moments' like the release of the IPCC reports, *The Times* picked individuals at the margins of respected science and magnified their opinions in order to sustain a certain view of the world and a certain social order. [. . .]
>
> In contrast, *The Guardian* and most authors in *The Independent* conveyed an image of scientific knowledge that emphasized the risks associated to climate change. Promoting confidence in science by emphasizing consensus and enhancing the reliability of knowledge, *The Guardian* and *The Independent* demanded a stronger political intervention on the problem. By re-configuring the state of scientific knowledge in ways that justify and promote preferred courses of social, economic and political action, newspapers discursively construct fields of action and fields of inaction. (Carvalho 2007: 237–238)

In such ways, then, the science of climate change became selectively appropriated and incorporated into the contending ideological outlooks of the British press. Carvalho's study underlines the importance of attending to the ways in which the news media actively embedded and inflected the claims and accounts of science and not whether the science of climate change was accurately represented or not. Though differing forms of knowledge circulate and migrate across different public arenas, on the basis of this study it seems that the news media occupy a particularly pivotal role in the public translation and elaboration of the science involved (see also Weingart et al. 2000).

It would be less than the full story to suggest, however, that sections of the British press worked alone in its amplification of climate change scepticism. George Monbiot (2007a: 20–42) has traced the corporate funding and support of organizations and individuals that denied the scientific basis of anthropogenic climate change. In so doing he also notes how the most prominent and shrill voices of dissent in the news media had in fact no scientific credentials and quotes the following to help make his case:

Global warming? It's hot air and hypocrisy
George W. Bush is right. The Kyoto Treaty is a silly waste of time. The Greenhouse effect probably doesn't exist. There is as yet no evidence for it. (Peter Hitchins, *Mail on Sunday*, 29 July 2001, cited in Monbiot 2007a: 23)

Does this prove that global warming's all hot air?
And if the climate is indeed overheating, that does not mean that manmade emissions are necessarily to blame. Indeed, it is extremely unlikely that they would be since carbon dioxide forms a relatively small proportion of the atmosphere, most of which consists of water vapour. (Melanie Phillips, *Daily Mail*, 13 January 2006, cited in Monbiot 2007a: 23)

As Monbiot points out, Peter Hitchins appears to confuse the naturally occurring process of the greenhouse effect with specifically human-induced global warming and, if Melanie Phillips' assertion about water vapour were correct 'we would need gills' (Monbiot 2007a: 23).

When delving deeper into the source of these and other sceptical claims, Monbiot finds that they often originated not with the newspaper commentators but with a number of US-based organizations funded by Exxon, one of the world's most profitable corporations based on oil. Together this select group of organizations set out to contradict the growing consensus of the world's scientists and advanced a consistent line: 'that the science is contradictory, the scientists are split, environmentalists are charlatans, liars or lunatics, and if governments took action to prevent global warming, they would be endangering the global economy for no good reason' (Monbiot 2007a: 27–28). Such sceptical interventions were frequently found to be based on out-of-date or simply poor science and publications that had not been subject to the usual exacting standards of scientific peer review. The claims of the sceptics nonetheless became widely circulated and repeated in the news media, creating the erroneous impression that there was indeed a continuing scientific controversy over climate change when in fact the consensus was growing ever stronger and more urgent. A memo written by a leading political consultant in the US in 2001, for example, maintained that 'should the public come to believe that the scientific issues are settled, their views about global warming will change accordingly' and he therefore advised political party leaders, 'you need to continue to make the lack of scientific certainty a primary issue in the debate' (Frank Luntz cited in Cox 2006: 346). One way of doing this, he went on, was to recruit experts sympathetic to the cause because 'people are willing to trust scientists'.

By all accounts, this strategy proved effective with the media. In Britain the BBC, says Monbiot, 'seemed incapable of hosting a discussion on climate change without bringing in one of the Exxon-sponsored deniers to claim that it was not taking place. On only one occasion did it tell its listeners that the "expert" it had chosen had been funded by an oil company' (Monbiot 2007a: 37). He concludes:

> By dominating the media debate on climate change during seven or eight critical years in which urgent international talks should have been taking place, by constantly seeding doubt about the science just as it should have been most persuasive, they have justified the money their sponsors spent on them many times over. I think it is fair to say that the professional denial industry has delayed effective global action on climate change by several years. (Monbiot 2007a: 39; see also Boykoff and Boykoff 2004; Antilla 2005; Cox 2006: 351–361)

Monbiot's analysis clearly identifies the media presence of this highly vocal group of climate change sceptics and underscores the necessity of attending to source aims and communication strategies targeting the news media. But we also need to address further why exactly the news media so readily granted this vocal minority so much weight in its news coverage, especially given the deep seated cultural resonance of environmental concerns already noted. A study by Maxwell Boykoff and Jules Boykoff (2004) argues that the answer lies in a fundamental norm of professional journalism: balance or telling 'both' sides of the story (Boykoff and Boykoff 2004: 129).

Based on a study of the US elite press, the *New York Times*, the *Washington Post*, the *Los Angeles Times* and the *Wall Street Journal* and a sample of relevant news stories from 1988 to 2002, Boykoff and Boykoff found that the majority of the coverage (52.65%) provided balanced accounts, giving roughly equal attention to the view that humans were contributing to global warming and the alternative view that natural fluctuations could explain the Earth's temperature increase. In the context of the growing scientific consensus at the time, 'this supports the hypothesis that journalistic balance can often lead to a form of informational bias' (p.129). A similar finding was also elicited from the sample in respect of the reporting of proposed political responses to global warming. Here over three-quarters of news reports (78.20%) featured approaches in roughly equal measure that included 'courses of action that ranged from cautious to urgent and from voluntary to mandatory' with only a strict minority (10.63%) of articles including views that 'pulsed with urgency' and which clearly favoured 'immediate and mandatory action' (p.131). The authors conclude:

> Even though the IPCC has strongly posited that anthropogenic activities have had a 'discernible' effect on the global climate (IPCC, 1996), urgent, mandatory action has not been taken. The central messages in the generally agreed-upon scientific discourse have therefore not been proliferated by the mass media into the popular arena. The failed discursive translation between the scientific community and popular, mass-mediatized discourse is not random; rather the mis-translation is systematic and occurs for perfectly logical reasons rooted in journalistic norms and values. . . . In the end, adherence to the norm of balanced reporting leads to informationally biased coverage of global warming. This bias, hidden behind the veil of journalistic balance, creates both discursive and real political space for the US government to shirk responsibility and delay action regarding global warming. (Boykoff and Boykoff 2004: 134)

In a more recent study Boykoff and Boykoff (2007) develop this argument further and explain deficient news reporting of climate change in respect of a number of professional norms and practices including 'personalization', 'dramatization' and 'novelty' that help to select and shape news content in terms of underlying news values (see earlier) as well as professional norms of 'authority order' (dependence on authority sources) and 'balance' (leading to unfair access being granted to minority sceptics). Reflecting on the US administration's adamant refusal to join the 140 nations which ratified the Kyoto Protocol to curb human contributions to climate change, and the fact that the US alone is responsible for 25% of the world's carbon emissions though only has 5% of the world population, the authors conclude:

> [A] number of important factors combine to account for this foot-dragging. However, one under-considered factor – the very norms that guide journalism decision-making – plays a crucial role in the failure of the central messages in the generally-agreed-upon scientific discourse to transmit successfully into US-backed international policy to combat global warming. This is not random; rather, the translation is systematic and occurs not only because of complex macro-political and economic reasons rooted in power relations, but also because of the micro-processes that undergird journalism. Rather than relying on external constrictions – such as overt censorship and editorial spiking of stories – the mass-media depend on internal constructions, disciplinary practices that produce the patterned communicative geography of the public sphere. (Boykoff and Boykoff 2007: 1201–1202)

Anthropogenic climate change has been studied and observed for years, even decades, before the latest IPCC reports (Monbiot 2007a). Scientific evidence steadily mounted from around the world as people experienced unusually severe, frequent or out-of-season weather events that far exceeded anything in living memory, including unprecedented heat waves, hurricanes, floods, forest fires, droughts, accelerating desertification, melting glaciers and mounting seas. The release in 2007 of the latest and most conclusive IPCC reports, based on a near consensus of the world's scientists, included dire predictions and calls for urgent national and international action at the G8 meeting and UN sponsored conference in Bali later that year (the most important since Kyoto).

Anthropogenic climate change could no longer be simply denied or dismissed or even debated as a *possible* problem. It has now gained the imprimatur of scientific credibility and is legitimated as a 'global crisis' in much of the world's news media – a crisis that now demands worldwide attention and concerted global action. The news career of climate change, it seems, has finally entered a new, post-sceptical, phase.

Climate change: spectacle and . . .

If news accounts of climate change have finally begun to move beyond the stymieing impact of the sceptics this has been helped in part by the increased circulation of spectacular images of the threat climate change poses to the world's ecosystems and human life. Editors and journalists, camera crews and photojournalists working in the mainstream media have collectively contributed to the *visualization* of climate change and they have often done so within crafted TV packages and elaborate press features. These 'performative' forms of news presentation are often doing more than simply reporting and recording the subject of climate change; they are actively inviting us to 'bear witness' to the environmental change and devastation it has already caused and its impacts on vulnerable communities around the world. A good news story, it is often claimed, demands 'good visuals' and, as we noted earlier, some see arresting news visuals as a news value in their own right. In the context of global climate change (and indeed a world where a sense of impinging 'globality' has already become pervasive, as discussed in Chapter 1) the role of images can prove crucial. An integral, possibly indispensable, part of the construction of social problems and their subsequent legitimation, mobilization and political action involves, then, first being able to *visualize* them. This is why symbols remain so important.

In order to form a 'view' of different issues and concerns we need, ideally, to be able to see what they look like – whether involving human subjects or not. Images more than formally communicated ideas, it seems, often encourage affective responses and possibly help lay a foundation for a sense of moral solidarity and shared commitment. Media images can play a powerful role in constituting our sense of who we are and our felt relationship to the environment and others (Macnaghten and Urry 1998; Szerszynski and Togood 2000; Urry 2002). When extended to the global environment, as this sensibility must in the context of global climate change, images may even help to support a sense of 'ecological citizenship' concerned with the rights and responsibilities of the citizen of the earth (Urry 1999: 315; Dobson 2007).

In western societies deference to authority and traditions has declined across recent decades (Giddens 1994) and both states and corporations, says Urry, have become regarded as less trustworthy. In this context 'media images can provide more stable forms of meaning and interpretation in a culture in which "seeing is believing" ' (Urry 1999: 319). They can also help to 'make sense of what would otherwise be disparate and apparently unconnected events and phenomena' and prove to be a key dimension in the success of staged, spectacular 'media events' (pp. 319–320). According to Martin Albrow (1996: 146), for example, mega-media events manufacture 'striking images which have become central to the iconography of global citizenship' – images that both depict and speak for the globe (Urry 1999: 320). The emphasis by Urry on visual imagery in the context of global communication flows certainly finds purchase on the news media's recent *visualization* and *spectacularization* of climate change.

Depictions of the globe in the context of news of climate change have become commonplace in the news media, as they have in the iconography of news journalism more generally. It is now commonplace, for example, for broadcasting corporations around the world to brand their news programmes, opening title sequences and logos with images of the globe and, invariably, with themselves depicted at the hub of world communication flows. Images of the globe also now proliferate in climate change reporting (see Image 1.1) as well as in (un)natural disaster reporting where satellite pictures track and capture, for example, the course of hurricanes, deforestation, forest fires and melting icesheets. These images that connote a shared planet and threatened environment serve as icons of globality and now abound in the media sphere.

Images that function, more indexically, to stand in for global processes of climate change also regularly feature across the news landscape. Consider the following: An image of a melting iceflow representing the breaking up of the Greenland icecap under the headline, 'On the edge: Greenland ice cap breaking up at twice the rate it was five years ago, says scientists Bush tried to gag' (*The Independent*, front page, 17.2.06); a picture of a sun-bleached animal skull, defoliated tree and scorched red desert with the banner headline, 'The century of drought' (*The Independent*, front page, 4.10.06); and a picture of an idyllic palm tree island surrounded by corals and green sea with 'SOS' emblazoned across it, followed by: 'On the front line of global warming, Pacific Islanders battle to save what is left of their country' (*The Independent*, front page 16.7.07). Such images, as I say, are now fairly typical. When put to work in the service of *The Independent's* campaigning editorial stance on climate change as just seen, such culturally resonate images arguably prove to be powerful allies. In images such as these, the abstract science of climate change is rendered culturally meaningful and environmentally consequential. Geographically remote spaces affected by climate change when *visualized* become literally perceptible and therefore 'knowable' places; as such, they can also potentially better become the object of political concern or even action.

Mainstream broadcasters, whether the BBC in the UK, ABC in Australia or CNN in the US have all commissioned special reports and/or dispatched correspondents to remote places, from the Arctic to the Amazon, in the wake of IPCC reports. They have done so to help record and visualize the consequences of climate change, as have many others broadcasters and journalists around the world. In 2007 the CEO of News Corporation, Rupert Murdoch, publicly committed his media outlets to reporting climate change as a real threat and reporting it in new vivid ways. He also committed his corporation to become carbon neutral (Nash 2007: 3). Climate change, it seems, has eventually come of age as a serious news issue. *The Times* newspaper, which, as we heard earlier, gave vociferous vent to the views and voices of climate change sceptics, now proves itself capable of producing a series of special Sunday magazine supplements, replete with free DVD produced by Discovery channel entitled 'Nature's Fury', pull-out posters of global warming and accounts of the 'fallacy' of climate sceptics (*The Sunday Times*, 4.11.07). The first of these posters proclaims, for example, 'Natural forces, illustrated here, control the temperature of the planet. But that fine equilibrium is now threatened by man's greenhouse emissions.'

The spectacular visualization of climate change is not confined to press or broadcasters' panoramic scenes of deserts, forests and icesheets or time–series photographs taken from high altitudes or outer space. It also encompasses the deliberate staging of spectacular 'mega-media events' and coordinated world wide demonstrations. Martin Albrow comments on the globalist values that underpin the staging of such spectaculars as follows:

> The possibility of performing live simultaneously to a world audience prompts the staging of spectacles which seek to accomplish ecstasy and, simultaneously, awe at the idea of the world viewing itself. This was the intended global village effect of the Live Aid concerts overtly designed for the celebration of globalist values. These staged global spectacles are unwilling to detach the musical performance from a celebration of the worldwide audience which the technology makes possible. They have for that reason been deliberately used to raise responses to global images, of poverty and starvation, where worldwide news manufacture equally relies on finding universal symbols of the human condition. (Albrow 1996: 146)

Taking its cue from the earlier Live Aid media concerts (see Chapter 8), Al Gore and the Alliance for Climate Protection staged Live Earth on Saturday 8 July 2007, a 24-hour series of nine concerts held on seven continents. The concerts were aimed at raising awareness about global warming and were watched by an estimated 2 billion people around the world. Such spectacular media events occupy something of a hybrid position between the planned ceremonial and celebratory media events discussed by Dayan and Katz (1992) and those unplanned exceptional media phenomena that include 'mediatized public crises' (Alexander and Jacobs 1998) and political scandals (Thompson 2000) which prove more disruptive or even challenging to the established social order. As we heard in the previous chapter, some forms of disaster reporting assume heavily ritualized forms where trauma, grief and sometimes anger become publicly circulated and performed. These mediatized disasters can turn into public crises and even political scandals as blame, culpability and ritual degradation and shame are seemingly demanded on the public stage. Staged spectacles, such as Live Earth, and Live Aid before it, in contrast, are planned spectacles designed to focus the world's attention on selected crises, building awareness and political pressures for change. They do so principally through the spectacle of live music, celebrity perform-ances and the global phenomenology of the event itself or its invoked sense of 'awe at the idea of the world viewing itself'. Their success is not a foregone conclusion, however, as far as the news media are concerned.

In the case of Live Earth, unlike Live Aid, much of the news coverage guaranteed by such a mega-spectacle did not translate into a full and enthusiastic endorsement of the underlying message of the event or the part played by the media within this. In the UK, the BBC alone scheduled over 16 hours, much of it live and gave prominent exposure to statements from Al Gore who encouraged the millions watching to: 'Put all this energy in your heart and help us solve climate change.' But Live Earth received at best mixed and often half-hearted news coverage. This was summed up, for example, in the following British newspaper headlines: 'Nice gig, shame about the footprint' (*Independent on Sunday*, 8 July 2007: 12), 'Rockin' all over the world (but just watch your carbon footprint)' (*Observer*, 8 July 2007: 17) and 'What on Earth? Political bias, lewd jokes, technical glitches and constant plugs for Microsoft . . . what possessed the BBC to air 15 hours of Live Earth?' (*The Mail on Sunday*, July 8:9).

The mediated politics of spectacle, it seems, is capricious and cannot always be predicted or relied on in advance. This is so no matter the good intentions of the organizers, the groundswell of concern about climate change prompted by the IPCC reports and reported widely in the news media, or even the Nobel-prize winning efforts of Al Gore himself touring the world and delivering his message and film 'The Inconvenient Truth'. Part of the problem, it seems, was that Live Earth was both too political and not political enough.

It was not political enough in the sense that the spectacular event appeared to subsist at the level of awareness raising, and did not move to target governments and corpor-ations or build a campaign based on explicit political demands (see Chapter 8 also). The spectacle and Albrow's 'awe of the idea of the world watching itself', in other words, was not capitalized on with a deliberate campaign of political action. And yet for others Live Earth was seen as too political. As we have already heard, sections of the British press clearly felt uneasy with the focus on the implicit politics of climate change which, whether explicitly articulated by the organizers or not, sees climate change as not only posing a considerable threat to the world's ecosystems but also to the organization of human life as we know it. This challenge to taken-for-granted notions of state sovereignty, goals of perpetual economic growth and consumer indi-vidualism, for example, were inferred by some commentators and felt to be beyond the pale of acceptable environmental concern, tipping over into 'radical politics'.

This interpretation of climate change as too politically 'hot to handle' appears to have also led the UK public service broadcaster, the BBC, to drop 'Planet Relief' – its planned day-long special on global warming. The head of BBC TV News declared, for example, that: 'It is not the BBC's job to lead opinion or proselytize on this or any other subject' (quoted in *The Independent*, 6.9.07:2) and a BBC news programme editor said: 'It's absolutely not the job of the BBC to save the planet' (quoted in *The Independent*, 6.9.07: 2). As many remarked at the time: 'The idea that one can remain "neutral" on the question of whether or not we should protect the habitable climate of this planet strikes me as both outrageous and absurd. This is cowardice' (Mark Lynas, quoted in *The Independent*, 6.9.07: 3). Again, it appears that the entrenched institutional and professional norm of 'impartiality' (exacerbated in a context of growing criticism of the BBC and its alleged failure to live up to its traditional standards) has tamed the corporation's preparedness to actively engage with, rather than simply document, global climate change. Although prepared to support other 'Comic Relief-type' events in support of Live Aid and, annually, 'Children in Need', evidently climate change and the devastation of the planet's ecosystems are seen as too political.

And yet, as noted earlier, the BBC like other major broadcasters has recently adopted a more proactive position on reporting the effects of climate change around the world and produced a succession of special news reports exploring these impacts leaving little room for doubt as to the disastrous consequences of climate change for the planet. And, in this respect at least, they have begun to rise to the challenge, identified in earlier research, to 'make the sheer scale of potential global damage that climate change may inflict a major and recurrent news story' (Hargreaves et al. 2002: 51). What they haven't done, and this is signalled in the BBC's decision not to continue with its planned Planet Relief day, is to overcome the evident *disconnect* between journalism's coverage of climate change as a world crisis and what audiences and publics can or should do with this new information and its affective charge.

If, at last, news of climate change has moved significantly beyond science and sceptics, how are we, the audience at home, meant to respond to the news spectacle of impending and actual climate-related disasters? How should we respond to the predictions of worse to come that now come thick and fast through the mainstream news media? It is this fundamental *disconnect*, publicly 'legitimized' by pronouncements of corporate timidity and misplaced professional norms such as those of the BBC and the US elite press that arguably threatens to position audiences as voyeurs of their own impending peril. George Monbiot (2007b) argues that the problem resides much deeper than the institutional timidity of public service broadcasting or the naïve 'apolitical' views of its news executives. It resides, fundamentally, he suggests, in the capitalist economy and consumer culture of contemporary societies that surround and shape the output of the mainstream media in their own image:

Who will persuade us to act? However strong the opposition parties' policies appear to be, they cannot be sustained unless the voters move behind them. We

won't be prompted by the media. The BBC drops Planet Relief for fear of breach-
ing its impartiality guidelines: heaven forbid that it should come out against mass
death. But it broadcasts a programme – Top Gear – that puts a match to its
guidelines every week, and now looks about as pertinent as the Black and White
Minstrel Show. The schedules are crammed with shows urging us to travel further,
drive faster, build bigger, buy more, yet none of them are deemed to offend the
rules, which really mean that they don't offend the interests of business or the
pampered sensibilities of the Aga class. The media, driven by fear and advertising,
is hopelessly biased towards the consumer economy and against the biosphere.
(George Monbiot 2007b, *The Guardian*, 30.10.07; *http://www.Monbiot.com/
archives/2007/10/30*)

Monbiot's biting comments find plentiful empirical support. His own newspaper,
The Guardian, though doing more than most to propel the issue of climate to the top
of the news agenda and keep it there with successive features and spectacular images,
routinely carries, for example, advertisements for petrol guzzling, carbon emitting
4×4s and glossy travel supplements inviting its readers to fly to distant destinations
extending their carbon footprints around the globe. The hold of commercial culture
throughout the media it seems is ubiquitous and it is definitely not carbon neutral.
  Conventional ways of reporting extreme weather disasters informed by the professional calculus of death as well as its ritualized forms of mediatization (Chapter 3)
are also part of the problem when it comes to the mega-disaster of climate change.
Whether unprecedented summer floods in the UK, prolonged droughts in Australia,
raging forest fires in California or exceptional rains and unusual storms across swathes
of Africa and Asia, the news media, it seems, rarely make the bigger connection with
climate change. No single weather event, no matter how extreme, say climate experts,
can definitely be accounted for in such terms – in spite of the fact that the recorded
increased frequency and patterns of extreme weather events that NGOs are clear
cannot be explained by any other means (Oxfam 2007). These bad news stories, then,
are treated for the most part as news as usual, and the opportunity for underlining the
reality and urgency of climate change becomes squandered in the news media. And, as
we have heard, the geopolitics infused in the priorities and parameters of national-
based news organizations is also no less relevant for understanding the western-centric
responses to the uneven impacts of global warming. As Monbiot astutely observes:
'The effort to tackle climate change suffers from the problem of split incentives: those
who are least responsible for it are the most likely to suffer its effects' (Monbiot 2007a:
21), a truism that registers in the regionally fractured responses of news organizations
to the differentiated impacts of climate change around the world.
  These formidable obstacles to the public elaboration of climate change in the news
media and its signalling as a problem demanding urgent political action and democratic participation notwithstanding, there are, as we have seen, signs of democratic
advance and even of engaged commitment by sections of the mainstream media to

propel the issue forward as a matter of the utmost importance. The politics of climate change moves over time and is conducted in and through a news media ecology, composed of differing outlets, media and editorial agendas and outlooks and the last is generally no longer impervious to the anthropogenic nature of climate change, its catastrophic consequences and need for radical, concerted action.

Science, sceptics, spectacle: where to next? Possibly spin. As governments and economies seek to adapt to and mitigate the realities of climate change and ratchet up their responses through international treatises and new protocols, committing to carbon trading schemes, emission reductions, fossil fuel energy efficiencies and the development of renewables and other new technologies, so the field of environmental issues and interests will complexify. New conflicts and contentions, new discourses and disagreements, inevitably, will open up on this increasingly crowded and cracked environmental terrain. Many already have and, following new international commitments to reduce carbon emissions pleaded at the Bali summit (2007), many more are poised to do so.

These include: the production of biofuels prompting the clearing of (carbon-sink) forests and substitution of biofuel crops for food crops in poor, under-nourished, countries; the 'carbon miles' involved in air freighting food exports from developing countries and the economic and social costs to those societies and communities of not doing so; the 'return' of nuclear energy as a preferred alternative to fossil fuels; the expansion of wind farms and the environmental costs of renewable energy schemes; the inconsistencies and contradictions of government taxation systems and differing systems of transport subsidies; the bureaucratic chicanery and corporate abuses of international carbon trading and offsetting schemes; the rise of China, India and Brazil as major carbon emitters alongside the US and the west; and the failure of major powers to ratify international protocols and/or meaningfully support processes of climate change adaptation as well as mitigation in developing countries.

These, and countless other conflicts and contentions, are all set to multiply in the years and decades ahead and, inevitably, they pose profound challenges to systems of governance and democratic politics from the local to the global levels. Here the 'argumentation craftsmen' (Beck 1999) or public relations experts and the politicians of spin are all likely to go to work, as vested interests and contending definitions of the global public good compete for public legitimacy and support. As they do so, most will seek access to the news stage and the media's evolving communication forms and platforms to put their messages and meanings across; and some may use these same means to strive for increased ecological solidarity with others around the planet. That is for the near future.

For the present, it seems ironic, to say the least, that just as climate change has eventually made it onto the news map and become visualized as a major threat – often spectacularly – so talk of 'eco-fatigue' has begun to be heard. We shall have occasion to question its elder conceptual parent 'compassion fatigue' later (see Chapter 7). Leo Hickman asks whether 'eco-fatigue' isn't in fact a classic symptom of denial:

The alarm clock is buzzing away, but we'd rather hit the snooze button than face the day ahead. All the classic signs are evident: transference ('our emissions are tiny compared to China's'); minimization ('personally I can't wait till it's 2C warmer'); falsifiability ('you can't prove 100% that we're to blame'); false memory ('summers were always much hotter when I was a kid'); diversion ('there are far more pressing things to worry about in this world than climate change'); and rationalization ('I work bloody hard, so I damn well deserve my long-haul holidays'). (Hickman 2007: 31)

Hickman is surely right to identify some of the responses and arguments made by individuals who resist changing their behaviour and consumption patterns in response to climate change. But do these argumentative stratagems add up to a named condition of 'eco-fatigue'? As we heard earlier, we know that processes of audience reception to environmental issues and concerns, including climate change, are complexly structured and negotiated by culturally situated audiences (Corner and Richardson 1993; Macnaghten and Urry 1998; Buckingham 2000; Hargreaves et al. 2002; Lorenzoni et al. 2006; Lowe et al. 2006; Etkin and Ho 2007). This complexity appears to be lost from view within the general assertion of a new condition and concept called 'eco-fatigue'. We certainly need to explore how exactly individuals (as well as corporations, organizations and governments) interpret and integrate into their practices the mediated discourses and depictions of climate change, but these representations, as we have seen, change through time, as well as across place and space, and have done so as climate change has become seen not only as a physical problem defined by science but a political crisis communicated and conducted in and through the media sphere.

The spectacle of climate change visualized through the news media helps to speaks to us all about this global threat and marks a crucial development in its media career. When presented in such spectacular ways, however, the news media can all too easily position us as voyeurs only of impending catastrophe. There is, in other words, a profound disconnect between the news mediated realization of climate change as a major threat to humanity and what exactly we as news readers, viewers and potential 'publics' can do about it based on the information, predictions and spectacular pictures offered to us of the world's ecosystems now under threat. Spectacular images can play a powerful role in 'bringing home' the threat of climate change but remain, for the most part, woefully disconnected from possible courses of collective engagement and political response. It seems foolhardy to interpret such a situation through an individualist prism of eco-fatigue.

To repeat, it is too early (or too late) to talk of eco-fatigue. The changing nature of the world's climate and its predicted impact on people and ecosystems around the globe can yet captivate attention and focus minds. Even fatigued people can stir from their slumber, especially when there's a growing storm outside that threatens their way of life . . .

5 | FORCED MIGRATIONS AND HUMAN RIGHTS: ANTINOMIES IN THE MEDIATED ETHICS OF CARE

The refugee challenge in the 21st century is changing rapidly. People are forced to flee their homes for increasingly complicated and interlinked reasons. Some 40 million people worldwide are already uprooted by violence and persecution, and it is likely that the future will see more people on the run as a growing number of push factors compound one another to create conditions for further forced displacement.

Today people do not just flee persecution and war but also injustice, exclusion, environmental pressures, competition for scarce resources and all the miserable human consequences of dysfunctional states.

The task facing the international community in this new environment is to find ways to unlock the potential of refugees who have so much to offer if they are given the opportunity to regain control over their lives. (UNCHR 2007; *http:// www.unch.org/cgi-bin/texis/vtx/events?id*=3e7f46e04)

Confronting the new global challenges posed by the changing nature of forced migration in the 21st century, the United Nations High Commission for Refugees (UNCHR) talks of a 'new paradigm'. Forced migration includes not only refugees and asylum seekers fleeing war, persecution and injustice but also growing numbers of internally displaced people. It is often the rural poor, for example, who are forced off their lands to make way for dams, agricultural and industrial developments or new cities in the name of 'progress' and 'the national interest' – projects that invariably benefit national elites. *Un*natural disasters, climate change and environmental pollution are now also beginning to propel movements of people both internally and internationally. And people trafficking by criminal gangs, including women and children for sexual exploitation and the illegal transportation of migrants across national borders, are also characteristic features of contemporary forced migration (Castles 2003: 15). Globally, more and more countries are now experiencing the simultaneous arrival of migrants from diverse countries and backgrounds, and migration has become increasingly politicized as policies of border control are tightened in the name of national security (Castles and Miller 2003). It is in this context that Stephen Castles has called for a new interdisciplinary sociology of forced migration – a sociology that aims to analyse the characteristics of forced migration in the epoch of globalization (Castles 2003: 17).

An important component of the study of forced migration, necessarily, must include research into how the media portray migrants, their past experiences and hopes for the future as well as the policies and politics that surround their arrival and shape their efforts to rebuild lives. To what extent and in what ways, for example, have the media communicated the lived realities of forced migration within their host societies? Have these representations helped prepare the ground that can begin to 'unlock the potential of refugees who have so much to offer' and sought to support their efforts to 'regain control over their lives'? Or have they problematized their collective standing, undermined claims for recognition and acceptance and compounded their plight? The findings of research studies from Canada, Australia and the United Kingdom first help to address such questions and, together, provide evidence of the news media's 'collective problematization' of the arrival of refugees and asylum seekers.

However, this is not the whole story. The chapter then moves to examine media representations that have gone beyond these established national frames of reference, sometimes challenging them and presenting a more complex and caring stance to the plight of others. These forms of journalism variously and professionally inscribe what can be termed a 'mediated ethics of care', an invitation to recognize, better understand and care about the plight of others. Often advanced against a backdrop of human rights law enshrined in international treatises and legislative frameworks as well the established normative culture of civil society, some news outlets and their journalists increasingly promote human rights issues and investigate and condemn their continuing abuse around the world. This chapter sets out to explore further this antimony or apparent contradiction between the 'collective problematization' of forced migrants and asylum seekers when reported within a national context, on the one hand, and the inscribed 'mediated ethics of care' also in evidence when reporting on human rights abuses from around the world, on the other.

News, migrants and collective problematization: three case studies

In the summer of 1999 four unmarked ships from Fujian province in China arrived at Canada's west coast transporting several hundred undocumented migrants. At the time over 30,000 immigrants and refugees were attempting entry to Canada each year. Joshua Greenberg and Sean Hier (2001), in their detailed study of the Canadian news media response to these latest migrants, document how the news media constructed a public image of the immigration and refugee system as being in a 'state of crisis'. They elaborate their position as follows:

> It is one of the core tasks of media analysis to address the involvement of news organizations in the construction of social problems. By selecting which events to report, interviewing and quoting experts who interpret those events, and assembling and distributing the final news product, news organizations create the discursive environment in which collective problematization about troubling events may occur. (Greenberg and Hier 2001: 564)

In many respects their study serves as an exemplary case study of the news media's part in the social construction of crises and how, in this instance, Chinese migrants became defined as a collective threat:

> The significance of crisis, therefore, rests not just in an ability to diagnose a problem at the structural or institutional level, but also in the capacity to construct a repertoire of narrative representations of that problem, which may then compete in the public sphere in terms of their ability to find resonance with the general population. . . . Thus, we argue that the immigration and refugee crisis spawned by news coverage of these events should be seen as part of a much broader process of 'collective problematization' from which the contours of the present and future of social and political life in Canada are and will be born. (Greenberg and Hier 2001: 564)

This stance on the social construction of social problems recognizes, then, their structural and institutional underpinning as well as construction through the discursive representations and elaborations of the news media. The news media are seen as operating as a *claims-making forum* for the *social construction and contestation* of reality and *structures of news access* as well as the *thematic structure* of news coverage becomes key focal points of analysis. Based on a systematic analysis of Canada's four main newspapers, the *National Post*, *Vancouver Sun*, *Toronto Sun* and *Victoria Times-Colonist*, the researchers document how:

> [T]he press generally gave prominent coverage to the idea that the migrants' arrivals posed a significant danger to the 'health' and 'security' of the Canadian state and its public(s). This portrayal encompassed three particular features: first, the migrants' arrivals would prompt a sharp increase in both international and domestic organized crime; second, they would bring with them infectious diseases that would harm 'legitimate' citizens; and third, Canada was only a stopover to the migrants' ultimate destination of the United States . . . Although the migrants were unambiguously represented in mainstream news discourse as the embodiment of such threat, blame was also attributed to a 'good intentioned' but 'flawed' refugee and immigration system. The threat to public health and security was thus accounted for in terms of Chinese migrants would bring with

them 'communicable diseases and violent political habits'. (Greenberg and Hier 2001: 572–573)

In these ways, news coverage enacted a process of *collective problematization* in which Chinese migrants became represented as the embodiment of danger, as a threat to the physical, moral and political security of the nation. These findings are not without historical precedents. The collective problematization of immigrant groups in terms of disease, health scares and dirt has long been noted (Butterworth 1967) as have other attributions of deviancy, whether crime, rioting, drug use, sexual promiscuity, welfare sponging or, more recently, religious fanaticism and terrorism (Cottle 2000b; Poole and Richardson 2006). What is particularly disturbing about these recent findings is how such 'historical' associations can be so easily resurrected and ascribed by the press in the present, suggesting that these stigmatizing outlooks hold wider cultural resonance as well as historical longevity.

Greenberg and Hier's study is also noteworthy in that it discerns how this particular case of news coverage *resonated* with broader concerns already expressed through the Canadian press about the disintegration of the Canadian welfare state, the perceived threat to territorial sovereignty by unwanted outsiders and the fear that the government can no longer protect the security of its population. Again, the ways in which minority groups through their representation in the news media can become a cipher for surrounding discourses and concerns or even a scapegoat for society's wider ills has long been observed in the research literature (Hartmann and Husband 1974; Hall et al. 1978), and underlines how wider processes of change can become refracted in and played out ideologically through the news media's responses to migrants.

Similar findings are reported in Australian research. Kate Slattery situates the news mediated 'children overboard' affair, an important moment in the vexed politics of Australian migration, in the context of escalating problems in the Middle East, global economic uncertainty and an increase in asylum seekers, refugees and migration worldwide (Slattery 2003). The 'children overboard' affair concerned the alleged preparedness of Iraqi asylum seekers intercepted by the Australian Navy north of Christmas Island to throw their children overboard as a way of putting pressure on the Navy vessel to pick them up and take them to Australian territory. As Prime Minister John Howard stated in a radio interview at the time:

> I don't want in Australia people who would throw their own children into the sea, I don't think any Australian does. . . . There's something, to me, incompatible between somebody who claims to be a refugee and somebody who would throw their own child into the sea. It offends the natural instinct of protection and delivering security and safety to our children. (cited in Slattery 2003: 95)

The story was relayed widely by the Australian news media and effectively served to demonize the asylum seekers as seemingly heartless, amoral and lacking in family values – collective representations that could only help legitimize the government of

John Howard's tough approach to border control and the incarceration of asylum seekers and refugees in remote detention camps (including mothers and children, often for years) before deporting them back to their countries of origin:

> The 'children overboard' incident, as a constructed 'media event', was used to reinforce public attitudes towards the asylum seeker 'other' and to reaffirm an Australian 'self' – that of a 'good', 'moral' Australian citizen. . . . this was done by pitting an Australian national identity – signified in media and political dialogue by the metaphors of family morals and responsibility, and the value of democracy – against a menacing and threatening asylum seeker 'other' – signified by Islamic extremist principles attached to the people who were apparently prepared to risk their children's safety. (Slattery 2003: 94)

We now know that the video footage and photograph images released by the government purporting to show children having been thrown in the water and circulated throughout the Australian media were untrue. They showed, in fact, scenes of adults and children fleeing their sinking boat that had been recorded some days after the government's initial claims (Saxton 2003; Marr and Wilkinson 2004). Other studies document how the negative framing of asylum seekers in Australia was not confined to this particular incident. The news media, it is argued, generally adopted the negative terms of reference deployed by the Australian government, whether in respect of 'threat' through 'other', to 'illegality' and 'burden' (Klocker and Dunn 2003). By such news mediated images and the largely uncritical reporting of government pronouncements and claims, the news media, argues Slattery, 'reignited tensions involving boundaries and borders, both geographical and cognitive' (Slattery 2003: 93)

A report produced by Article 19, 'What's the Story? Media Representation of Refugees and Asylum Seekers in the UK' (Article 19 2003), also examined how asylum seekers and refugees are represented in the news media and went further in exploring the extent to which refugees and asylum seekers feel able to participate in the public debate on asylum and immigration as well as the impact media coverage has had on their everyday lives. The report produced nine principal findings that bear repeating here:

1. Media reporting of the asylum issue is characterized by the inaccurate and provocative use of language to describe those entering the country to seek asylum. 51 different labels were identified as making reference to individuals seeking refuge in Britain and included meaningless and derogatory terms such as 'illegal refugee' and 'asylum cheat'.
2. Media reporting, particularly in the tabloid press, consistently fails to correctly distinguish between economic migrants and asylum seekers or refugees. The terms immigrant and asylum seeker are used as synonyms rather than as distinct terms to accurately convey the specific status and situation of individuals.
3. The asylum debate focuses overwhelmingly on the number of people entering

the country to claim asylum, but the numbers which are presented in print and broadcast reports are frequently unsourced, exaggerated or inadequately explained. Contextual analysis of the relevance and meaning of official statistics is missing from the debate.

4. Images used to accompany print and broadcast reports on the issue of asylum are dominated by the stereotype of the 'threatening young male'. Women and children are rarely seen and stock images of groups of men trying to break into Britain are used repeatedly.

5. News and feature articles on asylum rely heavily on politicians, official figures and the police as sources of information and explanation. Individual asylum seekers and refugees are only quoted when they themselves are the subject of a report and rarely contribute directly to the policy debate.

6. Asylum seekers and refugees feel alienated, ashamed and sometimes threatened as a result of the overwhelmingly negative media coverage of asylum. Many of the interviewees reported direct experience of prejudice, abuse or aggression from neighbours and service providers which they attributed to the way in which the media informs public opinion.

7. Asylum seekers and refugees are not hostile to the media, in spite of the negative coverage, and many describe their sense of duty to speak out and highlight human rights abuses in their own countries and counter the myths about refugees in the UK. Nevertheless they are wary of 'hidden agendas' and rely on trust established by refugee organizations to facilitate contact with the media. All insist on anonymity and very few are willing to be photographed or filmed.

8. Refugee women are frustrated by the lack of interest by the media which affect them and feel that misguided assumptions about their role in their own communities can act as a barrier to journalists approaching them for an interview. Both men and women think that the media fails to adequately reflect the experience of refugee women in Britain.

9. Asylum seekers and refugees are reluctant to complain about inaccurate or prejudicial reporting. Interviewees expressed a mixture of doubt that their views would be accurately represented and concern about the consequences of being seen to complain. (Article 19 2003: 9)

These studies, and many others conducted across the years, generally document how the news media have collectively problematized minorities in different ways (Cottle 2000b; Poole and Richardson 2006; Allen et al. 2007). Recent research documenting news responses to forced migrants in Canada, Australia and the UK are important and their findings follow in descent from earlier studies. Together they suggest that boundaries of inclusion and exclusion, of acceptance and denial, are not only represented and circulated in the news media but are constituted, in meaningful and detrimental ways, by them. Such representations, moreover, can enter into the course of social relations, influencing their conduct and entrenching identities and discourses of difference. In such ways, news representations and public discourses can help set the parameters of 'acceptable' social conduct, conditioning perceptions and practices and legitimizing the policies and politics of control. But is this the whole story?

A different story: journalism and the mediated ethics of care

If the news media can perform such a crucial role in the public definition and elaboration of the politics surrounding forced migrants, it is imperative that the more progressive openings and potential of the media are also carefully examined. How different news outlets, editorial outlooks, distinctive journalism forms and the increasing global interpenetrations of today's complex news ecology (see Figure 1.1) can help to sustain a more pluralized elaboration of the politics and personal testimonies of forced migrants demands in-depth exploration. In this respect, the Article 19 report is especially noteworthy in deliberately setting out to explore how refugees and asylum seekers relate to the media and what obstacles and difficulties need to be overcome if they are to secure access and put their points of view across.

Media representations of minorities including migrants, we know, have long involved demeaning stereotypes, discourses of denigration and symbolic annihilation. But this story, as argued elsewhere (Cottle 2006a: 167–184), is not necessarily destined to remain fixed for all time. Some sections and outlets of mainstream news media are, in fact, capable of producing representations that give voice to the voiceless and identity to image and these can perform an important role in the public rehabilitation of former 'others', accessing personal testimonies, visualizing past narratives and challenging dominant codes and discourses. By such means media audiences are encouraged to 'bear witness' to the difficult circumstances and hazardous journeys endured by asylum seekers, refugees and other forced migrants, and consider the politics of their collective plight.

Although often overlooked by researchers or buried within the statistical aggregates of content analyses, especially when based on generalized press findings, news media can and do sometimes produce more expressive, in-depth, contextualized and challenging news reports and features. The day on which I wrote this, for example, *The Independent* newspaper published its front page under the headline: 'Slave labour that shames America' and continued, 'Migrant workers chained, beaten and forced into debt, exposing the human cost of producing cheap food' (*The Independent* 19.12.07). This special investigation report continued on inside pages under the titles: 'How migrant workers are abused and exploited in the land of the free' and 'Slavery in America' (pp.2–3).

Not all mainstream newspapers, it seems, are editorially destined to reproduce discourses of denigration and the collective problematization of migrants; and some mainstream TV news programmes around the world, for their part, also routinely produce a minority of in-depth forms of reportage focusing, for example, on social justice issues (Cottle and Rai 2006). Current affairs and documentary programmes though increasingly squeezed in the TV schedules by reality TV formats also continue, as we shall see, to provide occasional in-depth programmes that go behind the headlines – and these journalistic interventions sometimes reverberate across the news media and wider society (for examples, see Cottle 2006a: 167–184). Ulrich Beck, fur-ther, alludes to the role of the mass media in what he terms the 'globalization of emotions' with its contribution to a new, transnational cosmopolitan outlook:

> The tears we guiltily wipe from our eyes before the television or in the cinema are no doubt consciously produced by Hollywood trickery and by how the news media is stage-managed. But that in no way alters the fact that these spaces of our emotional imagination have expanded in a transnational sense. When civilians and children in Israel, Palestine, Iraq or Africa suffer and die and this suffering is presented in compelling images in the mass media, this produces cosmopolitan pity which forces us to act. (Beck 2006: 5–6)

Beck continues: 'It is not necessary to isolate and organize human beings into antagon-istic groups, not even within the broad expanses of the nation, for them to become self-aware and capable of political action' (Beck 2006: 6). While we need to pursue further whether mediated 'cosmopolitan pity' necessarily leads us to act (and how) (see Chapter 7) we can agree, on the basis of findings reported earlier, that national news frames often militate against the development of a cosmopolitan outlook and mediated ethic of care especially when national news media report on 'their' national preoccupations. But contemporary forms of journalism, from the local to the global and deploying both argument and emotion, can also sometimes help to fragment stereotypes and 'flesh out' or humanize former 'others', repositioning them within the public universe of collective recognition and the mediated politics of care. The increased salience of human rights issues within a globalizing context helps to under-gird these more caring journalist treatments that go against the grain of 'collective problematization.' An example helps to make the point.

Rageh Omaar's documentary, 'This World: Child Slavery' set out to trace con-temporary child trafficking and slavery around the world (BBC2, broadcast 26.3.07). The programme's principal themes and subject treatment is encapsulated in Omaar's own summary publicized on the BBC news website:

> We do not see slavery as belonging to our world, not as something which is still happening today. . . . It is believed that there are nearly nine million children around the world today who are enslaved. There are international charters and covenants which try to come to a legal definition of what constitutes slavery. In essence these documents define slavery in the modern world as a situation where a human being and their labour are owned by others, and where that person does

not have the freedom to leave and is forced into a life which is exploitative, humiliating and abusive.

One of the characters in the film I have made for the BBC is Dalyn, a young girl from Cambodia, who after years of counseling and therapy was able and willing to talk to us about how she was sold into sexual slavery in a brothel when she was 12 years old. Dalyn represents just one of the estimated 1.2 million children that the International Labour Organization believes are trafficked every year . . .

Then there is the gentle and sweet 12-year-old boy Mawulehawe from Ghana who is sold by his mother to a fishing 'master'. Far from being the sadistic and immoral person you would expect, master Aaron is friendly and completely open about what he does and his motives. Mawulehawe sits and listens as he is haggled over, eventually being sold for £25 ($48). . . . In selling him to a fishing master, his relatives believe that far from being sold into anything approximating slavery, Mawulehawe is being given an apprenticeship, a chance for him to learn a trade . . .

Nearly three thousand miles away in Saudi Arabia, 6-year-old Ali was picked up by the authorities for begging on the streets of Jeddah. He was smuggled into Saudi Arabia from Yemen for this purpose. Ali says he ended up begging after being beaten with a metal wire when he said he did not want to beg all day. Ali is one of thousands of Yemani children sold to gangs and forced to beg each year. . . .

In this documentary, we get to see and learn about the world of modern slavery in which these children live, through them, and as a result it provides a complex, disturbing, surprising and vivid look into a world many of us adults are oblivious to. . . .

Poverty underlies almost all aspects of the phenomenon of modern child slavery. It is the one issue that most often lies behind the reasons and circumstances they were given up or sold into such conditions. (*http://news.bbc.co.uk/1/hi/programmes/this_world/6458377.stm*)

As intimated by Omaar's own account, his programme interweaves personal narratives, experiential testimonies, wider analytical frames and authoritative sources into a powerful (and visually arresting) indictment of contemporary child slavery and trafficking across the globe. As it does so, it provides a transnational and global perspective on a problem that both migrates across and transcends national frames of reference or explanation, exposing international interconnections, contextualizing motives and exploring both the scope of the problem and its human consequences.

The programme was also 'global' in its potential communicative reach. It was publicized extensively by BBC promotions and also featured in BBC news programmes at the time and it has since been broadcast and discussed by other broadcasters around the world. At the time of writing it has its own web pages on the BBC News website (listed earlier) and long after its first showing. The web pages also provides access to video extracts, further background and analysis, graphic depictions of world slavery, the latest International Labour Office (ILO) *Child Labour Report*, and internet links to UNICEF, ILO, Anti-Slavery International and the UK Human Trafficking Centre. Although one programme only, it registered widely in the media sphere and serves to remind us how some forms of journalism can and do recognize and publicize the collective plight of others, performatively intervening within the surrounding discourses of forced migration and promoting its message through transnational broadcasting and online networks – a global subject matter and global reach, then, that many media academic analyses have yet to match. Omaar's programme both embeds and encourages an evident mediated ethics of care.

Media representations of human suffering can assume different salience and forms within the communication flows and differentiated nature of contemporary news ecology. A number of scholars have recently turned to questions of mediated ethics and how the news media position us, the audience, in relation to reports and scenes of human suffering, those who suffer and the sorts of responses and obligations that are incumbent upon us when they do (Tester 1994; Boltanski 1999; Stevenson 1999; Cohen 2001; Seaton 2005a; Chouliaraki 2006; Silverstone 2007). Roger Silverstone (2007) has written eloquently of 'proper distance', for example, a concept that promises analytical purchase on the contemporary media and how it variously encourages or denies a mediated ethics of care:

> Proper distance refers to the importance of understanding, the more or less precise degree of proximity required in our mediated interrelationships if we are to create and sustain a sense of the other sufficient not just for reciprocity but for a duty of care, obligation and responsibility, as well as understanding. (Silverstone 2007: 46)

The news media are, in fact, capable of providing differing degrees of mediated proximity or distance when reporting others and, in so doing, variously inscribe the possibility of a mediated ethics of care. Depending on how journalists craft their news packages, involve different voices and narratives and reproduce scenes of human suffering, so the viewing/reading audience is variously invited to assume a position of felt connection and possible obligation to the news represented subject – though there is no guarantee that the 'invitation' or proposed reading position will necessarily be accepted, much less acted on. Nonetheless, there is a complexity and differentiation in news treatments and appeals here that demands to be looked at in more detail. As will be discussed further in Chapter 7, when addressing the 'CNN effect' and 'compassion fatigue' thesis, the 'communicative architecture' of journalism that variously organizes how news stories are told, deliberated and displayed (Cottle and Rai 2006) and the 'analytics of mediation' that embed different 'regimes of pity' (Chouliaraki 2006) are deeply entwined in the mediated ethics of care.

Here we turn, however, to how the political struggle for and institutionalization of human rights in recent decades has also begun to exert influence on western news agendas – a development that appears to run counter to the collective problematization of asylum seekers and refugees reproduced in national news frames already noted.

Human rights on the news agenda

> In recent years, it has become apparent to observers as well as practitioners of mass communications that human rights is more newsworthy than it was. The media have become interested not only in violations of human rights, but in the institutional apparatus that has been designed to promote and protect human rights. (International Council on Human Rights Policy (ICHRP) 2002:16)

Following the Second World War and the United Nations' Universal Declaration of Human Rights in 1948, governments have increasingly integrated humanitarian norms and human rights principles into their policy frameworks and, in the years since, numerous international protocols and conventions have become ratified in international law (ICHRP 2002; Kaldor 2003: 128–136; Benhabib 2004; Held 2004a: 119–136; Marks and Chapman 2005). In the last three decades especially, the discourse and promotion of human rights has become increasingly salient in public and political discourse: more and more human rights organizations have emerged to monitor human rights violations around the world and human rights has become a rallying call for social justice issues and the advance of democracy worldwide. The language of human rights has become established in the lexicon and policies of contemporary governance (Marks and Clapham 2005), in international tribunals and the establishment of the International Criminal Court, as well as in the justifications for 'humanitarian interventions' and new 'military humanism' (Kaldor 2003; Beck 2006; Hammond 2007). In this context, it is unsurprising perhaps that the media should discern human rights issues as increasingly newsworthy. And neither should we forget that the media themselves occupy a pivotal role in respect of human rights enshrined in the Universal Declaration of Human Rights as the 'freedom to hold opinions without interference and to seek, receive and impart information and ideas through any media and regardless of frontiers.' And yet, as we saw earlier, refugees and migrants are often reported in ways that distance or completely ignore related human rights issues. This demands further consideration.

Journalism, Media and the Challenge of Human Rights Reporting (ICHRP 2002), one of the few attempts to explore contemporary human rights reporting, observes how 'the media are more receptive to human rights issues today than at any time in the modern history of the media' (p.32). This is not to suggest, however, that many human rights issues do not remain under-reported:

> Issues that are less visible, or slow processes, are covered rarely. Human rights are still taken largely to mean political and civil rights, and the importance of economic, social and cultural rights is ignored widely by the media in their

coverage of economic issues, including the international economy, poverty, inequity and social and economic discrimination. (ICHRP 2002: 16; see also Ovsiovitch 1993; Fan and Ostini 1999)

One could also add that, in globalizing times, new conceptions of citizenship that stretch beyond the nation state also prompt new conceptions of human rights whether, for example, minority citizenship 'involving the rights to enter another society and then to remain within that society and to receive appropriate rights and duties' (Urry 1999: 315; see also Benhabib 2004) or ecological citizenship 'concerned with the rights and responsibilities of the citizen of the earth' (Urry 1999: 315; see also Dobson 2007: 132–134). According to the ICHRP report, however, three fundamental problems surface in current human rights reporting in western democracies.

The first relates to how journalists often have a 'superficial grasp of the institutional apparatus of human rights' which are 'taken to be rather arcane and specialist territory' and the second to how journalists often fail to provide sufficient context, whether historical, political, social or local, to human rights stories (ICHRP 2002: 19). Both, clearly, are important for understanding the delimited and less than in-depth reporting on many human rights issues. The third concern, however, relates more directly to our discussion of forced migrants and the collective problematization of refugees and asylum seekers, already noted, as well as those exceptional forms of reporting that periodically go against the grain of these nationally based findings. Here, importantly, the ICHRP report finds that the news media are generally disposed to conceive and compartmentalize human rights in ways that leave them blind to human rights abuses committed in their own countries:

> For the Western media, human rights are almost always seen as a dimension of foreign policy. Issues that have a strong human rights element may be addressed extensively in a domestic context but are seldom categorized in terms of rights. Child abuse, refugees and immigration, unemployment, sexual and racial discrimination and a host of other issues that are the daily staple of the media are generally covered in a manner that suggests that there are no external or commonly agreed standards to which governments must adhere. The effect of this is to weaken the media's own efforts to hold their institutions and other powerful interests in society to account. (ICHRP 2002: 19)

This observation helps to explain the apparent antinomy between the findings reviewed earlier concerning the 'collective problematization' of refugees and asylum seekers by national news media, on the one hand, and the growth of human rights news reporting that gives expression to the wider awareness and international promotion of human rights, on the other. The news media can variously provide a 'proximate' sense of understanding and sympathy for the plight of others, embedding a 'proper sense of distance' and mediated ethics of care, or they can effectively 'distance' the same through the news frames of collective problematization. Refugees and asylum seekers, as well as prisoners of war, torture, extra-judicial killings, child abuse, trafficking and racism, all occupy a core position in the historical formation of human rights discourse and international human rights law and yet, as we have heard, national news media often continue to report on many of them in ways that displace or effectively deny the validity and reality of human rights and their embodiment within international law.

The reporting of human rights issues, nonetheless, continues to evolve in response to its extension to different fields of conflict and social injustices as well as in respect of the changing international and global news ecology. As discussed by the global public sphere theorists (see Chapter 2), global and international news provision now inter-sects and interacts with national media systems and does so in ways that often com-plexify the notion of nationally constituted and hermetically sealed 'public spheres.' International communication flows and the importation of external news agendas into the 'domestic affairs' of other countries can sometimes exercise a powerful influence on the field of human rights recognition and protection, lending weight to arguments (and even humanitarian interventions) which assert that human rights increasingly trump national sovereignty (Benhabib 2004; Serra 2004; Gaber and Willson 2005) and even legality (Beck 2006). Two illustrations of how global and international news flows helped to 'trump' nationally based, sovereign news agendas and national news media help to make the point.

A study by Sonia Serra (2000) analyses how the killing of Brazilian street children by death squads in the mid-1980s at first went largely unreported in the Brazilian news media. She reports how there was no major public outcry against the murderous targeting of vulnerable street children. When a coalition of advocacy and religious groups staged a protest in Rio at the deaths of over 300 children this was still mainly ignored by the Brazilian news media which reproduced the dominant definitions and discourses of the police and courts dissimulating the extreme human rights violation by associating these children with drug trafficking and urban crime. In the early 1990s, however, growing pressure from advocacy groups such as Amnesty International, as well as the production of news reports and television documentaries that were shown around the world, shocked international public opinion. This combination of pressure from advocacy groups and the influence of international media reporting then, in turn, put pressure on the Brazilian national news media to take the issue seriously and adopt a more engaged reporting stance. This eventually pressurized the Brazilian authorities to recognize this violation of human rights and seek to bring the practice to an end.

Serra theorizes this interpenetrating environment of national and international communication flows and civil actions with the help of Habermas's later writings on the public sphere conceived as a site of institutional mediation between the state and civil society. She argues, 'public space in contemporary societies must be seen as a "highly complex network that branches out into a multitude of overlapping inter-national, national, regional, local, and subcultural arenas" ' (Habermas 1997, cited in Serra 2000: 155). She concludes her account of the rise of the international public sphere as follows:

> The historical reconstruction of the rise of the killing of Brazilian street children
> . . . clearly shows that the formation of the international agenda and its repercus-
> sions in the national arena involved complex mediation and representations and
> top-down, bottom-up and cross-wise relations between pressure groups, author-
> ities, civil societies and the media at the local, national and transnational
> levels. . . . the international public sphere . . . can represent a defense mechanism
> for groups outside the structure of power . . . this association of local movements
> with global public opinion is becoming increasingly common. (Serra 2000: 169)

Twenty or so years after the events recovered in Serra's detailed case study, her account
of the emergence of an international public sphere reads as extraordinarily prescient
(see, for example, Gaber and Willson 2005).

In September 2007, to take our second illustration, Burmese monks dressed in traditional saffron robes defied the Burmese authorities and led mass protests against the
appalling poverty and human rights abuses in their country (see Chapter 1, moment
seven). In 1988 when a similar popular uprising had been attempted it was brutally
suppressed by the Burmese junta with the loss of nearly three thousand lives. In 1988
little was known outside Burma of this crushed revolt as the witnesses to these events
had no way of communicating them to the outside world. In 2007, in contrast, the
so-called 'saffron revolution' palpably registered around the world; graphic scenes and
sounds, text and talk, became conveyed by the latest communication technologies,
including mobile phone cameras, weblogs and the internet.

Over the course of the first few days, the world witnessed the progress of the revolt
and then its brutal repression via smuggled videos distributed to news agencies and
television networks and by online blogs (weblogs) written by dissidents in Rangoon
and Mandalay. Images of troops beating demonstrators and firing into unarmed
crowds circulated widely. The world also witnessed the last moments of the Japanese
videojournalist, Kenji Nagai, being shot at point blank range by a soldier – giving the
lie to the official Burmese response that he had died from a stray bullet. The power of
these and other images as well as the graphic testimonies of the protestors posted
on the internet and picked up by the mainstream western news media, summoned
condemnation from the UN, political leaders and different publics around the world.
The words of one blog placed on the front page of a British newspaper, for example,
and superimposed over an image of a fleeing monk and subtitled 'Inside the Saffron
Revolution', read:

> Riot police and soldiers are beating monks . . . I saw a truck full of police with
> guns. . . . They are using tear-gas bombs against the crowd . . . Buddhist monks
> are now chanting: 'All humans be free from killing and torturing' . . . A monk was
> beaten to death while he was praying . . . the military have been ordered to
> shoot . . . About 200 people were hauled off on to the trucks and driven away . . .
> One patient died on arriving in hospital – four are still in a bad way . . . They are
> starting a crackdown . . . The junta is reducing the internet connection bandwidth

. . . I think they will cut off communication . . . We are so afraid. (*The Independent* 27 September 2007)

Visceral accounts such as these poured out of Burma at the height of the crackdown, demonstrating the capacity of the internet and its so-called blogosphere to infuse traditional mainstream media with firsthand, experiential accounts and vitalize global news reporting (Allan 2006; Pallister 2007; Reese et al. 2007).

This flood of powerful testimonies, accounts and images conveyed around the world by new and old means of communication undoubtedly caused consternation in the Burmese junta which quickly sought to regain control of the communications environment. The regime had quickly barred TV crews from entering the country, it then pulled the plug on all but the state-run television service, closed down telephone lines and the country's principal internet server and forced internet cafés to close under threat of reprisals. It finally set about tracking down computers and videocameras smuggled into the country by external dissidents. External dissidents and alternative news sites based in exile nonetheless continued to act as focal points for disseminating the reduced flows of information and images. The Democratic Voice of Burma, originally an opposition short-wave radio station, for example, continued to operate out of Norway; Mizzima News, established by a group of independent Burmese journalists in 1998, and based in Delhi, ran a news bureau in Thailand that provided an email news service and online video site with updates and eyewitness testimonies; and a Irrawaddy magazine also run by exiles in Thailand provided 'citizen reporter' accounts online – all in defiance of the regime's attempted stranglehold on Burmese communications (Pallister 2007: 5).

These examples further help to illustrate the complex communication flows between different regions and across national borders. While, in this instance, the Burmese junta managed to regain communication control relatively easily (only 1% of the Burmese population ordinarily have access to the internet, for example) this was not before some of the most damaging images and accounts of brutal repression had been captured, circulated internationally and condemned by the majority of world opinion.

Even though largely suppressed, the reporting of human rights violations in Burma at the height of the crackdown and covertly and intermittently since, underlines how an embryonic 'global public sphere' can emerge on the basis of multiple infusions from different communication technologies and the wider news ecology and communication networks that are no longer simply coincident with or confined behind national borders (see Figure 1.1).

Repressive regimes around the world are increasingly cognizant of the 'soft power' of this new communications environment with its capacity to capture and communicate human rights violations around the globe, potentially incriminating them and galvanizing world opinion and opprobrium (see Chapter 6, on 'hidden wars'). The power relations that constitute the foundation of all societies as well as those processes that challenge institutionalized power, argues Manuel Castells, 'are increasingly shaped and decided in the communications field' (Castells 2007: 239). This is not to suggest that this is only where relations of power are conducted and contested, as the images of indiscriminate shooting from the bloodied streets of Rangoon, attest. But it is to say that this is where such images can register with wider political force and impact, in the globalized media environment and its interlinkage with diverse national and transnational horizontal networks.

If Castells' general view is correct, what we are increasingly witnessing is the 'attempt by the holders of power to reassert their domination into the communications realm' and, at the same time, the rise of new social movements, insurgency politics and other forms of counter-power are seeking to mobilize – evidently with some success – new communication technologies and horizontal communication networks (Castells 2007: 258–259; see also Thompson 1995; Bennett 2003; Allan 2006). This broader picture of communicative struggle and complexity in the media field now includes the continuing 'transformation of visibility' (Thompson 1995), use of the internet by global activists (Bullert 2000; Bennett 2003; Opel and Pompper 2003; Donk et al. 2004; Jong et al. 2005) and evolution of online and other forms of citizen journalism (Allan 2006; Allan, Sonwalkar and Carter 2007). Attending specifically to the fields of forced migration and human rights reporting, however, has helped to reveal something of the differences and antinomies that currently structure news reporting and its mediated ethics of care.

These seemingly contradictory journalistic outlooks, variously informed by news prisms of 'collective problematization' and a 'mediated ethics of care' can be found across the range of news outlets and even within the same news media outlet and its expressed editorial views. While the globalizing discourse and promotion of human rights, evidently, now registers in the sensibilities of many professional journalists, mainstream news outlets and news agendas so also, demonstrably, does the continuing hold of national frames of understanding that inflect and, in more xenophobic expressions, infect the construction of representations of forced migrants in problematic or less than humanizing ways.

These antinomies are conveyed and reproduced in and through the news media. They may also give expression to the deeper political contradiction that emanates from today's post-Westphalian state system in which the sovereignty of nation states has become increasingly challenged by international systems of governance and law as well as globalizing processes such as transnational migrancy. The antinomies discerned may, in other words, ultimately be an index of the contradiction 'between the expansive and inclusionary principles of moral and political universalism, as anchored in human rights, and the particularistic and exclusionary conceptions of democratic closure' (Benhabib 2004: 19; see also Kaldor 2001; Goodhart 2005).

Nonetheless, the field of human rights issues and forced migrations are literally on the move around the globe and the antinomies discerned here need not be taken as inevitable or fixed for all time. As we have heard, human rights issues around the globe have made news headway in recent decades (ICHRP 2002; Kaldor 2003) and examples of journalism reporting that embed a mediated ethics of care and challenge the discourses of collective problematization are now also produced and circulated within the contemporary media sphere. Moreover, these forms of journalism can now also extend beyond the boundaries of the nation states in which they are produced, both in terms of their subject matter and wider global circulation.

Before we conclude, however, we must also consider that just as national news outlooks and national prisms can shape the construction of migrants in problematic and excluding ways, so the universalizing discourse of human rights can also carry a heavy western inventory and charge. 'Bearing witness', 'proper distance' and 'the mediated ethics of care', all referenced in this chapter, are not the same as adopting an external position of spectatorship only. They demand more than this. Neither can they presume to be based on the moral high ground or assume a position of ethical omniscience whether in respect of our relationship to news media subject matter, the accessed views and voices of others or the informing news narrative. No matter how 'caring' our standpoint may like to think itself to be, the mediated ethics of care ideally prompts us to respond to and engage with all these invited positions and perspectives while also reflecting on our own standpoint (see Chapter 7). So too must we constantly reflect on the place of human rights discourse (and its powered appropriations) in the wider power plays and structures of inequality that continue to shape both 'our' world and the world of 'others'.

NEW WARS AND THE GLOBAL WAR ON TERROR: ON VICARIOUS, VISCERAL VIOLENCE

When war becomes a spectator sport, the media becomes the decisive theatre of operations. (Ignatieff 2001: 207)

I share the view that there has been a revolution in military affairs, but it is a revolution in the social relations of warfare, not in technology, even though the changes in social relations are influenced by and make use of new technology. Beneath the spectacular displays are real wars, which . . . are better explained in terms of my conception of new wars. (Kaldor 2001: 3)

Processes of globalization, new information and communication technologies and developments in the field of warfare are some of the principal changes now transforming the media's relationship to and representations of war. How these and other changes position the news media with heightened significance in the reporting of war as global crises forms the main focus of this chapter.

The news media have long occupied a key terrain on which the battle for hearts and minds and propaganda war is fought and this has been extensively documented. But the media's relationship to the social organization of violence that we commonly call 'war' continues to develop and change. Increasingly the news media do not only communicate or *'mediate'* the events of war; they enter into its very constitution shaping its course and conduct. In this sense war becomes *'mediatized'*. Most wars, though not all (see later), are now *mediated*. They are reported widely and extensively in the news media and it is mainly by these means that the unfolding events of war become conveyed and, for many of us, 'known'. However, the communication of war, as suggested, now often exceeds this well documented sense of *mediated* war.

Consider the following: when war becomes a media spectacle and when symbolic war events are deliberately staged for news cameras; when combatants digitally record military actions and circulate them on the internet for their own and others' amusement; when inhumane acts and atrocities are choreographed in front of videocameras, uploaded to the internet and globalized by the world's news media; when Osama Bin Laden releases video cassettes to the media and when US political and military leaders send messages via CNN direct into the command bunker of their enemy; when the interim Iraqi government films the execution of Saddam Hussein for wider public consumption (see Chapter 1) and when suicide bombers prepare 'martyrdom videos' for wider media release. When these and countless other images and information releases enter into the course and conduct of war via the media, then clearly this is more than mediated war. This is war that is being *conducted in* and *through* the news media as well as being *communicated by* it. This is *mediatized* war (Cottle 2006a: 143–166).

In *mediatized war*, then, the involvement of media *within* war becomes heightened and, in different ways, constitutive of war itself, influencing its conduct on different fronts. Indeed it has often been observed that in war the news media can form a 'front' in their own right, but in mediatized war this becomes even more pronounced. Here the news media constitute a battleground of images and information, spectacle and spin constructed and communicated for home and global consumption. It is here, too, that relations of communicative power traditionally enacted between governments, military, publics and media begin to shift.

As discussed in this chapter, there are grounds on which to argue that what we are increasingly witnessing on our television screens, in our newspapers and within and across the overlapping vertical, horizontal and interactive communications flows of today's global news ecology is *mediatized war*. This should not be taken to somehow imply, however, that the systematic application of militarized and industrialized technologies of death and destruction are no longer directed at the bodies of others with anything other than terrifying and repulsive efficacy, or that somehow 'real war' and 'real deaths', miraculously, don't happen off screen. But it is to argue that real wars for those of us who are fortunate enough to escape them are often experienced vicariously through their media presentation. Even those who are caught up in war can now find themselves unwitting participants in symbolic events and spectacular displays of firepower and terror designed for wider media consumption and disseminatory effects.

The evolution of mediated and mediatized war should also not be presumed to be a simple outcome of the growing centrality of media in society, politics or culture, much less simply a consequence of the advent of new communication and information technologies – though both are clearly necessary preconditions for mediatized war. To recognize, for example, the 'spectacle of war' communicated in the contemporary news media simply begs further questions about the social relations of war and in particular the relations of communicative power that are enacted within and through it. Media spectacle in relation to the theatre of war, as anywhere else, is not sufficient unto itself (Cottle 2006a: 25–29). It demands to be contextualized, historicized, explained and better understood. Media war spectacle, then, raises questions about the evolving forms of socially organized violence as well as the latter's growing dependency on the media in processes of public opinion formation and public legitimation. Contemporary media representations of war as spectacle, as we shall see, may provide more visceral if ideologically opaque means of communicating war than in the past, but it is too soon to disregard the continuing efficacy of traditional forms of information management and propaganda war in the manufacture of consent and dissemination of fear. And some wars in the world today, evidently, shun both cameras and spectacle, preferring to go about their inhumane business by stealth, killing unseen and undeterred by the news media.

This chapter, then, seeks to explore the changing forms of contemporary warfare and its articulation with today's news media. To begin, it is first useful to briefly review what we know about the traditional role of the news media in war reporting, its determinants, controls and constraints. These basic findings are then augmented and updated in the light of more recent changes and the theorization and findings of recent scholars. Next we consider the technological paradox of 'hidden wars' in a global communications age of plenty. Oft heard claims about communication and information technologies collapsing time and space and their possible global omniscience in 'bearing witness' to inhumane actions practically anywhere on the planet notwithstanding, communication black holes evidently remain in respect of some contemporary wars. The chapter also addresses theories of so-called 'new wars' (Kaldor 2001), 'information wars' (Tumber and Webster 2006) and the 'new Western way of war' (Shaw 2005) and how each, in contradistinction to 'old wars', 'industrial wars' and 'total wars', theoretically posits the latest communication and media systems with added significance and centrality in their conduct. These differing theoretical claims are reviewed and their relevance for media and news reporting discussed. Finally, the chapter turns to debates about the spectacle of mediated war and does so principally in respect of the 'global war on terror' and the communication of global fears and terror.

Communicating war: controls and contingencies

Warring states have always made use of the latest communication technologies to pursue their aims, control the flow of information and engage in propaganda war. By such means they seek to bolster public morale and the war effort on the home front, protect their troops' safety and undermine their enemy's capacity to wage war in the theatre of conflict, and build alliances and secure legitimacy for their actions internationally. The integral involvement of media and communication systems in propaganda war, then, is neither new nor unexpected. When liberal democracies go to war the 'public's right to know' is destined to become pushed and pulled and, on occasion, pulverized by different strategic interests, information management techniques and a battery of military and governments controls.

In the field of media and war studies, a powerful confluence of controls and constraints have traditionally been identified to explain the documented tendency of national media to support government actions in times of war and insurgency, succumbing on occasion to cheerleading and displays of patriotism. Before we consider new forms of warfare and the global war on terror in terms of its mediatized communication, then, it is first useful to summarize these established principal findings. Most obviously, the news media historically have come under a battery of direct and indirect forms of government censorship and military control. Censorship and the control of information flows is often justified on grounds of safeguarding military lives and strategic objectives by withholding information of possible value to the enemy – but, in fact, frequently appears to be directed at massaging public opinion and generating public support for government war aims, especially when there is less than unanimous support for war. Military controls on journalists have also taken diverse forms in the past and these too are often justified on similar grounds, including concealing the whereabouts of troops and protecting the lives of the journalists concerned. Such military controls include curtailing access to the field of operations; restricting official releases to authorized press briefings and providing at most vague, imprecise and/or out-of-date information; the imposition of a system of military minders; the military's control of communication systems; the operation of a 'pool system' where news material is shared among selected journalists from different news organizations; and processes of journalist embedding with journalists assigned to specific military units (GUMC 1985; Taylor 1992, 2003; Harris 1994; Carruthers 2000; Knightley 2003; Wilcox 2005; Cottle 2006a: 74–85; Andersen 2006; Lewis et al. 2006).

Routine news deference to political and military elites (Elliott 1977) who thereby act as 'primary definers' (Hall et al. 1978) and define and set the parameters of news discourse is a further powerful explanation for the less than critical or independent nature of much war reporting. This 'authority skew' has been documented time and again in countless war studies and renders journalists vulnerable to, at best, partial information, at worst official deceit and deliberate misinformation (GUMC 1985). Journalists may be particularly susceptible to official source manipulation because of their working conditions including a competitive news environment, working to deadlines, journalist claims to impartiality and objectivity undergirded by a reliance on 'authoritative' (read 'authority') sources, as well as the practical and logistical difficulties of venturing into the war zone and/or the risks and dangers of attempting to communicate with the enemy and insurgents.

The incremental identification by war correspondents with military personnel in the field of combat (Morrison and Tumber 1988; Harris 1994; Morrison 1994) as well as their preceding national outlooks rooted within a culture of patriotism (Bromley 2004) have also been found to play their part in ensuring that reporting is 'on side'. And both these factors may help to account for the blind eye turned to military misconduct including the aftermath of troop atrocities (GUMC 1985). In times of war, the norms of civilian journalism are not immune to the corrosive impacts of systematized violence, death and destruction which, phenomenologically, can alter the outlooks and values of all those who experience it (Morrison 1994).

The operation of deep seated news values such as drama, conflict, violence, human interest and, in the case of visual news media, arresting images and spectacle, can further play their part in prioritizing and shaping the images and events of war and occluding others (Thussu 2003), as can the 'event orientation' of news that is geared to the daily cycles of news production and hence discrete news events and not the wider politics, oppositional debates and historical narratives of war (Boyd-Barrett 2004).

The political economy of corporate media underpins the operations and orientation of the news media in times of war, as it does in times of peace. In times of war the corporate pursuit of readers, ratings and revenue are no less muted and the logics of the marketplace can find ample opportunities to appeal to audiences and construct imagined national communities, building market share and profits as they do so (Boyd-Barrett 2004).

Perhaps, too, something of the nature of war is already encrusted in myth and disposed to archetypal themes of death and destruction, community and collectivity, heroism and victimhood. Such universal themes prove fertile grounds for journalists and their transcription of war into the 'war genre' replete with cultural myths, heavy symbolism and dramatic narratives – all rich in cultural affect and marketable potential.

These principal theoretical explanations, then, recur time and again across the field of media and war studies and, taken together, they provide a powerful set of explanations for the documented coincidence of media and state views in times of war (for a review, see Cottle 2006a: 74–99; and more detailed discussions GUMC 1985; Harris 1994; Carruthers 2000; Zelizer and Allan 2002; Knightley 2003; Taylor 2003; Thussu and Freedman 2003; Allan and Zelizer 2004; Miller 2004; Andersen 2006; Lewis et al. 2006). Even so, when generalized, these accounts can prove less than sufficient in theorizing and explaining the media's relation to war. We know, for example, that political dynamics and unfolding events on the ground as well as the types of war can also impact on the nature of new media representations, sometimes in unforeseen ways. Different types of war, for example, whether 'world wars' and 'total war', 'national wars' or 'partial engagements', 'civil wars' and 'insurgencies', 'our wars' or 'other people's wars', 'humanitarian wars' or 'degraded wars' can all powerfully shape and condition both the extent and nature of their portrayal (Carruthers 2000; Van der Veer and Munshi 2004; Sonwalkar 2004b). Reporting from different fronts, whether the home front, the international front or the enemy's front can also augment or close down the different perspectives and discourses of war in circulation (Hallin 1997).

The changing and/or fragmenting nature of elite consensus that can result as war unfolds over time and as body bags return home can further 'open up' or 'close down' what Daniel Hallin has coined the media's 'sphere of legitimate controversy' (Hallin 1986, 1994).The evident degree of elite consensus or dissensus can condition the extent to which the media feel emboldened to publicly air dissent and oppositional views or simply toe the establishment line (Hallin 1986, 1994; Zelizer and Allan 2002; Tumber and Palmer 2004; see Chapter 7). This more politically dynamic and contingent view, then, paves the way for empirically detailed and comparative studies sensitized to the complex interactions between political elites, media and publics and how these can shift through time and circumstance and variously condition news media practices and performance (Bennett 1990; Butler 1995; Wolfsfeld 1997; Robinson 2002; Entman 2004; Bennett et al. 2007) – and do so notwithstanding the powerful batteries of control and constraint identified earlier.

The increasingly complex, overlapping and interpenetrating flows and counterflows of today's global news ecology (see Figure 1.1), produced and circulated by western 24/7 global news providers (CNNI, BBC World, Fox, Sky), new regional corporate players including, most spectacularly in recent years Al-Jazeera, and multiple national public service and commercial news services within most nation states now generates a constant cross-traffic of news flows, images and information (El-Nawawy and Iskander 2003; Azran 2004; Rai and Cottle 2007; Thussu 2007). Much of this global corporate news output can also now be accessed via the world wide web, where it variously takes on some of the characteristics and possibilities of the medium including multimediality, interactivity and hypertextuality (Castells 2001; Deuze 2003). Surrounding online mainstream news services are now myriad interacting, constantly updating and emergent weblogs and web pages from wider civil society, posting different individual and institutional perspectives, commentaries and personal experiences both supplementing and periodically directly intervening into the world of corporate news (Allan 2006).

This complex communications infrastructure has now also become enmeshed in the communication of war and conflicts prompting researchers to attend, for example, to the nature of war reporting as corporate global infotainment (Thussu 2003, 2007), live modes of televisual spectacle (Hoskins 2004; Hoskins and O'Loughlin 2007), transnational counterflows and networks for dissent and war opposition (Bennett 2003; Iskander and El-Nawawy 2004; Murray et al. 2008) and, as mentioned, warblogs (Allan 2004, 2006). Today this globalized communications environment combines with changes in the nature of war and the practices of warfare, whether 'new wars' or 'hidden wars' – discussed next.

Hidden wars, new wars

Although the conflict in Afghanistan and Iraq has dominated news headlines around the world since their invasion in 2001 and 2003 respectively, major armed conflicts involving 1000 or more deaths caused by fighting are, in fact, declining and have been for the past decades (SIPRI 2004; Ploughshares 2007). Although major interstate wars fought for territorial conquest and control have declined in the world, civil wars and other forms of intrastate conflicts often involving extreme violence, including genocide and the deliberate targeting of civilian populations, continue. These bloody conflicts can last for years with varying intensity, often take place in failed or failing states and are conducted in relatively disorganized and sporadic ways by militias, mercenaries, criminal gangs and child soldiers as well as remnant armies and regular military forces. The extreme brutality associated with these new forms of intrastate and internecine warfare produces large numbers of internally displaced people and an exodus of refugees to neighbouring territories, sometimes extending the field of violence and embroiling outside powers.

In 2006, as in previous years, the majority of such armed conflicts occurred in Africa (41.5%) and Asia (38%) (Ploughshares 2007: 1). Many of them go unreported and unnoticed by the world:

> The thesis of 'symbolic annihilation' that was hitherto viewed in terms of the marginalization of news about women (Tuchman 1972) and other minorities can also be applied to the coverage of wars and conflicts that involve swathes of population in the developing world. There are countless wars and conflicts raging across Africa, Asia and elsewhere that figure only in small print research statistics of think tanks or when citizens of Western countries fall victim there. . . . the need to bring most – if not all – wars and conflicts into the international public sphere has never been more important than now. . . . The absence of news, or according low priority to the many 'invisible' wars and conflicts, means that they do not figure in the public agenda, within national public spheres or at the international level. (Sonwalkar 2004b: 207)

The structured silence of hidden wars, courtesy of the media, is all the more remarkable on a planet now constantly orbited by communication satellites and where conflicts and crimes against humanity can be communicated from almost anywhere on Earth shortly thereafter, if not in real time (see, for example, Human Rights Watch (*http://www.hrw.org/*); Chapter 4). We observed earlier the silent moral scream in the news media's selective reporting of *un*natural disasters around the world and its professional calculus of death (see Chapter 3) and we shall revisit these media constructions from the 'inside out' with the help of humanitarian NGOs later (Chapter 8). Here a further underlying factor evidently comes into play. When humanitarian emergencies are understood by the news media to be caused by people and politics, rather than natural forces and unforeseen calamities, so they appear to be regarded as less newsworthy or too complicated to receive the same amount of news interest. The professional distaste of politics in humanitarian disasters also, it appears, contributes to the news media's structured silences.

The war in the Democratic Republic of Congo, a country two-thirds the size of western Europe, is estimated to have killed over 4 million people since 1998 and has left countless thousands traumatized by rape, massacres and the extreme violence inflicted by machetes. Despite a formal end to hostilities in 2007, unrestrained violence continues in the Congo. It is the single most deadly conflict in the world in recent times, it is Africa's Second World War and yet it has barely registered on the world's media. A bloody insurgency that has run for 18 years in northern Uganda has uprooted nearly 2 million people, caused the deaths of hundreds of thousands and relies on an army of over 25,000 abducted child soldiers – and yet this too barely prompts a mention in the western news media. The genocide perpetrated in Darfur, in western Sudan, went unreported for years and has only found intermittent coverage following high-profile US declarations of genocide in 2004, celebrity calls for action and belated UN peacekeeping involvement. This is so notwithstanding the 200,000–400,000 estimated civilian deaths, the systematic rape of women and children and the 2.4 million people displaced from their villages and homes (Shaw 2007: 162–171).

These and many other conflicts around the world are routinely ignored by the news media. Humanitarian organizations such as Médecins sans Frontières and Reuter's news service, AlertNet, routinely provide updates and annual reports on the latest forgotten disasters and hidden wars in the world today (see *http:// www.doctorswithoutborders.org/publications/reports/topten* and *http://www.alertnet. org/thenews/emergency/index.htm*), but the mainstream news media's silent moral scream continues to reverberate around the world as deafening silence.

The Stockholm Institute for Peace Research (SIPRI) observes that, 'In a globalized world, intra-state conflicts are increasingly becoming international in nature and in effect,' and suggests, 'The complexity and diversity of these conflicts challenge the distinction between the "internal" and the "external" and calls into question the basis on which conflicts are classified and addressed' (SIPRI, 2004: 1). Mary Kaldor's *New and Old Wars: Organized Violence in a Global Era* (2001) goes further by boldly theorizing the evolving nature of war and warfare practices. A new type of organized violence originated in the 1980s and 1990s, particularly in Africa and eastern Europe, she argues, and this often in failed or failing states. Such conflicts exhibit high violence and brutality and are theorized as expressions of globalization – that some may see these conflicts as traditional civil wars based on ethnic and tribal enmities notwithstanding. As processes of globalization impact on centralized, rationalized, hierarchically ordered and territorialized modern states so this prompts new conflicts and new forms of warfare.

New wars, she contends, are principally about identity politics and political mobilization based on ethnic and national goals, rather than geopolitical or ideological goals. Methods of warfare are no longer principally oriented to the capture of territory and states or conducted through decisive battles but are directed at the control of populations by sewing 'fears and hatreds' and the use of systematic violence and collective expulsions (ethnic cleansing) – all targeted at civilian populations. The political economy of warfare also undergoes a fundamental shift from centralized and autarchic modes of state funding to decentralized and non-hierarchical means of securing war funding including émigré remittances, external government assistance, the diversion of international humanitarian aid, military plunder and criminality. The field of violence, for example, often supports militias and others who extort, plunder and kill and the distinction in new wars between criminal activity and military objectives often becomes indistinct.

New wars, therefore, are based on new forms of socially organized violence and the humanitarian catastrophes that result cannot be seen as aberrations or as simply excess violence; they are endemic to the nature of new wars, their goals, methods and means of funding. The increased calls for humanitarian intervention in the 1990s (so-called 'military humanism') are also theorized as part of the new global era and follow the humanitarian crises and human rights abuses endemic to new wars. New wars, argues Kaldor, express the contradictory pushes and pulls of globalization, between exclusivism and particularism, on the one side, and universalism and cosmopolitanism, on the other.

Kaldor's new war thesis appears to map onto a number of conflicts in the world today (SIPRI 2004; Ploughshares 2007) but to what extent it can adequately subsume and explain the evident differences and complexities of contemporary wars and forms of warfare, inevitably, is a matter of academic debate. Some challenge, for example, the explanatory reliance on 'identity politics' as the goal of new wars and point to the continuities as well as discontinuities within western forms of warfare. Both so-called 'information wars' and the 'new western way of war', discussed next, emphasize further attributes of contemporary warfare associated with western wars including their deployment of high-technology and sophisticated communications. This point appears to be conceded by Kaldor, at least in respect of weapons technology, in her later writing which now delineates not one but three forms of contemporary warfare: 'network warfare' (broadly coincident with 'new wars'), 'spectacle warfare' (mainly US and British warfare conducted at 'long distance' using high-altitude aircraft and missile weapons, such as the first Gulf War), and neo-modern warfare (exhibiting the evolution of classical military forces in transitional states) (Kaldor 2003: 119–128). Both 'spectacle war and network war', she now concludes, 'feed off each other and sustain themselves through fear and insecurity' (Kaldor 2003: 155). And new wars have also embroiled western military forces through humanitarian interventions once again suggesting that contemporary forms of war in the world today can often merge and bleed into each other.

None of this detracts, however, from one of Kaldor's depth insights into how and why genocide and the deliberate targeting of violence against civilians should have become a recurrent characteristic of contemporary warfare. Her analysis and argument is underpinned by the sobering fact that the ratio of military to civilian casual has been reversed from 8:1 at the beginning of the 20th century to 1:8 towards its close and the proportion of internally displaced peoples and refugees according to UNCHR and others has also risen dramatically across the same period (Kaldor 2001: 100–101; Castles 2003; see also Chapter 4).

In this context, the chilling possibility arises that contemporary 'hidden wars' and the failure to report their extreme violence may not simply be a representational oversight produced by the myopic, amoral gaze of the news media. A combination of political economy factors, the informing professional calculus of death and logistical difficulties and risks associated with reporting in dangerous situations may all help to explain the structured silences of the news media. But hidden wars and their extreme brutality targeting civilians may, in fact, be more closely related to the operations of the news media than many may care to think. If new wars are characterized by their extreme violence targeting civilians, in contravention of international humanitarian law and universal human rights, those who seek to systematically commit such acts will seek to do so out of sight of the world's news media (Rwanda, Darfur, Srebrenica, Aceh). In such moments, the *media's silent moral scream* unwittingly colludes with the dark side of contemporary warfare and, by its silence, encourages and enables its most inhumane expressions. Such barbaric, systematic and collective violations scream to be heard and demand to be 'witnessed' in a globalized world where every possible pressure must be brought to bear to bring them to an end. In a globalized media environment, the impact of news silence on the reporting of new wars and hidden wars, as paradoxical as it may sound, registers in the propensity to commit acts of systematic atrocity, killing and genocide (Shaw 2003, 2007) – entering into their bloody constitution.

In globally interconnected and mediated times and through their commissioned silence, the news media effectively set foot into the field of war; they do not remain outside it by simply reporting or not reporting from what may be professionally pre-ferred and seen as respectable moral distance. In a globalized media environment 'proper distance' (Silverstone 2007) shrinks to the killing zone. Whether news organ-izations and individual journalists recognize it or not, in today's mediated and human rights-aware world, the socially organized violence of new wars and hidden wars has become their responsibility in so far as the commissioning of atrocities and inhumane actions relies on invisibility in the news media. In today's globalized world, the news media have become the hinge between 'new wars' and 'hidden wars.'

Information war and the new western way of war

Mary Kaldor's theorization of new wars, as we have heard, helps us to understand the increased brutality of many wars around the world today, including the Balkans and Bosnia-Herzegovina, Sudan, Chad and Sierra Leone – to name just a few. The concept and theorization of 'information war' and the 'new western way of War', in contrast, serve to focus specifically on those characteristic attributes of war now waged by powerful western states. In *Journalists Under Fire: Information War and Journalistic Practices* Howard Tumber and Frank Webster distinguish between 'industrial war' and 'information war' (Tumber and Webster 2006). By industrial war they refer principally to earlier wars that:

- were conducted between sovereign national states often over territory
- involved the mobilization of mass populations to support the war effort on the home front and sustain high numbers of combatants in the theatre of war

- were centrally coordinated and geared the industrial economy to the military struggle
- were directed at controlling the media environment through censorship and the control of journalism to ensure public support and boost public morale. (Tumber and Webster 2006: 1–44)

Increasingly, however, industrial war has become superseded by information war. Building on ideas of the 'revolution in military affairs' (RMA), the authors recognize how so-called C3I technologies of 'command', 'control', 'communications' and 'intelligence' have 'fused information and firepower' with deadly military efficiency and effect. A graphic example from the invasion of Iraq in 1991 helps make their point:

> [L]inked satellites, observation aircraft, planners, commanders, tanks, bombers and ships, enabled the allies to get around . . . OODA (observation, orientation, decision and action) loops at breath-taking speed in a continuous temporal outflanking. A completely new air tasking order – a list of hundreds of targets for thousands of sorties – was produced every 72 hours, and updated even while the aircraft were airborne. Iraq's radar eyes were poked out, its wireless nerves severed. (Morton cited in Tumber and Webster 2006: 30–31)

Use of computer technologies to command and control the battlefield, directing overwhelming firepower with deadly effect, have understandably been regarded by many in the military as constituting a revolution in military affairs. But Tumber and Webster do not propose that information war is simply a technological determinism ushered in by the advent of computers. Rather, they theorize the shift to information war in relation to much wider and deeper forces of change, including: the decline of sovereign nation states as autonomous actors in the field of international relations; the porosity of nation states in terms of the migration of people, finances, images and ideas; and the development, following Anthony Giddens (1994), of so-called 'states without enemies' and 'enemies without states'.

When economic activity in a globalizing world is no longer dependent on territorial conquest or state control or is even based within a particular nation given the mobile flows of finances and capital, then states, argue Tumber and Webster, have fewer reasons to go to war. These same processes of globalization and 'de-territorialisation', also prompt, however, the emergence of new fundamentalisms opposed to the seemingly inexorable forces of global change and westernization. Transnational terror networks are themselves not rooted in particular places or aligned to particular nation states. They now assume fluid networks and transnational alliances, conducting sporadic and often highly symbolic actions.

Information war, in this context, becomes asymmetrical and conducted against enemies who lack comparable communication facilities and military fire power. Western military, based on its technological superiority and constrained by its democratic accountability, develops 'knowledge warriors' and conducts 'post-heroic warfare'. The overwhelming application of force can lead to so-called 'instant wars' that take place over days and weeks rather than months and years.

On the western home front the experience of war is distanced from most people and their everyday lives and is only known vicariously, through the media. In democracies the consent for war can be won or lost at the ballot box and the media engage with their audiences not as participants but as spectators:

> It follows that those who wage Information War devote great attention to 'perception management' for the population at home and, indeed, round the world. This is especially pressing in democratic nations where public opinion can be a vital factor in support for war. (Tumber and Webster 2006: 35)

When democracies go to war, Tumber and Webster suggest, government and military benefit from independent journalism: if they are to successfully manage public perception then it is important that the public do not dismiss everything they read and see as lies and propaganda. The rise of warblogs and the war blogosphere, and ease of access to the complex flows and counterflows of news and related war commentary across the global news mediasphere, also now means that overt attempts at censorship and crude manipulation of journalists are less likely to succeed and, when detected, can incur a high political cost. In this context, war as spectacle and entertainment, rather than as overt forms of propaganda and information manipulation, may prove to be a more effective way of controlling and containing the communications environment.

Tumber and Webster's theorization of information war, then, grants considerably more attention, rightly, to communications as a technology of warfare and to the news media as a means of 'perception management' in a context where audiences are addressed as spectators and not, as in industrial war, participants. As a theoretical contender designating the new form of contemporary war, however, its reach is less than universal and it cannot be regarded as sufficient when applied to particular wars. The ideas and practices of information war have less relevance for understanding the strategy and tactics of enemies who possess relatively unsophisticated weaponry and communication capabilities and, as such, there is a tendency to overstate the role of information war as a defining feature of contemporary wars.

As we heard earlier, new wars today produce extreme forms of violence much of it sporadic and delivered by relatively unsophisticated weaponry. The machete continues to exact a terrible toll in terms of mass death and mutilation on the continents of Africa and Asia, and small arms fire, not guided-laser bombs, kill most people in conflicts around the planet today. Asymmetric war, as the term implies, is characterized by unequal military capabilities, technological firepower, differing political goals and military strategies and tactics. 'Information war', as defined by Tumber and Webster, does not apply equally to all those involved. It is principally a western invention, deployed by western states and militaries and theorized by western academics. This is not to deny the deliberate use of spectacles of terror as a mediated weapon of war by terrorists and insurgents as well as by western states (see later), but it is to say that to focus on 'information war' in a context of asymmetric warfare is to conceptually inflate a particular dimension of contemporary westernized war and marginalize or occlude that which really needs to be placed centre stage: the motives and politics that animate war, terror and insurgency in the 21st century and the prospects of overcoming such global conflicts in the future.

Martin Shaw explicitly recognizes 'the new Western way of war' in his book of the same name (Shaw 2005) and, in so doing, also observes the increased dependency of western governments and military on the news media as well as their vulnerability to processes of global media surveillance:

> Wars must play much more by the rules of politics, markets and media; warmaking must *capitalize* on market relations, *exploit* democratic political forms, and *manage* independent media. In the end, armed actors must reckon not so much with global governance – which suggests a purely governmental even if broadly based process – but with the comprehensive surveillance of their military ventures by global state institutions, law, markets, media, and civil society. The best way of characterizing the new mode of war as a whole is therefore *global surveillance warfare*. (Shaw 2005: 55–56)

Shaw's thesis argues that the new western way of war is premised on risk transfer. That is, in western democracies, wars generate political risks to politicians as well as, of course, life risks to combatants and civilians. To manage war risks, Shaw maintains, they must become transferred, hence his designation of 'risk-transfer war'. The physical risks of war are transferred, as in most wars, from governments to the military but because of the political damage that can be caused by high military casualties these military risks also become minimized and in turn transferred, via high-altitude bombing for example, to civilian non-combatants. The new western way of war, or risk-transfer war, helps to explain the increased, albeit *regrettable*, incidence of civilian casualties in contemporary western wars and in this respect differs from Kaldor's thesis of 'new wars' with their endemic, *planned* and targeted violence against civilians.

Shaw's thesis of risk-transfer war also recognizes the increased importance of the news media in managing public perceptions of war as well as the added risks to the political legitimacy of states, politicians and military in war when subject to the surveillance of the global media:

> Because electorates are almost exclusively national, Western governments still think largely of national surveillance. However, even this element of surveillance is mediated through the global and the international. National publics take notice of what allied governments and publics think, as well as of broader international official and public opinion. National media are influenced by global media. National politics and media are affected by norms of international legality and by decisions and judgements in international institutions. Although governments think in terms of accountability in a national public sphere, this is never

autonomous to anything like the extent to which it was in the total war era. On the contrary, governments must always recognize how integrated global media, institutions and public opinion have become. Western nation-states are increasingly internationalized and, indeed, globalized. (Shaw 2005: 75)

For Shaw, then, the news media – national, international, global – operate a regime of surveillance that now enters into and conditions the new western way of war. His theorization of risk-transfer war highlights the public relations value of precision-guided weapons systems and the avoidance of close-up scenes of death and dying – attributes that others have examined through a prism of media war spectacle.

Spectacle and the global war on terror

The global war on terror unleashed by the US administration in the aftermath of 9/11 pitched the world into a new vortex of political violence and killing that has continued long after the 'successful' invasions of Afghanistan (2001) and Iraq (2003). Image war has become a salient feature of this bloody turn in world history, especially the global circulation of spectacular scenes and symbolic, staged events. As discussed and illustrated in *Mediatized Conflict* (Cottle 2006a: 152–166; see also Michalski and Gow 2007), the war on terror has become in large measure a war of media images, from the aestheticized spectacle of the opening of the war with the televised 'shock and awe' bombing of Baghdad to the chilling DiY 'shock and awe' of videotaped beheadings circulated by insurgents on the internet; from the US administration's no expense-spared staged announcement of 'victory' by the US president on the decks of the USS *Abraham Lincoln* to the choreographed violent symbolism of stripped, tortured and sexually degraded bodies produced by low-grade US military personnel at Abu Ghraib.

These and many other images point to the prominent role of images in today's global media ecology where insurgents and soldiers as well as states and military machines have access to media technology and the media sphere. Such images are often produced, circulated and harnessed in the furtherance of strategic war aims. In a world of global communication flows and images, the costs of not winning the image war can be high and efforts at control are not always successful. It appears that the historical 'transformation of visibility' (Thompson 1995) facilitated by new media and communications has recently taken a new turn in the field of mediated war, at once both democratizing and tyrannical. The widening, seemingly omnipresent lens of citizen media can now capture, store and upload images and pronouncements of the powerful and communicate these around the world either directly via the mainstream news media or more circuitously via the world wide web.

This extended gaze of the media can be taken as democratizing insofar as the availability of new digital technologies, ease of visual recording and access to communication systems seemingly enfranchises everyone, from ordinary citizens and human rights activists to foot soldiers and even torturers who can bear witness to their own and others' acts of inhumanity anywhere in the world. But it also proves tyrannical in so far as these same communication technologies and developments have produced a new 'amoral economy' in which the production and circulation of acts of violence have increasingly becomes staged and produced for the media in pursuit of strategic and tactical war aims – whether building public support and legitimacy for war (through aestheticized spectacles of war and other forms of *'symbolic violence'*) or the production and dissemination of public fears (through staged mediated acts of terror or *'violent symbolism'*) (Cottle 2006a: 155–162).

Andrew Hoskins and Ben O'Loughlin in their study *Television and Terror* (2007) argue that television news in particular functions as a key 'actor' in the communication and conduct of contemporary war and terror in the post 9/11 era. Television news discourse, they suggest, is in crisis. It amplifies terrorist threats through its characteristic appeals of liveness, immediacy and visuality:

> This economy of liveness and connectivity coupled with the textual and graphic enhancements of 'televisuality' is the most effective global delivery system for terror events and its discourses. (Hoskins and O'Loughlin 2007: 188–189)

On this basis, they conclude, 'it is not an exaggeration to state that the medium has become "weaponised" ' and television has become 'an actual constituent of terrorism' (Hoskins and O'Loughlin 2007: 188–189). As a medium and regime of meanings, television grants the acts and threat of terrorism prominent and sustained exposure and extends news space to speculative discourses and commentary that can only compound, they suggest, the sense of threat and amplify public fears.

But television also 'contains' and 'assuages' threats, they suggest, and it does so with its compulsion to repeat, recycle and reframe scenes from the live coverage of terrorist events that diminishes their shock value with each re-showing. Television fits new events into pre-existing and familiar templates drawing on the medium's growing archives and placing disruptive events into the more comforting parameters of the 'known'. And the prevailing professional and regulatory codes of 'taste and decency' also serve to sanitize the violence of war and terror, rendering reports about them less shocking or disturbing (Hoskins and O'Loughlin 2007: 188–189). In these ways, then, television as medium and regime of meanings modulates terror and trauma, moving precariously and uncertainly between amplification and containment.

This theorization, sensitive to the seemingly contradictory responses of the television medium to terror, improves considerably on *a priori* readings of television news as either simply the vehicle of elite propaganda aimed against insurgents and terrorism or simply as the conduit for the dissemination of fear based on mediated acts of terror. It is not entirely clear, however, why exactly this constitutes a 'crisis of news discourse' or for whom exactly. The analytical focus on *'televisuality'*, the characteristic presentational modes and forms of the television medium, certainly helps to focus attention on the *mediating* properties of television and how it shapes and colours the presentation of war and terror. But when theorized in such ways, the analysis inevitably tends toward *media centrism* and *television essentialism* and risks losing sight of how the surrounding field of sources and power actively seeks to structure public discourses of terror from outside the television medium. It is in and through this interaction that discourses and representations of terror also become shaped, signalled and sensationalized. David Altheide is quite clear, for example, that the 'politics of fear' in the field of terror (as in the field of crime), is principally about 'decision makers' promotion and use of audience beliefs and assumptions about danger, risk and fear in order to achieve certain goals' (Altheide 2006: ix) – a position that puts questions of surrounding political power more firmly centre frame in the media's representations of terror.

The crisis at the heart of news discourse, then, is arguably not medium specific. Rather, it is the global war on terror itself, with its continuing human carnage and exacerbation of deep seated enmities that will reverberate for generations that constitutes the real crisis. Questions of mediation are indispensable for improved understanding of the nature of war reporting, and are no less central to the conceptualization of 'mediatized war' outlined earlier, but they cannot be pursued without recourse to the surrounding forcefield of politics and power and how different interests seek to intervene within the news media. We also need to attend to how the news media's war on terror reporting becomes influenced, infiltrated and inflected from outside through, for example, the deliberate design and deployment of staged, symbolic and spectacular images by politicians, military and insurgents.

Philip Hammond in *Media, War and Postmodernity* (2007) goes even further in his theorization of media war spectacles. His thesis is that the Gulf War of 1991 can be understood as an instance of postmodern war and maintains this is 'not so much because of the way it was fought as a high-tech media spectacle, but rather because it was a response to the western elite's post-Cold War crisis of meaning' (2007: 17). He sets out, then, to considerably broaden the analysis and avoid any possible charge of media centrism by situating the evident turn to media spectacle in war reporting as an expression of a much deeper political malaise. He states his position as follows:

[W]ar and interventions since the Cold War have been driven by attempts on the part of Western leaders to recapture a sense of purpose and meaning, both for themselves and their societies. This in turn has led to a heightened emphasis on image, spectacle and media presentation. Yet it is not really the media themselves that are the problem, even though some reporters and commentators have actively colluded in the process. Rather, it is the changing character of war which is at issue, and behind that, a fundamental shift in the politics of Western societies, summed up as the 'end of Left and Right'. For that reason, although the staging of war, and of acts of terrorism, as media events make it important to examine media coverage, the analysis developed here attempts to reach beyond a critique of the media to examine the events themselves and the broader political changes that give rise to them. (Hammond 2007: 11)

This is a bold thesis and one that provides a good deal of empirical support for the ways in which wars have increasingly been reported through a lens of spectacle with war events stage-managed by western political and military elites for the news cameras (pp. 37–58). Hammond is also on strong grounds when he observes how media reflexivity, or the tendency of journalists and news media to increasingly reflect on and even turn a sceptical eye toward political and military attempts to stage-manage war images, possibly helps to neutralize the manipulative intentions and effects of mediated war images (Hammond 2007: 59–80). Whether it is also permissible, however, to generalize about the motivations of western governments for participating in different humanitarian interventions in the 1990s and the war on terror is another matter. Hammond argues that elite narcissism and the discerned western collapse of meaning can explain not only spectacle war, but also the propensity for western governments to go to war in recent years – from Somalia to Kosovo to Iraq. This meta-narrative is apt to be viewed more dubiously by many.

Spectacle war and the deliberate attempt to manufacture staged scenes and symbolic war events cannot be theorized adequately, it seems, either through a prism of focused media centrism or grand postmodern speculation. The changing circumstances and contingencies of war inevitably colour their media production, mediation and possible media enactment in processes of news mediatization. The journalistic reflexivity and scepticism towards image wars and war spectacle, noted by Hammond and interpreted as part of the western loss of meaning, may in fact be more politically contingent and dependent on unfolding events.

As I write, 5 years after the invasion of Iraq and 7 years after the invasion of Afghanistan, civilian and military casualties continue to mount with no seeming end in sight. According to Associated Press, the death toll in Afghanistan in 2007 alone reached more than 6500 people, including 110 US troops, 4500 militants, 41 British, 30 Canadian and 40 other nation troops (*The Independent*, 1.1.08: 22). According to Reuters, by December 2007, between 78,743 and 85,813 Iraqi civilians, 3896 US, 174 British and 134 other nations' coalition forces had been killed and between 4900 and 6375 Iraqi military (*http://www.alertnet.org/thenews/newsdesk/L20639455.htm*). Some sources put the true death toll of Iraqis as considerably higher (*http://www.justforeignpolicy.org/iraq/iraqideaths.html*).

In the context of military occupation, political siege and human attrition the bloody carnage and daily grind of asymmetric warfare has seemingly become much harder to valorize through spectacular visuals. Invasion rather than protracted occupation, aerial bombing rather than ground war, military advance rather than bloody attrition are all likely to produce a better supply of spectacular scenes and virtual 'bloodless' images than the protracted and bloody consequences of occupation. The means of visualizing and communicating war nonetheless continue to evolve and change and this, as suggested already, in both democratizing and tyrannical ways.

The 'views' of ordinary young soldiers recorded on the ground are now, for example, fast becoming circulated and consumed through the global media ecology that now disseminates a multitude of combat images and graphic scenes of war. This includes officially sanctioned television programmes documenting the lives of ordinary soldiers in the field interrupted by bursts of military action and also now includes TV documentaries such as 'Iraq Uploaded' by MTV or full-length feature films such as 'The War Tapes' based on soldiers' videos taken in the theatre of war. Raw video clips captured by ordinary soldiers on their mobile phones and uploaded to diverse internet sites have become widely available via the internet; whether uploaded to websites catering for military personnel (for example, Military.com) or interspersed on those collating shocking and prurient videos (for example, Ogrish), or simply included on leading online video sites (for example, YouTube) (see Glasser 2006). These 'raw' insider images provide a view of war from the ground up, often revealing the existential fear, excitement and terror of warfare as well as its brutalizing impacts on the soldiers concerned and their preparedness to capitulate to a media mindset that appropriates war as entertainment.

Vicarious, visceral scenes of war violence are now more accessible than ever before through today's global communication networks and communication flows. How these and other forms of circulating images of warfare express the changing social and communicative relations of war requires sustained, ethically informed, study.

THE 'CNN EFFECT' AND 'COMPASSION FATIGUE': RESEARCHING BEYOND COMMONSENSE

> Being a spectator of calamities taking place in another country is a quintessential modern experience, the cumulative offering by more than a century and a half's worth of those professional, specialized tourists known as journalists. Wars are now also living room sights and sounds. Information about what is happening elsewhere, called 'news', features conflict and violence – 'if it bleeds, it leads' runs the venerable guideline of tabloids and twenty-four-hour headline news shows – to which the response is compassion, or indignation, or titillation, or approval, as each misery heaves into view. (Sontag 2003: 18)

Across previous chapters we have heard how the news media variously communicate different crises around the globe. By signalling them as 'global crises' that demand recognition and response, the news media enter into their public construction and constitution. Today it is perhaps understandable that big claims are often made about the impact of global communications. Real-world crises seem to intrude into our everyday lives via the news media and the conduct of both politics and major conflicts, evidently, have become heavily mediatized (Chapter 6). Two claims in particular are often made about today's global news media. Although each takes up a contradictory position and both are based on a lack of robust empirical evidence they seem to have entered into media commonsense.

Adherents to the so-called 'CNN effect' hold that global broadcasting corporations, such as CNNI, transmitting harrowing scenes of human suffering from around the globe, prompt changes in foreign policy and can even galvanize governments into carrying out humanitarian interventions backed by military force. The opposite effect is claimed by those who hold to the 'compassion fatigue thesis'. Here it is argued that media reports and televised scenes of human suffering in fact have a diminishing capacity to mobilize sentiments, sympathy or sustain humanitarian forms of response.

Essentially, it is argued, audiences have become inured to the moral compulsion of such images and our capacity for compassion has become overwhelmed or 'fatigued' by their constant circulation in the media. Whereas the 'CNN effect' adopts a *morally benign* view of the humanitarian influence of global news media, the 'compassion fatigue' thesis discerns a *morally malign* impact in so far as our capacity for moral responses is undermined. What both positions share is an unquestioned media centrism and media determinism that, ultimately, undermines their respective claims and arguments. These positions and the debates they spark nonetheless are of relevance for thinking about global crises and the part played by the news media in their constitution.

This chapter sets out, then, to take a closer look at these seemingly contradictory positions and debates. In the process we can aim to secure a better grasp of some of the complexities and contingencies involved. As with so much else in the field of global crises reporting and today's enveloping global communications environment, however, simple or direct causalities are difficult to find. Still, by examining the arguments about the CNN effect and compassion fatigue and with the help of recent research we can become better equipped to understand something of the complex involvement of the news media in processes of global crisis recognition, expressions of moral solidarity and international humanitarian action.

The CNN effect: too good to be true?

Research about the 'CNN effect' can usefully be situated in descent from the so-called 'Vietnam War syndrome'. This refers to the US military and US state's belief that media images of US troops in the field in Vietnam and the scenes of carnage sapped public morale on the home front and undermined the commitment to continue the war. Daniel Hallin (1986, 1994) effectively rebuts this 'myth' and does so on the basis of a detailed historical account of the changing trajectory of the war, the growing elite dissensus that this produced within the US administration and the belated opportunities only that this created for a more challenging and questioning journalism. In other words, US media followed rather than led the establishment view. Although the 'Vietnam syndrome' may be based on a myth it has proved no less consequential for that: military elites and governments around the world continue to produce tight media controls based on their belief in the 'Vietnam syndrome' (Knightley 2003; Cottle 2006a: 74–99; Lewis et al. 2006). The point here, however, is that Hallin's study as well as other models of media-elite 'indexing' (Bennett 1990; Bennett et al. 2007) prompt a more historically contingent and politically dynamic approach to the role of media in conflict reporting and humanitarian emergencies. As such, they qualify generalizing claims of a media-led causality, a causality that is also posited at the heart of the so-called CNN effect.

Even so, some commentators have argued that in today's 24/7 'real-time', global news environment and under certain circumstances the media can and do exert influ-ence on decision makers. Examples often cited are the US humanitarian intervention in Somalia in 1992 ('Operation Restore Hope') and US and coalition efforts to support the Kurdish refugees fleeing the revenge of Saddam Hussein's troops in 1991, following the first US invasion of Iraq ('Operation Provide Comfort'). In the case of Somalia, for example, Bernard Cohen writes that television 'has demonstrated its power to move governments' and continues:

> By focusing daily on the starving children in Somalia, a pictorial story tailor-made for television, TV mobilized the conscience of the nation's public institutions, compelling the government into a policy of intervention for humanitarian reasons. (cited in Gilboa 2005: 35)

In respect of the Kurdish refugee crisis, Martin Shaw also appears no less certain about the power of televised images:

> The central agencies of global civil society in the Kurdish crisis, the institutions which forced the changes in state policies which constituted 'humanitarian inter-vention', were in fact television news programmes. Television – not newspapers, not social movements, certainly not the traditional representative institutions – took up the plight of the Kurds and in an unprecedented campaign successfully forced governments' hands. . . . Television news' role in the Kurdish crisis is all the more surprising, at first sight, since it contrasted so clearly with the managed medium which they had represented during the Gulf War. (Shaw 1999: 231)

Others remain less convinced. Even in respect of these seemingly strong cases, they argue, underlying geopolitical interests are often the most likely cause precipitating these and other US 'humanitarian interventions', not the 'CNN effect'. Adopting a realist approach to international relations, David Gibbs points out how in the case of Somalia, the humanitarian justifications circulated by government officials at the time notwithstanding, strategic US interests were, in fact, involved. Somalia, he notes, is close to shipping routes in the Red Sea and the important Bab-el-Mandeb straits. Conoco, a US oil company, was also investing in oil explorations in the region. And, furthermore, the US administration's relation with the warlord Mohammed Aideed had already fluctuated previously depending on his ability to protect these interests (cited in Gilboa 2005: 35). When taken together, strategic factors such as these, he suggests, better account for US involvement, irrespective of how officials may like to publicly legitimize them. When these admittedly circumstantial claims are com-bined with empirical analysis of US media coverage preceding and during the Somalia operation, the basis for a strong CNN effect begins to crumble. Piers Robinson elaborates:

> The decision to deploy 28,000 US troops in Somalia was not prompted or 'caused' by media attention to the starvation in Somalia. In fact, the media did not pay any

significant level of attention until after Bush had decided to send in US troops. Other factors, such as aid agency and congressional lobbying and President Bush's own personal convictions, offer more immediate and empirically substantiated reasons for the intervention. . . . If . . . the media played any significant role at all *vis-à-vis* the policy process it was as an enabler and then as a builder of support. . . . If the media played such a supportive, not pressuring, role in what was apparently an easy case for the CNN effect, the question is raised as to the validity of the thesis. (Robinson 2002: 62–63)

In respect of the Kurdish refugee crisis sparked by the first Gulf War, on closer inspection this too appears less convincing as a 'strong case' of the CNN effect. Piers Robinson argues that geo-strategic concerns rather than media-inspired humanitarianism are better able to explain the US intervention as Kurdish refugees sought sanctuary on Turkey's Kurdish borders. Turkey's membership of NATO and, particularly, its loyalty during the Gulf War to the US as well as its ongoing 'problem' with Kurdish separatists in the southern part of the country are all, for example, raised as possible factors informing the decision to intervene. At the very most, suggests Robinson, 'the critical and empathy-framed coverage would have had an enabling effect, helping to explain and justify the deployment of ground troops in Iraq to the US public, but the decision itself was most likely motivated by non-media related concerns' (Robinson 2002: 70–71).

Robinson is notable among a number of scholars who have sought to develop more analytically nuanced accounts of the CNN effect (see also Gilboa 2005). Through detailed and comparative case studies he has sought to identify the precise conditions under which a CNN effect, whether 'strong' or 'weak' (determining or enabling), may, occasionally, take place. He concludes that a CNN effect in fact rarely occurs and then only when there is elite dissensus, a high degree of policy uncertainty and when media coverage has involved emotive pictures and empathetic and critical framing. Even under these stringent conditions, as we have just heard, however, the operation of strategic and geopolitical interests as well as other possible factors 'behind the scenes' may be the key drivers of humanitarian intervention and today's so-called 'military humanism' (Beck 2005: 65). Too often claims about a CNN effect are deduced from policy outcomes and based on a simple correlation with empathetic media coverage (Shaw 1996), rather than in-depth and insider studies of policymaking personnel, institutions and processes (Gilboa 2005).

More recently Robinson has revisited the CNN effect in the post-9/11 context (Robinson 2005). Under the 'war on terror', humanitarian concerns have been marginalized if not displaced entirely from the US foreign policy agenda. In this context of relative policy certainty, the CNN effect, he argues, is now even more unlikely given that the US media have become noticeably more deferential and constrained (as often happens in times of major conflict and war), reducing the openings for an adversarial or oppositional media (Robinson 2005: 346). Post-9/11, the concept of humanitarian intervention has itself become debased following its use in political rhetoric justifying invasions in Afghanistan and Iraq. He also suggests that contemporary approaches to media management have become much more pronounced and this has strengthened the ability of foreign policy elites to influence media and not vice versa. In the particular political conditions of recent years, therefore, Robinson argues that the rare conditions which may have supported the case for a CNN effect in the past have, if anything, become even rarer and more unlikely today (Robinson 2005: 348).

Seen through a wider optic some theorists also argue that the CNN effect essentially misses the point (Jacobsen 2000; Hawkins 2002). By focusing its gaze on particular conflicts, argues Victor Hawkins, the media ignore many others (and the massive amount of human suffering that they cause) and this systematic media silence thereby excludes these as possible influences on public and policy agendas (Hawkins 2002). These 'forgotten disasters' (see Chapter 3) and 'hidden wars' (see Chapter 6) represent the principal failing of today's news media, though implicitly Hawkins' position seems to thereby grant the CNN effect at least some residual validity and potential use value. However, in a context in which conflicts and war have become not just *reported* or *mediated*, but actively *conducted* on the media stage and thereby *mediatized* (see Chapter 6), it becomes even more difficult to separate out *causal effects* given the enveloping and *constitutive role* of media within different global crises. The debate continues.

Behind the claims of the CNN effect, then, with its alleged causality operating from news media to publics to policy formation, lies a more complex reality (Hoskins and O'Loughlin 2007: 53–73). The news media are enmeshed within a wider and moving formation of political, institutional and cultural relationships, both registering and in part reproducing them. It is in closer approximation to these complex relationships and the changing historical contexts and politics of the time that the news media's public elaboration of images and ideas can sometimes make moral claims on our compassion and influence our propensity to act. Though we may want to question, therefore, the validity of the benign media centrism of the alleged CNN effect, the debate nonetheless usefully forces attention on how the news media have become a key resource for understanding and possible courses of action – which is not to suggest that they are the sole drivers in such processes. The role of emotive images performs, as we have heard, a key role in the claimed CNN effect; they are no less central to claims about the so-called 'compassion fatigue' thesis. Here, however, the *morally benign* media centrism of the CNN effect gives way to a *morally malign* media centrism in so far as the surfeit of media images of human suffering that bombard our senses through TV and other screens are thought to have sapped our capacity to care. This also demands closer examination.

Compassion fatigue: too bad to be right?

The notion of compassion fatigue has gained popular and media currency across recent years (see, for example, *The Guardian's* front page 'This is no time for compassion fatigue', Chapter 1). Some time ago, Anthony Giddens referred to social processes involving a 'double hermeneutic', processes in which concepts originally forged by academics for analytical purposes, say 'stereotype' or 'moral panic', subsequently enter into lay knowledge and even inform the thinking and actions of those caught up in the phenomena that such concepts were originally designed to make sense of (Giddens 1976: 79). The same, perhaps, can now be said of the concept 'compassion fatigue'. This is not to suggest that the phenomenon the concept refers to actually exists, but rather that the belief that it does exist *is* real, and that this belief in turn can have real consequences – as we have heard, for example, in respect of the so-called 'Vietnam syndrome' and CNN effect. Whether used by general commentators or scholars, however, the concept of 'compassion fatigue' often betrays a distinct lack of analytical precision. Too often it serves as a woolly blanket term covering diverse facets and features of contemporary news reporting and alleged impacts. Consider the following:

> Compassion fatigue is the unacknowledged cause of much of the failure of international reporting today. It is at the base of many of the complaints about the public's short attention span, the media's peripatetic journalism, the public's boredom with international news, the media's preoccupation with crisis coverage. (Moeller 1999: 2)

Susan Moeller in her study of the same name argues, then, that compassion fatigue is responsible for many of the woes of contemporary journalism, including the nature of its international crisis reporting. Specifically, she maintains that 'compassion fatigue' acts as a prior restraint in so far as editors and producers don't assign correspondents to possible stories; it abets American self-interest; it reinforces simplistic, formulaic coverage; it ratchets up the criteria for stories that get coverage; it tempts journalists to sensationalize; and it encourages the media to move on (Moeller 1999: 2). As this encompassing list suggests, the concept of compassion fatigue in fact is being asked to do a great deal, from explaining the failures, practices and forms of international news reporting to audience-based questions about levels of news engagement and interests. As we know, however, matters are a good deal more complicated on all these and other fronts (see Chapters 2 and 3).

Humanitarian aid organizations, for example, generally prefer the term 'media fatigue' to the more generalized concept of 'compassion fatigue' and do so on the basis of their dealings with the news media and its operations (see Chapter 8). And, as we heard in Chapter 3, the 'professional calculus of death' as well as the political economy of western and national news media can help to account for the systematic, selective myopia of the news media's treatment of humanitarian disasters and can do so without recourse to a generalizing claim about compassion fatigue. That said, for the most part the debate about compassion fatigue is not conducted in respect of professional news producers or news organizations, but rather news audiences and more particularly how audiences respond to mediated images of human suffering. Here the debate, until recently at least, has tended to produce relatively speculative statements rather than empirically sustained argument and theorization.

Michael Ignatieff has written, for example, that:

> Through its news broadcasts and spectaculars like 'Live Aid,' television has become the privileged medium through which moral relations between strangers are mediated in the modern world . . . television has contributed to the breakdown of the barriers of citizenship, religion, race, and geography that once divided our moral space into those we were responsible for and those who were beyond our ken. (Ignatieff 1998: 11–12)

In other words, Ignatieff suggests that in the modern world television and other media may have helped to break down former barriers of social distance and physical space and, on this basis, it may now be possible to sustain a sense of moral solidarity with distant others (see also Chapter 4; Beck 2006: 5–7). He is also careful to emphasize, however, that media images alone cannot guarantee that audiences will necessarily respond in this way, arguing: 'Images of human suffering do not assert their own meaning; they can only instantiate a moral claim if those who watch understand themselves to be potentially under obligation to those they see' (Ignatieff 1998: 11–12). Our capacity to care and sense of obligation to others expresses, according to Ignatieff, much deeper and historically developmental processes in which former 'others' becomes progressively recognised and incorporated into the category of 'people like us'.

Keith Tester, no less eloquently, takes a more media-centric and less historically progressive view.

> Certainly the media communicate harrowing representations of others, but the more the face of the other is communicated and reproduced in this way the more it is denuded of any moral authority it might otherwise possess. Increased visibility of the gaze seems to go hand in hand with increasing invisibility from the point of view of the responsibility of moral solidarity. Media significance means moral insignificance. The image of the other, and therefore the face of the other, which should be so compelling . . . becomes commonplace and incapable of attracting a thoughtful or deliberate second glance. Even less is it capable of demanding any kind of a second thought. (Tester 1994: 130)

Speculative views on the role of televised images of human suffering and their capacity to move us demand to be taken seriously and each of these positions in their own terms make for persuasive reading. But if we are to move beyond the seeming impasse of these contradictory views and debate there are further complexities to be discerned and better understood. Here recent work incorporating empirical investigation and analysis helps. Studies of the news media's 'spectacle of suffering' (Chouliaraki 2006) as well as 'discourses of global compassion' (Höijer 2004) productively recover important complexities buried beneath the nebulous term of 'compassion fatigue'. Together they point to the need for closer empirical engagement, refined concepts and further analytical distinctions.

Birgitta Höijer (2004) observes in her audience-based study how feelings of 'compassion' are often highly dependent on visuals and involve 'ideal victim' images – typically, women, children and the elderly. The media's 'ideal victims' are seemingly informed by geopolitical outlooks that either highlight or ignore 'worthy' and 'unworthy' victims depending on whether the countries concerned are regarded by national western media as hostile or friendly (Herman and Chomsky 1988: 38; see Chapter 3). Changing sociocultural outlooks and values also shape 'ideal victims':

> That the ideal victim is a cultural construction becomes apparent if we consider historical and cultural variations in the victim status of women. Women who are assaulted by men are not always seen as victims, in some cultures not at all. Without any feelings of compassion from people an elderly woman could be burned to death in a witch hunt trial some hundred years ago in Scandinavia. And it is only recently that male soldiers' systematic rape of civilian women from the enemy side have been condemned. During the Second World War it was more or less accepted that Russian soldiers, for instance, committed massive rapes of German women immediately after the capture of Berlin. (Höijer 2004: 517)

Höijer also makes the case for a more analytically precise and disaggregated understanding of the term 'compassion'. This in fact involves very different forms of compassion: 'tender-hearted', 'shame-filled', 'blame-filled' and 'powerlessness-filled' (Höijer 2004: 522–524). As she explains, *tender-hearted compassion* focuses on the suffering of the victims and one's own sense of being a spectator filled with empathy and pity and is documented in such audience reflections as: 'It breaks my heart when I see refugees. They are coming in thousands and they tell what they have been through. It's so terrible.'

Blame-filled compassion in contrast registers a sense of indignation or anger that such suffering could have been allowed to happen and may variously be directed at people or political authorities thought to be responsible: 'I became angry when I saw the many innocent people and civilians who died and who were stricken by the conflict.'

Shame-filled compassion involves the sense of having failed to act on one's sense of obligation to those whose suffering is witnessed: 'I had such a bad conscience and I almost did not manage to watch any more terrible scenes on television. And they weren't just scenes, it was reality.'

Finally, *powerlessness-filled compassion* involves the recognition in the spectator that one may not have the power to do anything about the scenes of suffering and alleviate the hurt endured by the victims: 'You feel so helpless and there is little that you can do. You can of course give some money but that will not stop the war.'

In such ways, audience responses to reports and images of human suffering can exhibit wide variations and express their own complexities and contingencies. These demand further exploration and explanation. Just as we know that international news reporting is shaped and conditioned by a complex of constraints and imperatives, including market imperatives, professional norms and cultural outlooks, so perhaps we should not be surprised that audiences and their responses to images of suffering will also display wide variations and register biographical differences, differing contexts of reception and changing social and cultural realities. These complexities of audience reception and response, then, inform the intersection between audiences, humanitarian organizations (see Chapter 8), news images and international news organizations. They are not usefully collapsed under the catch-all concept of 'compassion fatigue' especially when the latter shortcircuits the complex ways in which individuals, social groups, cultures, professional news workers and different institutions make sense of and variously respond to images of human suffering and humanitarian disasters.

Höijer's empirically informed analysis, therefore, points to some of the more subtle and differentiated responses of audiences to images of suffering and demonstrates how 'compassion' can in fact encompass multiple and different responses. Others have also observed how meanings cannot simply be read off images of suffering, even when they depict scenes of the worst violence. 'Scenes of an atrocity', remarked Susan Sontag in her essay *Regarding the Pain of Others*, 'may give rise to opposing responses. A call for peace. A cry for revenge. Or simply the bemused awareness, continually restocked by photographic information, that terrible things happen' (Sontag 2003: 11–13). A position not so different from that of Ignatieff, as we saw earlier, when arguing: 'Images of human suffering do not assert their own meaning; they can only instantiate a moral claim if those who watch understand themselves to be potentially under obligation to those they see' (Ignatieff 1998: 11–12).

How exactly the news media may encourage or help to elicit a sense of obligation to those they see has recently been explored by Lilie Chouliaraki in her major book, *The Spectatorship of Suffering* (2006). This also helps us to move beyond the speculative impasse noted earlier. Based on a sophisticated semiotic reading of three different 'regimes of pity' that she sees based within distinct types of news reporting, Chouliaraki pursues how each variously invites, or distances, a sense of obligation in the TV viewer. Like Höijer, then, she discerns important differentiations and distinctions at work in the mediation of human suffering though these are now embedded in the forms and narratives of their media presentation and telling. Specifically, the obligation to see, feel and act are encoded in three sub-genres of news that she labels, respectively, *adventure*, *emergency* and *ecstatic* news. It is through these different forms of news that the mediated ethics of care first introduced in Chapter 5 becomes variously enacted and conditioned. On the basis of a close analysis of each of these distinct types of news, Chouliaraki manages to gain empirical as well as analytical traction on the spectatorship of suffering and how audiences are addressed to feel pity or, following Luc Boltanski (1999) 'a generalised concern for the "other" ':

What I seek to study is the choices made when creating the news text concerning how the sufferer is portrayed on screen and how the scene of suffering is narrated. Even though such choices are part of everyday journalistic routines rather than ideologically motivated calculations, they always carry norms as to how the spectator should relate to the sufferer and what we should do about the suffering. It is these ethical values embedded in news discourse, that comes to orientate the spectator's attitude towards the distant sufferer and, in the long run, shape the disposition of television publics vis-à-vis the misfortune of faraway others. (Chouliaraki 2006: 3)

So what are these three regimes of pity and how do they variously position us as spectators of suffering? To take *adventure news*, or 'news without pity', first. This typically comprises short, relatively simple news reports that restrict the emotional and ethical appeal of scenes of suffering (p.97); they present as distanced reports of 'an alien world'. More semiotically, she argues, they comprise descriptive narratives that only register facts; they are based on singular space–times that restrict the spectator's proximity to the suffering (by presenting the event as a disconnected and random singularity, without antecedents or aftermath); and they lack agency which in turn dehumanizes sufferers and suppresses the possibility of action in the scene of suffering (p.98). With the help of examples of such 'adventure news' – reports of shooting in Indonesia, a boat accident in India and 'biblical' floods in Bangladesh – Chouliaraki maintains that 'compassion fatigue – the audience's indifference towards distant suffering – may have less to do with the fact that people are tired of the omnipresence of suffering on their television screens and more to do with the fact that television is selective about which sufferings it dramatizes and which ones it does not' (p.97).

Emergency news, unlike adventure news, produces pity and does so by providing visually and verbally complicated narratives with affective power. Here news reports provide concrete, specific, multiple and mobile space-times (chronotopes) and these more complex narratives place suffering in the order of lived experiences and often give suffering historical depth and future perspective. The presentation may even connect the suffering with the 'space-time of safety and propose a frame of action to the spectators themselves' (p.119). This type of news report also involves agency, whether active and personalized sufferers and/or the news presence of benefactors and persecutors. These forms of represented agency, then, may imply that the sufferer has limited agency him or herself and may be positioned in a relationship of dependency to an outside interventionist force. But the type of presentation, this regime of pity, nonetheless provides differing opportunities for spectators to discern, and therefore possibly to act, on the basis of a sense of obligation to those who are depicted as suffering.

Finally, *ecstatic news* breaks through normal news conventions and invites, according to Chouliaraki, identification with the sufferer. These media events such as, for example, the first few hours of televised coverage of the September 11 terrorist attacks, produced a succession of different forms or genres of reporting that rolled into each other. Here Chouliaraki describes her selected extracts and how these combined to produce a further regime of pity as follows:

> Each extract enacts a specific mode of representing suffering, a specific topic of suffering. The first evokes empathy with the sufferers, the second is a denunciation of the persecutors and the third an aesthetic contemplation of the spectacle of suffering. I argue that these alternating topics and their genres are characteristic of live footage, the master genre of instantaneous and global transmission. As a result the live footage establishes a regime of pity and a manner of moralizing the spectator that we have not encountered so far. The moral disposition of the live footage is grounded in a sense of space-time as ecstatic, in a conception of the sufferers as sovereign agents on their own suffering and in a relationship of reflexive identification between these sufferers and the spectators. (Chouliaraki 2006: 157)

Chouliaraki's analytical distinctions and examples help us to move beyond the relatively abstract and generalizing statements about mediated images of human suffering and their possible impacts on audiences – whether supportive or critical of the compassion fatigue thesis. Her position also provides a sophisticated demonstration of how a semiotic reading of different media texts can seemingly recover different 'regimes of pity' encoded into their forms of representation, narratives and modes of address. Though an undoubted advance, a number of problems remain.

As with semiotic analyses and interpretative readings of particular media texts more generally, the author's conjectures about how audiences will read these different news items according to the discerned regimes of pity encoded within them, remain untested. We know, for example, that audiences can display remarkable variations in terms of their cognitive understanding and processing of news information and story frames while also maintaining a degree of interpretative latitude that expresses their particular circumstances, outlooks and political and other commitments. In other words, different 'regimes of pity' may, or may not, register and resonate with actual audiences. And, as we heard on the basis of Höijer's work, when audiences do respond to calls for compassion embedded into news packages and visuals of human suffering so they may be doing so in differentiated and quite distinct ways.

To raise questions about audience reception in interaction with news texts, also raises questions about the extent to which it is sufficient to focus analysis, no matter how semiotically sophisticated, on particular news items. News texts including visuals of suffering do not exist in a social and media vacuum but are part of a wider and enveloping culture of circulating signs and meanings already plied by today's ever present and surrounding media ecology. Here, then, we may need to move beyond the analytics of mediation confined to particular news items and seek to situate these within the surrounding cultural flux of particular societies at particular moments in time (see, for example, the discussion of Tierney et al. 2005; Chapter 3).

As we know, some issues can become 'hot' topics of concern for a period and disappear off the news agenda at others (see Chapter 4). Is it conceivable that how we respond to particular news representations in such moments may depend on how we have already been positioned by preceding and surrounding texts to do so, including the wider circulation of particular cultural templates and narratives found in the wider media ecology? Issues of intertextuality, of how the meanings read off a particular news item may be influenced by audience involvement with other media texts, dents the predictive capacity of semiotic analyses confined to particular news items.

This, in turn, invites us to step beyond the media centrism and media determinism embedded in the compassion fatigue thesis (as well as the CNN effect) and aim to situate audiences within a preceding historical context and changing political landscape. In most societies in the world today, the majority of which now proclaim their democratic credentials, the universalizing discourse of human rights has become wedded to processes of democratic advance and the pursuit of social justice issues, challenging the racisms and national parochialisms of the past (see Chapter 5). As categories of the 'other' as alien become incrementally dismantled through processes of globalization, democracy and the international regime of human rights (which is not to say that this is a one-way street) so the cultural and political environment which we inhabit also informs how and what we see and feel and, arguably, our sense of obligation to act. Civil society, including new social movements, NGOs and some sections of the media all contribute to and help register these wider processes of change and the cultural shifts that permeate the 'cultural air that we breathe' (Keane 2003; Beck 2005; Alexander 2006).

Chouliaraki's 'analytics of mediation' provides a microscopic view of how selected news reports and their modalities of presenting and telling stories of human suffering address audiences and how these variously demand or distance an ethical stance concerning how the spectator should act. She also observes, however, that news texts are, in fact, communicating through powerful codes of 'deliberation' and 'theatre':

> Whereas the agora mobilizes the rational and deliberative sensibilities of the spectators vis-à-vis the suffering, the theatrical model enacts the emotional identification of the spectators with the sufferers. Impartial deliberation and the arousal of emotion are, as we know, the two constitutive properties of the politics of pity, which seeks to construe suffering as a moral cause by presenting the suffering as an objective fact to be contemplated. (Chouliaraki 2006: 208)

A recent study lends support to how these twin modes of 'deliberation' and 'theatre' or, to use the authors' preferred terms, 'deliberation' and 'display', are infused within the repertoire of forms routinely organizing and presenting news stories (Cottle and Rai 2006). Based on a systematic analysis of 25 news networks, 56 news outlets, 280 news programmes and 9662 separate news items broadcast in six different countries and internationally by satellite global news providers, the 'communicative architecture' of television news, argue the authors, exhibits far more complexity than Chouliaraki's discerned three sub-genres of news and their associated 'regimes of pity'. Television news, in fact, deploys a wide repertoire of established communicative frames or ways of organizing and delivering news stories, all of which can prove consequential for the public display and deliberation of views and voices as well as how news stories become invested with expressive meanings and emotional force. These communicative frames, moreover, prove pragmatically useful to producers in terms of the logistics, technical capabilities and pressurized environment of news production and are more firmly grounded in the world of news production than readings of news presentation and output alone are sometimes inclined to think (Cottle and Rai 2007: 52–54, 2008: 88–92).

The point here, then, is that television news exhibits a wide range of ways of telling and organizing stories and that these have become institutionalized and naturalized in today's TV news ecology. These 'communicative frames' of presentation pre-exist the communication of particular news events or issues – including humanitarian disasters. On closer inspection they also exhibit more variety and complexity (and occasionally open-endedness) in terms of how they variously inscribe and invite a mediated ethics of care than claims of three encoded 'regimes of pity' may suggest. The following describes some of these conventionalized ways of telling and delivering news stories.

The instantly recognizable, but discursively thin, *'reporting frame'* is journalistically positioned at the heart of conventional TV news programmes and delivers basic de-scription and information about 'news events' – including humanitarian disasters. But a number of more elaborate communicative frames also routinely communicate news stories. These can be analytically differentiated, in deliberative terms, as *'dominant'*, *'contest'*, *'contention'*, *'campaigning'* and *'exposé/investigative'* communicative frames (see later). However, not all news is communicated in such propositional and argu-mentative, that is, 'deliberative' ways, with some communicative frames displaying 'news' more expressively and aesthetically, often making use of compelling visual scenes and affective images (see Chapter 4) (Cottle and Rai 2006).

An in-depth communicative frame, termed here the *'reportage frame'*, has now also become part of the established repertoire of TV news frames around the world and proves capable of providing 'thick descriptions of reality' (Geertz 1973). It can do so by 'bearing witness' and recovering something of the lived, experiential reality of news subjects and/or providing depth background and analysis that purposefully seeks to move beyond the temporal/spatial delimitation of news event reporting. Such crafted packages can draw heavily on both analytic/propositional and aesthetic/expressive or *deliberative* and *display* modes of communication. Although we cannot necessarily assume how exactly they will be received or responded to in advance, their capacity to address audiences and represent those depicted through more in-depth and often humanistic treatments often reveals an inscribed mediated ethics of care.

To conclude this chapter, then, it is useful to consider two different communicative frames and how each presents the 'same' disaster story and humanitarian emergency. Each, as we shall see, provides very different resources either distancing or supportive of a mediated ethics of care. Consider first, then, the *news reporting* frame.

Nightline, Channel 9, Australia
13 September 2004

(News presenter voiceover) The Cayman Islands has become the latest victim of Hurricane Ivan, suffering widespread damage and flooding	Video: waves crashing down violently Video: destroyed houses on the verge of collapse Video: people walking through devastated areas filled with debris
The so-called 'super storm' has already left at least 46 people dead across the Caribbean. Cuba is the next in line	Video: car driving through metre-high floodwaters Video: backstreet filled with floodwater and wreckage Video: tree crashed down onto a vehicle, extensively damaging it Video: building with roof damage
1.3 million people have been evacuated from the path of the storm	Still: close-up shot of storm over regional map Video: distance shot of Fidel Castro examining map

This standard *news reporting frame*, as we can see, functions principally in terms of information conveyance and the surveillance of news events and does so consonant to the daily production cycle of television news. As illustrated here, such news reports are also often of short duration and can help to underpin journalism's professional claims 'to inform' and even 'objectivity' through the provision of facts and details. But, as we can also see, this communicative frame provides at best 'thin' accounts of events that are presented without context, background or competing definitions or in-depth accounts. There is little in this report that can encourage an empathetic response given the complete evacuation of any human subject behind the reified category of the 'Cayman Islands which has become the latest victim'. Here the personal tragedy and trauma of those who have lost their lives is simply buried and rendered invisible behind the brief reference to the '46 dead'. Notwithstanding the factually documented enormity of the disaster resulting in the evacuation of 1.3 million people, this three-sentence news report and its 'distancing' scenes of depersonalised destruction provides minimal resources for sustaining a mediated ethics of care.

The *reportage frame*, in contrast, communicates the same event through a considerably more in-depth, analytically elaborate and emotionally inflected package. Consider, then, the following excised but still much longer and qualitatively different news treatments of the 'same' emergency.

World News, CNNI, Satellite TV
13 September 2004

(News presenter to camera) Hurricane Ivan's category five strength is moving steadily toward Cuba. From the Cayman Islands no official reports but radio operators say that power is out throughout Grand Cayman. Water nearly two metres deep swept through some homes forcing residents to their rooftops	*(News presenter in studio)* Video: animated graphic map identifying regions affected by Hurricane Ivan
(News presenter to camera) The western half of Cuba is under hurricane warning the other half a hurricane watch. Lucia Newman looks at last minute preparations	*(News presenter in studio)*
(Correspondent voiceover) Unwilling to lose everything they have like they did a few years ago during Hurricane Isadora the six thousand residents of La Coloma in western Cuba are rushing to leave, taking as much with them as they can	Video: man pushing a wheelbarrow full of possessions Video: woman hurrying down a street carrying some household items Video: two men loading a mattress onto a horse-drawn cart Video: a boat filled with people sailing across the sea Video: horse-drawn cart loaded up with people and possessions
'You have to try to preserve your belongings' says this woman	Video: woman carrying various possessions
Absolutely everything is being evacuated	Video: man leading his pigs
People who live in low-lying areas or whose homes are too feeble are going to shelters set up in schools and other sturdy buildings. Hundreds of thousands of Cubans are being evacuated	Video: women and children getting off a bus Video: younger woman assisting an elderly woman to climb up stairs Video: people and children inside a makeshift shelter
People like Myra Perez who lives in Havana. She and her children were sleeping, when their roof was blown off exactly one month ago, when Hurricane Charlie ploughed through here so she's understandably frightened 'You can replace your walls', she says, 'but not your life'	Video: woman directing camera through the skeletal remains of her house Video: house with several walls and roof missing Video: woman being interviewed by reporter

On state-run farms workers are rushing to harvest the banana crop before it's destroyed	Video: workers piling bunches of bananas onto trucks Video: close-up of banana leaves
And in a country where so many people have so little and where home and property insurance is unheard of, most here will tell you that the worst part is how they're going to recover from the aftermath	Video: dilapidated building *(Correspondent on site in Havana, Cuba, to camera)*
As they try to take down the statue of Neptune the Greek god of the seas, workers grumble that not even he seems to be safe from Hurricane Ivan. Lucia Newman, CNN, Havana	Video: men attempting to harness and secure statue Video: distance shot of statue standing tall against a cloudy, blue sky Video: statue being picked up and moved by machinery
(News presenter to camera) In Jamaica at least seventeen people died on the island as a result of Hurricane Ivan. In one of the worst hit communities where at least eight villagers were killed, grieving parents told Karl Penhaul about the horror of the storm. This report contains graphic images which some viewers may find disturbing	*(News presenter in studio)*
(Correspondent voiceover) The storm has passed but the time for grieving is just beginning	Video: crying woman holding a screaming toddler Video: toddler taken from woman's arms Video: distraught woman, hands covering her face
Minutes before we reached the fishing community of Portland Cottage villagers had just found three more bodies killed when Hurricane Ivan whipped up a tidal surge	Video: group of villagers stand in a semi-circle Video: another woman looking sombre Video: a man pulls aside a collection of tree leaves to reveal three dead bodies Video: the group disperses one woman walks through the crowd
One of the dead, two-year-old Lisa-Anne Thompson was snatched right out of her mother's arms by the raging floodwaters	Video: woman bent over, gently stroking the body of a lifeless child
Lisa's mother: 'The big water came again and just flushed her out of my hand. She disappeared out of my hand and I cannot find her because it was night and the place was very dark'	Video: woman talking directly to camera

(*Correspondent voiceover*) Her husband Uroy was carrying their other daughter Tiffany she drowned too when the tide dragged her from her father's arms	Video: a crowd of people. An elderly woman crying Video: close-up of two hands being held together and then separating
Uroy Thompson: 'I had three babies. One on my right arm, one on my left. She was behind me and had a little baby in her arm'	Video: man talking directly to camera
(*Correspondent voiceover*) Through their tears and pain the true horror of that night becomes clear Imagine this, it's pitch black outside, close to midnight and the floodwaters are already waist high and then a huge wave comes rushing in from the sea	Video: villagers covering the dead bodies with blankets News presenter on site in Portland Cottage, Jamaica, in front of dilapidated house, talking directly to camera
(*Correspondent voiceover*) This is what's left of the village	Video: close-up of red-coloured muddy waters Video: dilapidated houses, debris littering the surrounds
Edwards and her husband take us back to the ruins of their wood home. She finds her only surviving son Jerome playing in the receding floodwaters	Video: man standing outside the remains of his house Video: woman and child walking through ankle-deep floodwaters
Their possessions were wrecked by the wind-lashed waves	Video: woman and child stand in the doorway of the shell of their house. Man leans against a remaining wall
A zip-lock bag failed to protect the birth certificates of her dead daughters Tiffany and Lisa-Anne's tiny shoes still lay in the corner	Video: close-up shot of documents. Video: close-up shot of children's shoes and toys strewn in a corner
Neighbour Dawn Williams also tried to flee to safety the night the hurricane struck She survived, her eight-year-old son Anton-Wayne drowned	Video: distance shot of house surrounded by floodwater Video: a pile of broken branches surrounded by floodwater
Dawn Williams: 'The water was high, high, high so we still don't know what to do. So we was trying to turn but the water was coming very fast and I had my little boy in my hand, holding him very tight and a wave of water come and splash him away, out of my hand'	Video: woman talking directly to camera

(Correspondent voiceover) She says she spent eight hours in the water clinging to a tree branch, holding on for dear life. Her mother drowned	Video: panning distance shot of high floodwaters and floating branches
The police come and stretcher away the corpses	Video: two men carrying a corpse on a stretcher.
Nobody seems to know what's next for the living or the dead. Karl Penhaul and the camera of Neil Hallsworth, CNN, Portland Cottage, Jamaica	Video: man wading through floodwaters

As we can hear, see and possibly feel, in this instance, the television news *reportage frame* moves considerably beyond the 'thin' descriptions of the standard *reporting frame*, providing in relative journalistic terms 'thick' descriptions of reality (Cottle 2005). Here we are invited to relive the experiences of Hurricane Ivan as it unfolded through time and to do so through an array of personal testimonies and witnessed tragic events, most relayed direct to camera in the emotionally charged voices of survivors. Visually a succession of 'moving scenes' (in both senses of the term) direct the viewers' gaze from distancing, contextualising shots, to progressively personal, close-up and intimate scenes 'bearing witness' to the human hurt, distress and loss of loved ones – including the covering over of bodies. Through this professionally produced choreography of visual scenes, personal narratives, displays of emotion and organizing voice-over, the news presentation acts performatively. That is, it actively seeks to encourage our empathy and sense of identification with victims and survivors, even commanding us at certain points to imagine what they must have felt and experienced: '*Imagine this, it's pitch black outside, close to midnight and the floodwaters are already waist high and then a huge wave comes rushing in from the sea.*' As the news narrator also states. '*Through their tears and pain the true horror of that night becomes clear*' and we, the viewers, are positioned and encouraged to recognize and even feel something of this pain and horror through its journalistic mode of telling.

On the basis of this capacity for elaborate, empathetic framing, the established communicative frame of *reportage* can also potentially 'move' (performatively, diachronically and emotionally) from the *indicative* to the *subjunctive* in its story treatment, from telling how things are to suggesting how they should be (Alexander and Jacobs 1998; Cottle 2004, 2006b). In this instance, however, the news item focuses principally on retelling and re-enacting the tragedy and trauma brought in the wake of the hurricane, seeking to 'bring home' something of its human impacts and consequences. The referencing of everyday familial possessions left behind by the bereaved is a poignant device for creating this sense of ordinary lives ripped apart ('*A zip-lock bag failed to protect the birth certificates of her dead daughters. Tiffany and Lisa-Anne's tiny shoes still lay in the corner*'). On the basis of this crafted, performative elaboration of the tragedy and trauma brought in the wake of the hurricane, it is not difficult to see how this could also easily move into a more questioning, interrogative and critical journalistic response in the days and weeks ahead. As the correspondent concludes: *'The police come and stretcher away the corpses. Nobody seems to know what's next for the living or the dead.'* And this, as discussed earlier (Chapter 3), is precisely what can happen in some mediated disasters. Here we have simply indicated how the crafted fusion of deliberative and display forms of journalism found in the reportage frame inscribes a mediated ethics of care and it is through this means that the viewer is summoned to recognize the hurt and pain of others.

We have attended to only two of the recurring communicative frames routinely deployed by TV news programmes around the world when covering humanitarian disasters. Journalists can also report humanitarian disasters and emergencies through deliberative frames that are structured around a dominant defining voice, a structured contest between opposing views, or a more complex contention involving many competing views and voices – items that may, or may not, deliberatively and rhetorically invite our compassion. Or journalists may, on occasion, devote time and resources in proactively pursuing a humanitarian disaster story in terms of an expose/investigation as can happen when disasters tip over into scandal and political dissent or celebrate and affirm supposedly timeless values of human endurance, heroism and resilience in the face of adversity by seeking out and communicating 'mythic tales' of individual survivors and rescuers (Chapter 3).

How, when and with what efficacy journalism differently inscribes and invokes a sense of moral compassion and thereby mediates an ethic of care in its telling and visualizing of news stories has generally been overshadowed by established academic interests (see Chapter 5). These have generally tended to be more preoccupied with how dominant messages and meanings are framed in the news media and how these serve interests of power. But, as the work of Höijer, Chouliaraki and others has begun to suggest, there is, in fact, an underlying relational and ethical dimension embedded within televised scenes of suffering. This can assume quite different and potentially consequential forms. How ethical demands become embedded or dissimulated within the communicative forms and appeals of journalism are also, of course, profoundly relational and powered. The mediated relationship between the viewer and the seen, between us and distant others, demands sustained empirical research as much as theoretical speculation (Beck 2006). The relational ethics professionally embedded within news texts, but relatively under-researched by news academics, goes to the heart of claims about the role of the news media within a globalizing world and possible cosmopolitan outlook.

8 | HUMANITARIAN NGOs, NEWS MEDIA AND THE CHANGING RELATIONS OF COMMUNICATIVE POWER

Despite our ongoing hard work on trying to generate media interest, we will simply have to wait for the 'magic wand' of international news services before we can have a chance of profiling terrible tragedies. What I am describing here are two prominent symptoms ... one of them is that there will always generally be a lack of interest in (. . .) media outlets for places that an average person in this country may not be able to find on the map; and the other is the general 'pack' mentality of all the global media – if somebody else is reporting on it, we may as well do it too. (communications manager, Oxfam Australia)

Whether humanitarian emergencies are routinely signalled in the news, sensationalized as spectacular media events, or simply buried along with countless imageless victims in 'forgotten emergencies' and 'hidden wars' depends, as we have heard across previous chapters, on the practices and priorities of global reporting. We know, for example, that the media spotlight is apt to roam quickly from one disaster/emergency to another and does so in a competitive media environment informed by the pursuit of readers, ratings and revenue. Such fleeting coverage, at best, generally provides sparse context or historical background and even less follow-up coverage of post-conflict, post-emergency communities or longer term processes of development. The news media, we also know, are drawn selectively to images of distress rather than issues of structural disadvantage or the forces that determine and shape the scenes of skeletal figures that appear like ghosts on our TV screens. In these respects, the news media lens is peculiarly insensitive to the distant suffering of others and, based on geopolitical outlooks and historical legacy, it is apt to see through a prism of ethnocentrism and western-led interests now normalized within a professional 'calculus of death' (Chapter 3; see also Harrison and Palmer 1986; Benthall 1993; Philo 1993; Minear et al. 1996; Rotberg and Weiss 1996;

Beattie et al. 1999; Moeller 1999; Carruthers 2004; Ross 2004; IFRCRCS 2005; Seaton 2005a).

This much, then, is generally known and has been documented by earlier research. It is not the whole story, however. As we have also heard, the news media can sometimes perform a more progressive role in publicly visualizing and even humanizing the suffering of distant others, positioning victims and survivors within a mediated ethics of care and alerting publics and power-holders to their plight (see Chapters 5 and 7). And, as we have also seen, the news media can play a central role in the public ritualization of catastrophes, performatively enacting tragedy and trauma and channelling public emotions into moments of ritual solidarity, imagined community and/or political contestation and dissent (see Chapter 3). We have yet to explore in detail, however, how organized sources within the field of humanitarian action seek to further their aims and goals in interaction with the news media, the sorts of communication strategy that they deploy and the difficulties and dilemmas that they encounter and must seek to overcome. It is in and through this critical nexus with the news media that humanitarian NGOs, such as Red Cross, Oxfam, Save the Children, World Vision, Care and Médecins sans Frontières, and their aims and appeals, images and ideals are principally disseminated and become known, and it is by these same means that public sympathies and support are periodically galvanized in humanitarian appeals.

This chapter first contextualizes the contemporary field of humanitarian NGOs in relation to the rise of new forms of global crises, the changing organizational field of humanitarian aid organizations and the rapidly changing global media and communication environment. How these changes impact the work and communication strategies of NGOs are then explored in more detail with the help of professional and experiential accounts from communication managers and professionals working in some of the leading world aid agencies. Here we learn firsthand of some of the difficulties that aid NGOs grapple with in their attempt to get their message across within today's global communications environment. We then move to consider attempts by NGOs to regain the communications initiative through proactive communication strategies and coalition campaigns, including Make Poverty History, designed to mobilize publics and governments. The chapter concludes by considering how new communication technologies are helping to reconfigure relations of communicative power between NGOs, governments, news media, donors and recipients of aid – changes that look set to continue in the years ahead.

Humanitarian NGOs in the global age

Humanitarian NGOs such as Red Cross, Oxfam, Save the Children, World Vision, Care and Médecins sans Frontières historically have played an important part in establishing the discourse and regime of universal human rights (Benthall 1993; Ignatieff 1998; Höijer 2004; Beck 2005; DeChaine 2005). Many did so long before academic debates about globalization, the global public sphere, global citizenship and global cosmopolitanism became so current. These and other NGOs further humanitarian principles and practices by bearing witness, raising awareness and funds, lobbying powerbrokers, delivering short-term aid and emergency relief as well as providing longer term development assistance and advocating on behalf of distant others. Social theorists increasingly regard them as important agents in the transition to a more global civil society. Ulrich Beck, for example, sees them as leading actors in the transition from 'a nation-state to a cosmopolitan world order' and as a potent force in the 'meta-power of global civil society' (Beck 2005: 64–71, 236–248), and D. Robert DeChaine, more discursively, has argued that they define the contours of 'a new global social landscape' and 'rhetorically craft a new global community' (DeChaine 2005: 23, 37–65).

In the post-9/11 political environment and the ensuing global 'war on terror', how-ever, NGOs have had to negotiate their position, practices and even their principles when conducting their work in occupied territories:

> The relationship between humanitarian actors and the military has become increasingly fraught, and the campaigns in Afghanistan and Iraq have only made it worse. Most NGOs have, at one time or another, coordinated with military forces in the execution of their aid activities. This is done with varying degrees of caution and reluctance; US organizations are typically the most amenable. Agen-cies have not yet found a comfortable way to position themselves *vis-à-vis* the counter-terror agenda. Some have tried to distance themselves, while others take the aid funds available to them and the context of their provision as simply political realities that define their operational universe. (Stoddard 2003: 3)

'New wars' (Kaldor 2001) target civilian populations with extreme, systematic violence including 'ethnic cleansing' and 'genocide (Shaw 2007: 113–130) and western 'risk-transfer war' (Shaw 2005) produces civilian 'collateral damage' through high-level bombing and the deliberate destruction of civilian infrastructure (see Chapter 6). Intrinsic to these new forms of warfare, therefore, is the systematic creation of large numbers of internally displaced people as well as, often, an exodus of refugees seeking safety in bordering territories. The rise of western military interventions, ostensibly conducted in the name of protecting human lives and human rights, also pose extreme challenges to contemporary NGOs in the field, though the propensity of western powers to engage in such 'military humanism' appears for the moment to have been dented by the political debacle and human carnage of Iraq and Afghanistan in the protracted post-invasion phases of the 'global war on terror' (Robinson 2005; Shaw 2005; Beck 2006; Hammond 2007).

As well as the human fallout from the global war on terror and new forms of military conflict, NGOs also confront an array of formidable challenges, intimated at the outset of this book as the dark side of globalization. These include growing num-bers of forced migrants and environmental refugees; increasing extreme weather events and associated humanitarian disasters; the deterioration of sustainable human habitats through climate change; the threats of global pandemics (Ungar 1998; Wilkins 2005; WHO 2007) as well as future conflicts based on predicted food insecurity and water shortages exacerbated by world population growth, urbanization and climate change. The Intergovernmental Panel on Climate Change (IPCC 2007) estimates, for example, that 75–250 million people across Africa face water shortages by 2020; crop yields could increase by 20% in East and Southeast Asia but decrease by 30% in central and South Asia in the same period; and agriculture fed by rainfall in some African countries could also drop by 50% by 2020. In 2008 over 1 billion people already suffered from water shortages and 30 countries got more than one-third of their water from outside of their borders, figures that are destined to rise with continuing climate change. Food insecurity and water shortages now look set to produce new conflicts and humanitarian emergencies in the years ahead.

The organizational field of NGOs has also changed across recent years. Aid agencies now co-exist and compete for media attention and donor funds within an increasingly crowded field (Stoddard 2003; Cottle and Nolan 2007). Currently there are 3000 to 4000 internationally operating NGOs based in the west (Stoddard 2003: 1), with a handful of large and influential NGOs predominating including: Red Cross, Save the Children, Oxfam, World Vision, CARE and Médecins sans Frontières (Doctors without Borders). Some NGOs continue to be motivated by religious beliefs though today religious affiliations are often downplayed in general publicity. Some focus exclusively on disaster and short-term emergency relief and/or particular forms of humanitarian assistance – specific medical needs, food, or shelter – while others engage in long-term development work, seeking to adopt a more holistic approach to community needs and empowering local communities in participatory modes of development. And some publicly champion human rights, naming and shaming offending states and individuals and advocating for social justice, while others steadfastly protect their stance of impartiality and neutrality and seek to maintain access at all times to those in need (Kaldor 2003: 128–136; Gaber and Willson 2005).

Permutations on all this are found in the proliferation of NGOs working in the humanitarian aid field today, a field which also gives expression to the changing politics and cultural outlooks of wider civil society and the rise of human rights issues and the institutionalization of human rights in international law (Chapter 5; Beck 2006). NGOs based in western countries also operate within a political environment characterized by a decline in traditional political allegiances and the rise of new social movements, single-issue campaigns and a professionalized approach to public communications (Kaldor 2003: 78–108; Sireau and Davis 2007).

NGOs depend on communications media and access to get their message across and must seek entry to today's complex global news ecology to do so (see Figure 1.1). Global news corporations (CNNI, BBC World, Fox), new regional news formations and proliferating local to global news services and 24/7 'real-time' news capabilities all present new opportunities, as well as new challenges, for NGOs seeking to publicize their work and pursue their aims in an increasingly competitive, commercialized and accelerating news environment (Gaber and Willson 2005). 'Global surveillance' (Shaw 2005, 2007) and the 'transformation of visibility' (Thompson 1995) brought about by this global communications network has also produced an increased media proclivity for scandals (see Chapter 3) – a phenomenon that can prove disastrous for the public reputations of NGOs and their capacity to raise donations and carry out their humanitarian work.

The rapidly changing communications environment, however, also affords NGOs new opportunities including: tailoring new communication technologies (mobile telephony, videophones, satellite linkups, the internet and networked coordination, communication and information systems) to their needs and requirements in the field and when communicating with different stakeholders. These are some of the new global challenges and opportunities confronting humanitarian NGOs today. Here it is useful to see from the 'inside out' how humanitarian NGOs engage with the news media and how they seek to signal global crises and communicate their messages in and through the global news media.

Aid NGOs in interaction with the news media

Based on the accounts and experiences of communication managers and professional working for five of the principal NGO organizations (Red Cross, Oxfam, Save the Children, World Vision, Care and Médecins sans Frontières), a recent study documents how the 'critical nexus' between aid NGOs and the news media noted earlier, is undergoing further evolution and change (Cottle and Nolan 2007). These changes, argue the authors, can be seen in many respects as detrimental to humanitarian NGOs' projected ethos and aims of global humanitarianism. The following summarizes key findings.

The crowded aid field and organizational branding

The increasingly crowded NGO aid field produces a situation where more organizations are now chasing public and government funds. This can also affect the organizational standing of established NGOs as well as the quality or accuracy of information that finds its way into the public domain via the news media:

> The big organizations are also competing in a way with each other for media coverage and obviously we sometimes may have different agendas. The Red Cross may be working on a particular crisis which is related, for instance, to the Congo, or some other organizations are working on something else, and that does not necessarily help us in terms of generating media interest and media coverage . . . the big element there is that the media, as insatiable as they are for information,

will not always resort to traditional channels, but will accept an opinion or comment from any available source, which can create some additional problems for us. (national communications manager, Australian Red Cross)

The crowded field of NGOs also generates a sense of competition which, in turn, leads to the pursuit of organizational profile in the media. This profile can more readily be termed a market 'brand' in so far as it purposefully deploys associations, meanings and values to distinguish itself from its nearest competitors in the media marketplace. The use of the word 'brand' has itself become part of the lexicon or 'corporate speak' that aid agencies now use to describe themselves and their activities and it tells us something about the extent to which NGOs have incorporated the models and principles of corporate promotion and marketing into their communications practice: 'We do want to get awareness of the organization out there as much as possible, we want to get brand awareness (communications manager, MSF Australia).

So-called 'brand awareness,' by definition, seeks to differentiate the public's awareness of particular organizations. While MSF has often traded on the uncompromising idealism of its youthful volunteers delivering vital medical assistance in the field, the Red Cross deliberately seeks to promote its established 'reputable brand' identity which, as already suggested, is felt to be under threat from the proliferating agencies that are prepared to usurp its standing as an authoritative media source. This can happen in the context of today's 24/7 news environment, which demands constant updates and information on request and where some journalists may not necessarily wait for considered, accurately sourced and verified statements. All are now concerned to promote and protect their brand and ward off potential media criticism, a point returned to later: 'As far as I'm concerned, that's the role of the media officer to have to try and find out what they [the media] are going to do and offset any potential risk to the brand and the people that we work with and the way they're represented' (national media coordinator, Oxfam Australia).

How aid organizations respond to the need for media profile is not confined to considerations of branding however, but also informs their strategic use of communications and how they facilitate media access to the field, discussed next.

Packaging media reports and facilitating the field

Through experience and routine media interactions, aid organizations know exactly what the media require and incorporate this into their professional practice and communications strategies. Packaging information and images in conformity to the media's known predilections has now become institutionalized *inside* aid agencies. For example, 'Tricks of the trade: how to sell forgotten emergencies' (IFRCRCS 2005: 134–135) advises NGO communications personnel on how to get emergencies news coverage in the following terms:

World Disasters Report: How to Sell Forgotten Emergencies

- *Invest in media relations*: communications training and expertise, down to the local level.
- *Keep up a dialogue with the media*: provide background material on complex emergencies, but not 15 minutes before deadline.
- *Put a number on it*: death tolls give journalists pegs to hang their stories on.
- *Bring in the big names*: it's controversial, but enlisting celebrities can work. The press follows the famous face and ends up reporting the cause.
- *Make it visual*: nothing sells a story like a good picture. In disasters, aid agencies may have the only photos available.
- *Be creative and proactive*: tell the bigger story through the eyes of individuals. Fit what you are doing into the news agenda. Organize trips for reporters.
- *Never give up*: in this game, persistence really does pay off. (Tim Large, Deputy Ed. Reuters *AlertNet*, reproduced in IFRCRCS 2005: 134–135)

An Oxfam communications manager states, similarly: 'Our strategy is geared towards fulfilling the needs of the media and offering them what they are looking for, in as simple and "easy-to-use" way as possible' (communications manager, Oxfam Australia).

In addition to pitching and packaging stories in conformity to known media needs, aid NGOs also seek to 'facilitate the field' to the news media by arranging access to their field delegates and remote locations. Media field trips according to NGO representatives, however, are becoming increasingly rare, not least because of the news organization costs involved and the decline in foreign correspondents (see Chapter 2; Utley 1997; Hamilton and Jenner 2004). The advantages of 'facilitating the field' at different stages of the emergency cycle, however, are generally recognized by NGOs:

> At least in the initial emergency phase of the operation, there is this sense they need us as much as we need them and I think the global media organizations will often work with the likes of the Red Cross . . . We've met many journalists that we had to have bedded down if you like, literally bedded down with Red Cross workers in conflict situations and they understood the role of the Red Cross much better than most. (international communications officer, Australian Red Cross)

More routinely, aid agencies now seek to capture the media spotlight by other means – if only fleetingly. To do so they seek to engage the known event orientation of news as well as the media's penchant for celebrity:

> HIV and AIDS: nobody really wants to write or talk about that and, unfortunately, the only time that you can try and pitch those kinds of issues is either by a natural disaster or specific days in the year, like 'world disaster reduction day' or 'HIV and AIDS day', where we know generally the media will have some leniency in terms of allowing a story or two to appear about that. . . . In a way it's a compromise, but the bottom line is we really have to be realistic. (national communications manager, Australian Red Cross)

While 'event days' are designed to deliberately chime with the 'event orientation of news' (Galtung and Ruge 1965; Halloran et al. 1970), there is no guarantee that the media will always run with them and some NGOs now detect a growing media reluctance to report such NGO 'pseudo-events' (Boorstin 1961). A further strategy to capture media interest is to make use of celebrity, a known predilection of today's media culture. This can become tactically deployed in some NGO communications strategies:

> I think some media outlets just won't run some stories . . . then perhaps you get a Cate Blanchett or someone to go in there and advocate on behalf of it. So if it's a female genital mutilation or something that some outlets are going to cringe at, you do it through a celebrity possibly. So we have different ways to do it, and that's all about the mix and packaging. (communications manager, MSF Australia)

Although NGOs benefit from facilitating the field and embedded journalists these opportunities have become increasingly infrequent in the competitive, cost-cutting media environment where broadcasters and newspapers are increasingly reluctant to support correspondents in the field. Event days and celebrity, then, are used tactically to try and prise open the stubborn gates of media attention but these tactics, as we have seen, are already shaped by the news media culture and some may question its fleeting and shallow representations at best.

Regionalizing 'global' humanitarianism

In addition to celebrity, there are other statuses and hierarchies at play in the global universe of NGO–media interactions and these too are significant in shaping humanitarian media coverage:

> The peak of coverage about the Sudan crisis back in 2004 followed a BBC report. It was only then actually that the UN Secretary General, Kofi Annan, decided to visit the area as well as Colin Powell. And that then created an opportunity for us to cover that. But it was all very much driven by one single report coming out of the BBC which was then obviously replicated here. So that is one element of media globalization, I think, which includes reducing resources of media organizations which means that they don't have as many correspondents as they used to have in every part of the world so they're relying on global media networks such as CNN, BBC or wire services such as Reuters and AFP to pick up on the stories and then run them. (national communications manager, Australian Red Cross)

Evidently a global media hierarchy, as well as global elite figures, can prompt responses from nationally based media in respect of the hidden humanitarian disaster of Darfur in Sudan (see Chapters 3 and 5). While the debate about the capacity of the global media to galvanize political and policy responses, the so-called 'CNN effect', rolls on (see Chapter 7), there is little doubt that national news media often take their cue from world news services. In the field of humanitarian emergencies and relief operations these act as powerful agenda setters, periodically cascading reports of humanitarian disasters down through national news media networks. As the opening statement to this chapter from the communications manager, Oxfam Australia, observes humanitarian NGOs must now, it seems, bide their time and follow the lead of the international news services.

Powerful regionalizing (and personalizing) forces are also at work in the reporting of humanitarian issues and distant suffering. Reaffirming the underlying geopolitical parameters of selective news interests (see Chapter 3), the news media seek out, and for the most part NGOs happily render up, stories and personnel that regionalize and 'bring back home' the relevance and cultural proximity of the events portrayed. Australian NGOs describe, for example, how the media routinely request and receive 'regionalized' material for their media reports:

> In 90% of the cases the media will want to talk to us as long as we have an Australian person involved in any shape or form. If we don't have that, it's becoming increasingly difficult to portray something which is in any case probably remote to the Australian public if we are talking about places in the Middle East or in Africa or in former Soviet Republics. If there is a genuine crisis happening for instance in Chechnya and you want to talk about it, no matter how good a story it is, if there is no Australian angle you can almost forget it. (national communications manager, Australian Red Cross)

All the NGOs interviewed spoke about this regional media emphasis with its pursuit of 'home' connections in disaster reporting and all now deliberately incorporate it into their communication strategies:

> So it's very much about responding to disasters and crises as well as trying to raise the profile through the media of the work of Australian Red Cross and the wider Red Cross Red Crescents movements and there are many ways for us to do that but primarily we try and focus on the work of our Red Cross delegates, the delegates that work with the International Red Cross overseas. They're the stars of our organization in many ways and usually our best bet in securing media coverage, you know, 'A local hero from your neighborhood is now working in a disaster zone or conflict zone'. (international communications officer, Australian Red Cross)

This media logic to regionalize and 'bring back home' reports from global disaster zones by finding local personnel and accounts, now assimilated by NGOs, has implications for ideas of 'global humanitarianism'. When we are invited to see the world of disasters and human need through a mediated national prism that splinters the category of global humanity into 'us' and 'them', 'nationals' and 'foreigners', 'active saviours' and 'passive victims' then this inevitably underplays the active agency of indigenous aid workers (and survivors) and reinforces a western-led and western-centric view of humanitarianism. Arguably this does little to sustain the 'proper distance' required in our mediated interrelationships with others and necessary for 'a duty of care, obligation and responsibility, as well as understanding' (Silverstone 2007: 47).

Risk, reputation and mediated scandals

Across recent years humanitarian NGOs have become increasingly sensitive about and reflexively respond to the media tendency to pursue scandals and therefore seek as matter of course to 'offset any potential risk to the brand'. Mediated scandals have long been associated with politicians, celebrities and even the moral violations committed by ordinary people (Lull and Hinerman 1997; Thompson 2000), but recently it has also encroached on such formerly 'sacred' and 'inviolable' institutions as the church and humanitarian aid agencies. A number of mediated scandals have recently rocked the humanitarian aid sector, including the high-profile UN 'oil for food programme' debacle and allegations of UN peacekeepers involved in sexual misconduct in the Democratic Republic of Congo (DRC) and Liberia. Both the Red Cross and MSF have also become embroiled in scandals, the former in respect of allegations of mishandling public donations following the Bali bombing in 2004 and the latter following media claims that MSF had asked the public to cease giving donations for relief in the tsunami of 2004. Whether based on misconduct or misunderstanding, the claims and counterclaims that swirl in the media sphere can cause massive damage to that prized asset of high-profile aid organizations: public reputation. NGO reputation, based on public trust and an organization's credibility, is a bankable currency in the competitive field of humanitarian NGOs where each is dependent on public (and government) good will and donations for the continuance of its humanitarian work:

> In the past you could entertain the idea that the media are there to report on a certain event or issue, whatever it is, and to cover the work of aid organizations and that it will always be a feel-good story. That is no longer the case and this is something we are rapidly beginning to understand. We make sure that whatever we do with the media we have completely covered the risk elements . . . that we go consciously into an agreement with a media outlet knowing that they may turn on us, and that we have prepared strategies to deal with that. (national communications manager, Australian Red Cross)

In the context of the 2004 tsunami, for example, aid agencies predicted that the media would inevitably have high expectations that emergency relief, following the unprecedented wave of public donations, would result in tangible improvements such as new housing in the short to medium term, an expectation that was always going to be unattainable given the scale of devastation involved and the massive destruction to so much infrastructure. Aid organizations managed to head off at the pass this likely media response by collectively reinforcing the dimensions of the problem and the necessary timescale involved:

> If you look at the tsunami case it was going to be such a competitive field and the media would be overtly critical of aid agency's responses, so we needed to have a proactive strategy instead of just hoping for the best because we've invested so much and people have given so much to us and we don't want that jeopardized by a bad media report or just omission of us as a main player. (national media coordinator, Oxfam Australia)

This concern with possible media misrepresentation has led some agencies to stipulate that they will now only allow their key personnel to be interviewed live, thus minimizing the possibilities that post-interview editing and packaging will misconstrue their words and messages. Aid agencies reflexively respond to this latest 'media logic' (Altheide and Snow 1979) which pursues scandals with communication strategies deliberately aimed at safeguarding their brand and minimizing the risks of unfavourable publicity. Once placed in the media sphere, negative claims can continue to circulate and live on in public memory or perhaps, more importantly, journalist memory as 'media templates' (Kitzinger 2004: 54–78) that can become recycled in new scandals. The pursuit of scandals, then, has become an inextricable part of today's media environment and informs the media's selective focus on humanitarian disasters:

> We were pitching a story about the Democratic Republic of Congo, it's one of our big objectives this year to get that story out there, and the interview was with a particular person and it went very well. Then at the very end the journalist wanted to know how we were going with the tsunami because it's always a question that the journalists are going to ask this year and next year, maybe in the next five years. And so we told them how we were going, we told them how much money we'd raised and how much money we'd spent and what we were doing about that and why we stopped fundraising and the next day it's a front page story about what we were doing with the tsunami and they completely disregarded the whole point of the interview which was about the DRC. (national marketing and communications officer Save the Children Australia)

The contemporary field of humanitarian NGOs, then, is characterized by risk, reputation and a media logic now disposed to mediated scandals. NGOs find themselves obliged to respond in ways that are designed to 'protect the brand' through professionalized communication strategies:

> So I guess there's been a move towards the third sector, the aid sector, pulling its socks up if you like and employing professional communicators to ensure that it

isn't just about writing fluffy stories or trying to get good positive coverage for appeals and crises around the world; it's also about risk management ... we have a reputation to uphold and maintain. (international communications officer, Australian Red Cross)

This part of the discussion, based on insider testimonies from some of the major humanitarian aid agencies, has documented how NGOs have become increasingly dependent on the news media to publicize and pursue their humanitarian objectives.

This relationship of dependency increasingly insinuates the logic of the news media inside the communications strategies of NGOs. These include, as we have heard, the deliberate pursuit of media space to promote 'organizational brands' in the crowded media marketplace; the pitching and packaging of stories in conformity to the known dispositions of target media outlets as well as the general event orientation of news and the media's penchant for celebrity; the regionalized (and personalized) inflection of humanitarian disasters by forefronting 'home-based' issues and NGO delegates as media 'stars' and 'talent'; and the reflexive responses, that now consume resources, time and energy, to the perceived heightened risks of media scandal. In all these inter-related respects, humanitarian aid organizations are now working *within*, not simply sourcing, today's media regime and the public representation of global humanitarianism enshrined in the actions and agency of humanitarian NGOs increasingly becomes shaped by the dispositions of the news media.

However, other developments in the field of NGO communications practices provide evidence of more positive developments. These include the development of collaborative NGO media campaigns and the customized uses of new communication technologies that are now contributing to the reconfiguration of the relations of communicative power in the field – the subject of the final two sections.

Make Poverty History: campaign dilemmas behind the scenes

The Make Poverty History (MPH) campaign was launched in 2005, a year that also included the meeting of the G8 in Scotland, the UK's presidency of the European Union, the World Trade ministerial meeting in Hong Kong and the *Live 8* concerts. A wide coalition of groups including international development and aid organizations (Oxfam, Christian Aid, Action Aid, Cafod, Save the Children and others) campaigned for the governments of the richest countries to make political decisions that would deliver increased justice for the world's poorest people. The campaign challenged the UK government to take a leading role internationally at the G8, the UN World Summit and at the World Trade Organization, to make radical changes to its own economic policies and push for longer term changes internationally on three linked areas: injustice in global trade, the huge burden of debt levied on poorer countries and ineffective aid (*http://www.makepovertyhistory.org*).

According to the Make Poverty History website, the UK coalition grew rapidly, representing over 540 organizations and, after just 6 months, 87% of the UK population had heard about the campaign; 25,000 people took part in an overnight vigil at Westminster for trade justice; over 500,000 people contacted the prime minister and over 800,000 activists campaigned online; 8 million people wore the campaign symbolic white band and a quarter of a million people marched in Edinburgh ahead of the arrival of the G8 leaders (over half of whom joined a protest for the first time). Moreover, no fewer than 31 million people from 84 national coalitions around the world united in the 'Global Call to Action against Poverty' and participated in three days of coordinated White Band Days to put pressure on their respective governments (*http://www.makepovertyhistory.org*). The *Live 8* concerts around the world helped to introduce the campaign to a huge global audience and thereby put pressure on governments in key G8 countries (see also Nash 2008).

Behind the scenes, however, the Make Poverty History coalition experienced disagreements and dilemmas about communications strategy and these, according to Nick Sireau and Aeron Davis (2007), expressed basic choices that are intrinsic to all communication campaigns. Three fundamental decisions, they maintain, confront all interest groups in their communication strategy: (1) choice of target audience, (2) the position occupied or adopted by the campaigning group in respect of government and/ or other power-holders and (3) whether to use private or public means of communication. Each of these choices generates potential risks, costs and benefits, as Sireau and Davis explain:

> Is change better effected by placing a group closer to, or further from, centres of power and decision-making (an 'insider' or 'outsider' approach)? Is it better to orient campaigns towards mass media and mass opinion, or, to focus communication on active memberships and elite decision-makers? The rewards of greater private or public influence may be offset by the threat of institutional or media co-option/assimilation and, possibly, the alienation of group members. (Sireau and Davis 2007: 131–132)

Some organizations within the Make Poverty History coalition evidently pushed for a more 'insider' strategy, aiming to influence the UK government by adopting a more consensual, moderate and pragmatist stance. This approach won out in the run-up to the important G8 summit, publicly calling for the cancellation of debt, increasing foreign aid and alleviating suffering but without directing blame at the government. Others argued for an 'outsider' stance and didn't want to compromise their political independence or capacity to champion justice issues and to criticize both government and the economic system as part of the problem. The risks of political cooption were thus highlighted by some groups within the coalition, political isolation and ineffectiveness by others. The risks of media cooption were also at the forefront of campaign deliberations and disagreements:

> For those coalition NGO members with a significant, professional marketing contingent, the goal was to simplify the representation of issues and make extensive use of celebrity endorsement. For those NGOs that were more campaign-led, such strategies threatened to weaken and confuse campaign messages, alienate activist members and hand too much control to the celebrities themselves. All these tensions and division came to a head during the Live 8 music event and G8 Summit. (Sireau and Davis 2007: 138)

As the campaign progressed, the government increasingly associated itself with it and even suggested that the campaign represented public support for its policies. Members of the government, for example, frequently referred to the campaign's key triad of terms – aid, trade and debt – and even adopted its symbol of the white hand. Market research undertaken at the time suggested that some sections of the public were beginning to see the campaign itself as government inspired and controlled. This was a source of concern for the Make Poverty History Coordination Team.

According to Sireau and Davis, the larger insider members of the coalition ultimately won out and had more input into the framing of public messages up to the G8 Summit. Critics argued that this resulted in a less than robust engagement with the government on the key issue of trade. The *Live 8* concerts, organized by Bob Geldof and independently of the Make Poverty History campaign, were successful in generating public awareness but threatened to overshadow the mass demonstrations staged in Edinburgh on the same day and confuse the public message, with some members of the public seeing the concerts simply as a fundraising event and not as part of a wider campaign calling for political action. An article headlined 'Do stars really aid the cause?' in the magazine *Red Pepper* voiced a number of the core differences buried beneath the media success of Live 8 and Geldof's public pronouncements:

> There has been little coverage of how bitterly most MPH (Make Poverty History) members feel about the concerts, which were organised separately by Geldof and Curtis but with the full knowledge of Oxfam, Comic Relief and the Treasury. This is not just because they overshadowed MPH's rally in Edinburgh on 2 July. . . . Their focus was not on global poverty, but Africa. And their demands were not those of MPH, but of the Commission for Africa, a Government sponsored think-tank committed to free-market capitalism. (cited in Sireau and Davis 2007: 148)

Sireau and Davis summarize how the Make Poverty History became progressively coopted by the media, as well as political elites and was shaped and simplified by this encounter – an encounter which nonetheless generated mass public exposure and contributed to an unparalleled campaign that continues to this day (*http:// www.makepovertyhistory.org*):

> Just as political co-option hung over the campaign so did the threat of media co-option. In an attempt to engage and mobilise mass opinion, campaign advisors

found themselves having to accede to mass news values: simple sound-bites over complex policy, short-term events over long-term issues, and celebrity endorsement over NGO pleas. As the campaign evolved so Make Poverty History lost control of its frames, messages, celebrity spokespersons and news coverage. The campaign lost support among a number of its activist members and struggled to compete with the media's more traditional 'primary definers': politicians and celebrities. (Sireau and Davis 2007: 149)

Nick Sireau and Aeron Davis's behind-the-scenes analysis of this mass-mediated campaign is instructive. It demonstrates the indispensable role that the mass media and news media can play in the furtherance of coalition campaign aims but also the complex negotiations, compromises and disagreements that are likely to result (see also DeChaine 2005; Gaber and Willson 2005; Nash 2008). To what extent and in what sense Make Poverty History can be deemed, in retrospect, to have been a political success or failure will depend on the criteria used and political vantage point adopted (for an informed critique, see Nash 2008); but there is little doubt that the Make History Poverty campaign managed to secure mass media attention.

According to an independent commissioned analysis, the campaign reached 72% of adults in the UK (34 million people) with 87% of people aware of the campaign overall; based on a sample of press and magazine coverage, over 1 billion opportunities to read about the campaign were created; and the campaign generated over 3 days of broadcast coverage peaking around the G8 in July when campaign spokespeople featured in over 700 broadcast interviews (MPH 2006). The Make Poverty History campaign generated popular support and channelled political demands upwards to political elites and it did so both nationally and transnationally. In such ways, if only momentarily, the established relations of top-down communicative power between political elites, mainstream news media and popular opinion became destabilized and the communicative flows of politics, popular culture and protest were temporarily reconfigured.

The adoption and adaptation of new communications technologies in the current field of humanitarian NGOs also points to how established relations of communicative power are becoming reconfigured in the everyday work and practices of NGOs and between the different stakeholders involved.

New communication technologies: reconfiguring communicative power

The development of news communication technologies affords new applications in the world of humanitarian communications and relief efforts, shifting and sometimes reconfiguring established relations of communicative power. Whether concerning communications between NGOs and the news media or governments or publics and donors or direct to disaster victims and the recipients of humanitarian aid, communication technologies variously facilitate flows of information, coordination and control between different stakeholders. The following text message that arrived simultaneously on the mobile phones of two United Nations officials in London and Nairobi helps to illustrate the point:

> My name if Mohammed Sokor, writing to you from Dagahaley refugee camp in Dadaab. Dear Sir, there is an alarming issue here. People are given too few kilograms of food. You must help. (cited in *The Economist* 26.7.06)

Mohammed Sokor, a refugee in a northern Kenyan camp, had got the numbers of the two UN officials by surfing at the camp's improvised internet café and sent his desperate message to them on his mobile. The usual flow of communication and authority had momentarily altered. Since 2007, for the first time in human history, more than half the world's population now lives in cities, and urban refugees some of whom will have mobile phones are becoming more common (Brown 2007). With increased penetration of mobile telephony within even some of the world's poorest regions, such communicative encounters as the one above are likely to become more common – encounters that seemingly overcome former divides of distance and social geography (see 'Migrants and colliding worlds' in Chapter 1 and Chapter 5). This is not, of course, the only way that new communication technologies are now becoming enmeshed within humanitarian operations.

Aid workers have long made use of mobile telephony, communicating with each other, coordinating the delivery and arrival times of supplies, sharing information with other NGOs in the field and communicating their needs with their respective organizations and, occasionally, 'bearing witness' for the news media. Major relief operations now seek to set up as a matter of priority communications networks that can coordinate the efficient and targeted delivery of aid. The United Nations Foundation's 'Rapid Response Emergency Telecommunications' project, for example, works with UNICEF, the World Food Program and the UN's Organization for the Coordination of Humanitarian Affairs (OCHA) to improve access to life-saving technology and telecommunications tools in natural disasters, conflicts, and famines (*http://www.unfoundation.org*). It helps fund Télécoms sans Frontières (TSF) which provides rapid response teams to join UN missions anywhere in the world and aims to do so within the first 48 hours of an emergency to set up vital telecommunications centres. The latter are essential for assessment, logistics and coordination of planned and effective responses. Field operatives on the ground can access the latest security reports, study satellite maps of the affected areas and send and receive emails. Later on in the course of a disaster, victims and survivors can access collated online datasets and seek information about the possible location of missing family, friends and relatives and post communications to them (see *http://www.familylinks.icrc.org*).

The Global Disasters Alert Coordination System (GDACS), set up jointly by the United Nations and the European Commission, aims to provide the international disaster response community with the means for communicating disaster alerts and essential information quickly, interactively and in a structured and predictable manner to assist relief efforts (*http://www.gdacs.org/*). This online system provides immediate disaster alerts, media monitoring, map catalogues and a virtual onsite operations coordination centre.

Satellite phones, which are sometimes the only ones to work after a major disaster in the area, are now lightweight and communicate visual images as well as speech and transmission speed are increasing year on year. These new communication technologies also assist interagency communications and, as we have heard, the NGO aid field is now more crowded than ever. In the tsunami of 2004, for example, no fewer than 14 different countries in Asia and Africa were affected and over 400 different NGOs were working in Aceh alone (*The Economist*, 26.7.06). Coordination and shared communications in such potentially chaotic circumstances is clearly essential and new online forms of communication and coordination systems are now regarded by many as indispensable.

Communications systems directed at disaster avoidance have also become implemented in many regions throughout the world. Following the 2004 tsunami, Sri Lanka's largest telephone company implemented an early-warning system that will deliver SMS messages to every mobile phone in the area in the event of an imminent flood. Amnesty International has also paid satellite-imaging firms to take high-altitude pictures of the burning of villages in Darfur to document the continuing massacres in Sudan, contrary to the Sudanese government's denials, as well as to collect evidence for legal action against Robert Mugabe, the Zimbabwean President responsible for the forced destruction of people's homes. The UN's Food and Agricultural Organization (FAO) now routinely compiles detailed maps charting who is vulnerable to food shortages in so-called 'poverty mapping' and the United Nations Environmental Program (UNEP) hosts the website of APELL, the Awareness and Preparedness for Emergencies at the Local Level (*http://www.unep.fr/pc/apell/disasters*), which provides information and advice to local communities on how to prepare for and/or avoid natural hazards.

In all these ways, then, new communication technologies are being deployed and put to work in the service of humanitarian objectives and can sometimes shift established relations of communicative power. The development of new websites and portals such as Reuters' *AlertNet* (*http://www.alertnet.org/*) and the UN's *Relief Web* (*http://www.reliefweb.int/*) as well as the websites of humanitarian NGOs aim to address the information poverty associated with 'forgotten wars' and 'hidden disasters', discussed in Chapter 3, and provide up-to-date, accessible background reports and statistics on current disasters around the world. Some also provide interactive journalism training modules as well as links to related NGOs and other relevant bodies in the field. *AlertNet* even provides an interactive facility, 'World Press Tracker', to enable users to measure and compare the world's press coverage of self-selected major disasters (mapped since 2006) and generate graphs of the same (*http://www.alertnet.org/*). Here, then, not only are reporters and others provided with relevant information and data but interested parties can access the site and 'research' for themselves the world's press priorities and parameters of disaster coverage both across time and comparatively.

Some NGOs now also seek to bypass traditional news media to ensure that they get their intended message across to their intended audiences without the risk of mediated scandals. They can do so by aiming to communicate directly with donors and potential sponsors by email, targeted letters and communications incorporated into the commercial marketing of mainstream businesses. And neither should we forget how the development of new communication technologies feature within and across the humanitarian donor field more generally, including the electronic remittance of financial gifts and support from diasporic communities via electronic banking systems to relatives and friends 'back home' in afflicted countries.

In all these different ways, then, the communications environment of humanitarian aid is fast changing and as it does so it helps to reconfigure the established relations of communicative power within the humanitarian field. One futuristic scenario has gone so far as to suggest: 'In the humanitarian operation of the future beneficiaries of emergency aid will use technology to tell us what they need – cash, food or education – find out from us what to expect, and track its arrival, just as we can track an order from Amazon.com now' (a representative of Save the Children quoted in *The Economist*, 26.7.06). While this consumerist model of aid receipt possibly conceals more than it reveals about the remaining structures of benefactor power and control that remains structured within humanitarian operations, it is clear that the aid field and its relations of communicative power are nonetheless moving in subtle and sometimes obvious ways, and that new communication technologies, from mobile phones to virtual coordination and control systems online, will play an increasingly important and facilitative role in such processes in the future.

In summary: humanitarian organizations today confront a globalizing, increasingly competitive, media environment characterized by unprecedented 24/7 'real-time' capabilities and they also confront new forms of humanitarian crisis including the military use of starvation, systematic terror and flows of refugees as well as the human fallout from extreme weather events, climate change and potentially globalized pandemics, food insecurity and water shortages. NGOs co-exist and compete for media attention and donor funds within an increasingly crowded humanitarian aid field and must seek public profile through organizational branding in the news media while packaging their stories for the known predilections of the news media attracted to celebrity, regionalized and personalized stories and scandal. In the field of humanitarian disasters, it seems, the national news media are apt to follow global (western-dominated) news agendas. But so too have we heard how NGOs seek to proactively regain control over the news communication environment through collaborative campaigns and communication strategies designed to get their message across. And the fast changing communication technologies now embedded in the field of humanitarian aid are also facilitating possible shifts in the established relations of communicative power.

9 | GLOBAL CRISIS REPORTING: CONCLUSIONS

[I]t is the *reflexivity of world risk society* that creates the reciprocal relationship between the public sphere and globality. Regardless of all the borders and rifts that separate nations, the constructed and accepted definition of planetary threat and its global mass-media-projected omnipresence create a common arena of values, responsibility and action which, analogously to the national arena, *can* (though need not necessarily) give rise to political action among strangers. This is the case when the accepted definition of threat leads to global norms, agreements and common action. (Beck 2005: 38–39)

A number of global crises have been addressed across the preceding chapters, although others could also have featured (see Chapter 1). World poverty exacerbated by climate change, food and water shortages leading to social unrest, looming energy crises and the devastating HIV/AIDS pandemic around the world (but especially in Africa), among others, can all, for example, be regarded as no less humanly pressing or complexly dependent on the news media. Interstate political rivalries and the world's current political 'trouble spots' are also often construed as 'global crises' especially when threatening to escalate into regional conflicts and/or embroiling multiple state powers. Indeed, it is often these state-based forms of political crisis that have been taken to exemplify 'global crises' in the field of international relations in the past. But this book has deliberately sought to broaden its conception of 'global crises' from a delimited concern with 'political crises' to a more encompassing conception that better relates to the interconnected, interdependent and inegalitarian nature of the global age. Global crises, seen in this context, erupt from the dark side of a 'negatively globalized planet' (Bauman 2007: 25; see also Chapter 1) and contemporary journalism performs a crucial role in constituting them as such on the news media world stage.

The global nature and media dependence of many of today's crises has yet, however, to be taken seriously by journalism researchers, scholars and students – substantively, theoretically, methodologically. As earlier chapters have indicated, many of the most pressing threats in the world today are transnational and global in nature, both in terms of their impacts and responses and, importantly, in their *constitution* in the global flows and formations of the news media. Transnational terrorism and its bigger deadly twin, the global 'war on terror', forced migrations, virulent pandemics and market crashes can move around the globe at speed, some with devastating impacts, and climate change and other ecological threats threaten the planet's ecosystems and life as we have known it (with those least responsible already paying the human costs). *(Un)*natural disasters, humanitarian emergencies and human rights abuses also variously summon global responses, whether through the United Nations, structures of regional and national governance or the work of NGOs and the culture of humanitarianism and normative views about universal human rights that help constitute 'global civil society'. All are critically dependent on the flows and formations of the world's news media in terms of how they become defined and deliberated – or disappeared and denied.

Global crises both emanate from and obtrude into a globalized world forcing themselves *ontologically* into the public eye of the media. They are principally constituted *epistemologically* as 'global crises' through the news media where most of us get to know about them and where they are visualized, narrativized, publicly defined and sometimes challenged and contested. These processes of mediation (*social construction*) are, as we have seen, multidimensional and involve multiple interactions between different institutional agencies and contending social actors. Methodologically processes of social construction, it seems, cannot be easily ringfenced and confined to processes of news representation, neither perhaps should they be (Philo 2007). Contending claims makers, public performances and rhetorical and argumentative strategies as well as pre-existent media templates and cultural myths can *all* variously enter the news frame, as we have heard across preceding chapters, as can professional journalist codes of conduct, national outlooks and infusions from the wider (news-monitored) global news ecology.

But processes of 'social construction' do not only enter into and shape the construction of global crises discursively in the media. In a globalized world processes of social construction infuse crises from *the outside in, and inside out*, turning predictable hazards into devastating disasters (see Chapter 3), changing nature and climates (Chapter 4), compelling forced migrations and cosmopolitanizing emotions in response to human rights abuses (Chapter 5), generating failed states and new forms of warfare that systemically target civilians (Chapter 6), positioning some humanitarian emergencies and their victims as more worthy of help than others and galvanizing public sympathies and, possibly, political policies (Chapter 7), and shaping the professional communication practices of humanitarian NGOs (Chapter 8). Neither a *social constructionist* approach to global crises delimited to a media-centric and discourse-based epistemology, nor a position of *crisis realism* that remains ontologically blinded to the dynamics of journalism practised in the global age, therefore, is sufficient on its own to engage with the complex interplays between different crises and their public signification in the news media.

Some crises along with their victims are symbolically annihilated in the news media, becoming lost from public view in 'hidden wars' and 'forgotten disasters' (Chapters 3, 6 and 8). In a world of globalized media surveillance, annihilation by way of the media is not always only symbolic (Chapter 6). The absence of news cameras in different conflict zones today contributes to the unheard moral scream of all those who become victims of atrocity committed in part *because* the world's news media aren't there to bear witness to it (which is not to say that there are not good reasons why journalists do not venture into the killing zone) (Leith 2004; Tumber and Webster 2006).

In an interconnected globalized world, a world in which rapid communications are now generally recognized by major social theorists as foundational for processes of globalization and a defining characteristic of our global age (see Chapter 1), global crises are the dark side of a *'negatively globalized planet'* (Bauman 2007: 25) and they are no less dependent on global flows of information, ideas and images.

Researching complexity and contingency

The news media are not only capable of 'hiding' and 'forgetting' crises, they can also sensationalize them, literally investing 'sensations' into their public elaboration and wider circulation. They can do so through spectacular visualization and by embedding personal narratives of tragedy, trauma and despair. The news media can also perform an indispensable role in amplifying mega-media events and transnational protests, events that originate in civil society and are designed to capture the public imagination and put pressure on governments to act. So too can the news media variously give vent to the contention and conflicts that surround and shape crises. This includes the different views and voices that aim to define and prescribe courses of action on the news stage and which thereby seek to further their preferred projects, outlooks and, often, vested interests.

When conducted through the circulating flows and communications cross-traffic of today's global media ecology (see Figure 1.1), an expanded array of views and voices – global–local, west–rest, elite–ordinary, expert–lay, military–civilian – can now sometimes enter the frame and challenge the parameters and preferred terms of public discourse – though often with differing degrees of access and possibilities of success. The blogosphere is not coincident with the mainstream news media, neither does it simply map onto the traditionally conceived 'public sphere'. Transnational activist networks are certainly not comparable to transnational corporate news organizations in terms of organizational power, available resources or routine public reach, and neither do they aim to be. They nonetheless sometimes manage to inject new flows and forms, agendas and arguments, experiences and accounts into the transnational news media ecology and may even, on occasion, infiltrate and influence mainstream public discourse and debate.

The research findings and discussion outlined across the preceding chapters support these claims. Evidently, *complexity* and *dynamism*, *contention* and *discursive openings* as well as *dominance* and *stasis*, *consensus* and *representational closure* can *all* variously characterize the field of global crisis reporting in respect of different crises and their mediation across different media outlets, space and time. This is not to suggest, however, that all is cultural chaos, a matter of contingency, flux and indeterminacy (McNair 2006) or, more optimistically, that it represents a globalized 'culture-on-demand' (Lull 2007), seemingly overcoming the economic formations of the mass media and their 'corporate push' – as discussed at the outset of this book (Chapter 2).

When we get down to empirical cases and examine close up the determinants and dynamics, causalities *and* contingencies of global crisis reporting, as we must if we are to avoid succumbing to the seductive generalizations of empirically unsubstantiated theory, we find that research is, in fact, capable of recovering some of the principal determinants and dynamics at work. In other words, although complexity and difference are certainly in evidence across the field of global crisis reporting, this is not necessarily best encapsulated in terms of 'cultural chaos' and neither, given the evident power struggles and vested dominant interests at work in many of them, can we generalize about the influence of 'cultural pull' and the media's contribution to global processes of cultural deliberation. Politics, power and vested interests remain stubbornly implicated in global crises reporting (and how could they not) and they enter through the pores of the news media as well as occupy commanding positions on the surrounding terrain – as we have seen.

We have observed, for example, how geopolitical interests and the professional calculus of death are infused in the routine production of disaster news. We saw how prominent sections of the mainstream news media granted prominence to a small group of climate change sceptics at a critical juncture when the majority of the world's scientists had concluded that anthropogenic global warming was a reality. We heard how asylum seekers, refugees and forced migrants often become subject to processes of 'collective problematization' in different national news media and represented as a threat to national identity and national ways of life. And we also heard how news media deference to political elites and attraction to 'war spectacles' also conditions war reporting and marginalizes opposing views. In these and other findings reported across this book, global crises, demonstrably, are powerfully shaped and conditioned by economic, corporate and elite interests.

But so too have we encountered research findings that support a less closed and elite-driven construction of global crises. To take the same examples, we have observed how ritualistic appeals to moral community and nationhood informed the 'exceptional' news reporting of the Asian tsunami and how political critique, dissent and even biting satire were disseminated through the wider global news ecology and shaped the public representation of Hurricane Katrina. We saw how performative forms of journalism including the spectacular visualization of climate change have compelled audiences in the post-sceptic phase of press and broadcast reporting to 'see' global warming and take it seriously. So too have we heard how the discourse of human rights, now normatively established across most societies and institutionalized in international treatise and national systems of law, becomes journalistically inscribed within a 'mediated ethics of care'. And we have also seen how new developments in the field of warfare – 'new wars', 'western risk-transfer war', 'information war' – when combined with forms of global media surveillance potentially throw a spotlight on the increased civilian casualties that these latest forms of warfare produce.

In these and other ways discussed across the preceding chapters, complexities, dynamics and contingencies demonstrably inform global crisis reporting and variously reconfigure relations of communicative power. Only by empirically examining different instances of global crisis reporting are we able to develop a more grounded and encompassing understanding of the multiple and mediating roles performed by journalism in the constitution of global crises in the global age.

Global crises, nations and public sphere(s)

According to Ulrich Beck, it is the common and increasingly mediated perception of global threats, not universalizing statements about shared humanity, that serve to underpin and mobilize ideas about global cosmopolitan citizenship and an emergent global public sphere (see Chapter 1). It is in this context that Ulrich Beck calls for the social sciences to move beyond 'methodological nationalism'. It is time, he suggests, to question the presumptions that equate society with nation state societies and which see states and their governments as the cornerstone of social science analysis, as the 'containers' of all that is of sociological interest.

The charge of methodological nationalism could also be directed at much of the field of journalism studies and research today. Researchers continue to generally train their analytical sights on particular national media systems and the representations of crises and conflict that they produce, even when these same crises are better conceived and theorized in a context of global change and also in respect of the wider flows and formations of today's global news ecology. This is not an argument, then, for simply more comparative national research studies but the necessity to take 'global issues' seriously – theoretically, methodologically, ontologically. Important studies of 'race' and migration, the global war on terror, environment and ecology, for example, are often conducted *inside* particular national contexts and *through* national prisms, but few have sought to track and theorize these and other mediated global phenomena beyond the borders of particular nation states and with reference to the wider flows and formations of globalizing communications. Where are the studies today of journalism and international governance, journalism and international law, journalism and the normative discourse of human rights, journalism and forced migrations, journalism and ecology, journalism and poverty, journalism and energy, journalism and pandemics – all theoretically conceived and methodologically approached transnationally and globally?[1]

Part of the explanation for this continuing methodological nationalism in the field when addressing conflicts and crises that can only fully be apprehended transnationally or globally has at least two answers. Most obviously, at a practical and logistical level, it is simply easier to deal with one's 'own' media and inhabit the 'comfort zone' of a known culture rather than try to map transnational and global flows or fathom their differing cultural inflections and resonances as they move around the world. But it is also the case, as we have heard, that the news media themselves for the most part remain steadfastly wedded to national outlooks and see through national prisms and frames of reference. This stubborn *banal* nationalism (Billig 1995) has been encountered time and again across earlier chapters and, as we have also seen, these everyday, naturalized forms of news nationalism can also transmute into something far less banal (see Chapter 5). This is not confined, moreover, to how national news players frame and inflect global issues and crises but also colours the reporting of ostensibly 'global' news players such as BBC World or CNNI.

When reporting on distant disasters and humanitarian emergencies, for example, national news media seek out stories populated by their own 'nationals', whether through stock categories of hero, saint and saviour or victim and celebrity. These national 'representatives' regionalize, personalize and 'bring back home' to imagined and actual national audiences the meaning of distant events and tragedies (Chapters 3 and 8). When flows of forced migrants, including asylum seekers and refugees, eventually make it to foreign shores or cross national borders, so they are often subject to representational processes of 'collective problematization' conveyed and conducted through nationalistic news frames and discourses that denigrate, demonize and implicitly deny claims to human rights (Chapter 5). The global crisis of climate change has now moved into a new phase of contention as countries, corporations and citizens seek to negotiate their respective responsibilities whether in terms of national policies of mitigation and adaptation or through governmental support of developing countries confronting the worst effects of global warming. But again these various actions and contentions are frequently reported in and through national news prisms and coloured by national parochialisms. And the global war on terror, inevitably, becomes reported through blood-tinted glasses inflected by national interest, political national commitments and returning coffins draped in the national flag.

It would be hard indeed to overestimate the continuing 'pull of the national', 'the nation-on-demand,' that *claws back* global crises and frames these in ways consonant to national news prisms or the formidable stumbling block this poses to Beck's envisaged 'cosmopolitan vision', even when the latter is forced on the world through the intensifying 'interdependency crises' of ecology, terror and economy – to name but a few. Even so, counter-trends and transnational developments simultaneously point to the possibility at least of an emergent global public sphere and these endorse, in part, Beck's claims concerning the 'meta-power of global civil society' (Beck 2005: 64–71).

Significant examples of this embryonic cosmopolitanism have also been illustrated throughout this book. They include the following: staged mega-media events taking place simultaneously on different continents and in different countries designed to raise global awareness or prompt political action in respect of major global threats – world poverty, HIV/AIDS or climate change; mediated transnational protests coordinated around the world and challenging, for example, the global war on terror or condemning gross human rights abuses by authoritarian regimes (Sudan/Darfur, Burma, China/Tibet); and the infusion of international public opinion into national public spheres through circulating forms of condemnatory journalism in support of national campaigns against human rights abuses. Often facilitating and intertwined within all of these is, of course, the internet, as well as the rise of citizen journalism, the blogosphere and new means of interactive communications which are now contributing to emergent, diffused, transnational communications networks. Here different alliances, identities and even perhaps transnational solidarities can be pursued, enacted and performed and directed at issues and agendas of transnational and global concern. This is not, according to Beck, a question of *either/or*, of national or transnational, but *both/and*, of national and transnational, of how new social forms and modalities of political expression become conducted through extant and new experimental modes of political action in the global age (Beck 2006: 62).

And yet, emergent forms of transnational/global counter power and talk of a 'global public sphere' must also recognize that the concept of the public sphere itself remains indebted to a national-based (Westphalian) view of public deliberation in which processes of communicative action, public opinion formation and citizenship are enacted within a political jurisdiction that formally recognizes them as such and which can, to some degree, respond through corresponding structures of governance. As Nancy Frazer observes, transnational manifestations of public opinion and political will as yet, have no formal citizenship status or comparable means of influencing corresponding levels of governance: 'Failing major institutional renovation, neither transnational social movements nor transnational public spheres can assume the emancipatory democratizing functions that are the whole point of public-sphere theory' (Frazer 2005: 7).

How different global crises become communicated, contested and *constituted* within the world's media formations and communication flows – within its evolving global news ecology – may not only be the harbinger of a new (forced) cosmopolitanism but also prompt the *re-imagining of the political* within an increasingly interconnected, interdependent and *crisis-ridden* world.

Note

1 A series of titles under the '*Media and Global Crises*' series edited by the author and Peter Lang Publisher aims to begin to redress this conspicuous silence with forthcoming titles focusing on: *Human Rights, Humanitarian Aid, Terror Post 9/11, New Wars, Climate Change, Disasters, Migrations, Citizen Journalism, Global Protests, Pandemics, World Trade*, and *International Governance*.

GLOSSARY

breaking news   news that is reported live as it happens, or at least as it becomes communicated by a news source to the news organization. Often associated with the emergence of live 24/7 'rolling news' but which, in fact, constitutes a small fraction of routine daily output. Most 'news' remains 'olds', that is, predictable, routinised, pre-planned stories.

civilizational community of fate   Ulrich Beck's (2006) deliberately singular concept, developing on David Held's plural 'overlapping communities of fate' (2000a) which registers the ways in which today's global threats, such as climate change, transnational terrorism and world financial crashes are the outcome not of nature but the unwanted effects of globalized world society which affect us all. Such world 'inter-dependency crises' compel us to recognize our common plight and prompt forms of global cosmopolitanism and cooperative responses.

communicative power   the capacity to advance interests and influential ideas through access to and control of the communications environment. This can encompass the rhetorical and argumentative strategies deployed in the 'micro-politics' of news interviews to the 'macro-politics' of media ownership and control and different levels of communicative power in between.

contraflows   flows of media products and information, including news and other forms of journalism, that move from the less economically and powerful nations and regions to the more economically and politically powerful ones, countering the historical dominance of western-led flows.

cosmopolitanism   generally taken to be the ability to be at home in a world of different cultures and communities, transcending traditional outlooks, nationalism and cultural exclusivism. Philosophically derived, cosmopolitanism can be criticized for its idealism or wishful thinking; based on processes of globalization and the emergence of global crises that demand cross-cultural understanding and cooperative responses, cosmopolitanism becomes founded on real-world processes and trajectories of world crises (see Beck 2006).

cultural imperialism   an earlier theoretical perspective that maintains that capitalist expansion and political dominance in the world order is facilitated through the importation of western ideas, values and consumer-based aspirations by western cultural products and media. More recently adherents to the cultural imperialism thesis are inclined to see this in terms of transnational and regionalized corporate power, world flows of finance and the general commoditization of culture rather than as nationally based western dominance.

cultural industries   originally conceptualized by the Frankfurt School theorists as 'the culture industry' to refer to the ways in which processes of cultural production and creativity become commoditized and organized into industries for mass consumption. By such means, the culture of capitalism, based on false dreams and consumerist ideology, serves to reproduce the capitalist social order.

cultural studies   a major theoretical approach oriented to the study of how power and the constitution of social relations and identities are represented and reproduced, challenged and changed through language, text and discourse. As such, it tends to explore how meanings are generated in and through these mediums. Although sharing similar critical roots it contrasts with **political economy approaches** oriented to the structuring determination of the marketplace and forces of corporate competition and media ownership as the principal means by which dominant ideology and discourses are promulgated.

cultural templates   *see* **media templates**

dumbing down   a derogatory and sometimes contested term applied to discerned processes of popularization or 'tabloidization' that are thought to have undermined the informational, educational and/or political seriousness of traditional journalism and other media forms more widely.

ethnographic news studies   studies that have deployed an in-depth anthropological approach to the study of processes and practices of news manufacture and based on considerable time in the news 'field' and involving immersion in the cultural milieu of working journalists. Only by becoming familiar with and analysing the worlds of news organization and production, say news ethnographers, can we better understand and explain the nature and forms of news output, qualifying generalizing theoretical claims of **political economy** and **cultural studies** approaches.

forced migrants   those increased numbers of people forced to leave their homes and countries and who move around the globe seeking safety and sanctuary. Forced migrants include refugees and asylum seekers avoiding conflicts and oppression, increasing numbers of internally displaced people forced to move from their homes within their own countries because of, for example, national development projects and urbanization or those who have become ensnared by traffickers and people smugglers as illegal migrants, prostitutes and child slaves.

forgotten disasters   humanitarian disasters that have failed to attract the news media spotlight, public recognition and political response notwithstanding the scale of human tragedy, death and devastation involved and availability of portable communications technologies that can now communicate from virtually anywhere on the planet.

global public sphere   an expansion of Jurgen Habermas' original historical and conceptual formulation of the 'public sphere' (1989) as a public space or arena in which citizens can publicly confer, discuss and deliberate and arrive at consensual opinion formation about the public good. In today's complex and overlapping communications environment, global media flows are regarded by some as contributing to a global public sphere. Both the original and extended conception engenders debate. Habermas' original conception, say some, was based on an overly rationalist, deliberative and consensual view of public opinion formation and fails to properly take into account the imagistic, emotive and entertainment-driven nature of contemporary media forms and communication processes – concerns that can equally be applied to today's global media sphere. The notion of a global public sphere, closely correlated to global citizenship and global civil society, also raises distinct issues about the degree to which such a concept can have validity at the global level without corresponding forms of political representation and structures of governance, translating processes of world opinion formation into action with accountability. For others, global communications are undoubtedly facilitating new forms of global connectivity and trans-national politics that substantiate claims of an emergent 'global public sphere'.

global village Marshall McLuhan's (1964) celebrated image to describe the ways in which new electronic means of communication overcome barriers of geography and time and connect people around the globe, enhancing understanding and a sense of belonging to a shared place or community. Much criticized at the time, the concept appears to have found new purchase in today's global communications environment and discussion of a **global public sphere**. This is not to suggest, however, that the comforting metaphor of a 'global village' is no longer challenged for providing a far too rosy view that flattens out the continuing inequalities, power differentials, conflicts and enmities that inform global forms and flows of electronic communications today.

hidden wars wars and conflicts that disappear, like **forgotten disasters**, off the national and global news radar. Geopolitical outlooks forged on the basis of historical associations, contemporary national and political interests, the operation of a **professional calculus of death** and reliance on western **news values** have all been cited as contributing factors.

hotel stand-ups literally, correspondents (or **parachute journalists**) in foreign countries giving commentary to camera and communicated via satellite linkup from the roof of their hotel. More critically, a term that suggests that correspondents are not reporting from 'the field' but are simply feeding back information that has been fed to them from local sources or even, on occasion, from their own news organization back home – all to create the impression of news organization presence in the world's hot spots.

indexing model Lance Bennett's (1990) model of press–political relations that hypothesizes that the news media take their cue from political elite opinions and the degree of consensus or dissensus that this displays at particular points in time. In other words, press views are indexed to the surrounding and changing nature of elite views.

market determinations *see* **political economy**

media centrism the occupational hazard of media scholars and students alike who tend to regard media as a self-sufficient object of inquiry, empirically decontextualized and theoretically divorced from wider society, polity, economy and culture and which thereby grants contemporary media with inflated explanatory significance in the life and conduct of societies.

media sphere a concept that registers Habermas's **'public sphere'** but which affords the media increased theoretical and empirical significance as a central means of public representation and communication and which thereby also encourages a less rational, information-based and strictly deliberative understanding of such processes by recognizing the more expressive and entertainment-based forms of media communication.

media templates pre-existent media frames of cultural understanding that can be applied to new circumstances, whether they are strictly appropriate or not and which thereby enter into the public constitution of different issues and reported events, affecting prescriptions, actions and outcomes. Media templates often represent a potent sub-class of wider cultural templates.

mediascape one of five 'scapes' or cultural global flows described by Appadurai (1996) signalling disjuncture and difference in the global cultural economy and identifying the 'mediascape' as constitutive of these transformative global processes.

mediated deliberation how the communicative forms of media facilitate and enable public speech, argumentation and the public advancement of differing points of view and perspectives about public issues and political processes. *See also* **global public sphere**

mediated scandals the increased propensity of the news media to seek out, pursue and publicize scandals in the contemporary era, sometimes precipitating public crises of trust and confidence in power-holders or governments and contributing to loss of deference to political and other authorities.

mediatized disasters a term used to signal the ways in which the media on occasion do not simply report disaster events but actively and performatively enact them on the public stage by, for example, choreographing personal stories, encouraging public performances by public officials and others, and directing public flows of emotion, including trauma and grief. Mediatized disasters are often represented through highly ritualized forms, both affirming collective identities and imagined solidarities. They can also, sometimes, be channelled in more disruptive ways as power holders and authorities become subjected to public criticism and wider media flows and critics take the opportunity to focus on deep seated societal ills.

mediatized war war that is not simply communicated and conveyed by the media (mediated war) but actively conducted and constituted in and through the media. This can include, for example, image wars, spectacles and staged public relations all designed for the benefit of cameras, viewing publics and viewing enemies.

mega-media events a term that builds on the notion of 'media events' (Dayan and Katz 1992) and its influential theorization of those exceptional moments that interrupt the normal schedules of broadcasting and which serve to electrify national audiences. In today's globalized communications environment, 'mega-media events' include major media spectacles and transnational communication events. Such mega-media events are often broadcast simultaneously transnationally and/or involve multiple events in different countries around the world (Live Aid, Live 8, Live Earth). Such events are normally pre-planned and organized to fit media schedules and timelines and revolve around extensive forms of media attention.

military humanism military interventions and actions ostensibly conducted in the name of humanitarian objectives and human rights to safeguard human lives.

multimedia news production the convergence and/or simultaneous production of news for different media using digital technologies. Journalists, for example, in a TV news room could be producing news items for radio, television and online. Associated with multimedia news production are new professional practices which have sparked debates about 'multiskilling' and 'deskilling' when trying to ascertain the impact of multimedia production on traditional skills, professional demarcations and newsroom hierarchies.

network society an influential theory centring on how new information and communication technologies are facilitating fundamental changes in the organization and conduct of society including questions of politics, culture and identity (Castells, 1996, 1997, 1998). More recently, Manuel Castells' elaborate social theorization of the network society has possibly become more muted in more generalized claims about how online communications provide for new forms of connectivity, interactivity and decentralized and relatively fluid forms of participation.

news domestication   processes by which news stories reported from or about different countries become journalistically shaped and told in ways that conform to the cultural expectations and/or journalistic conventions of domestic news organizations and their audiences.

news ecology   a concept that refers to the complex and differentiated forms and flows of news in today's local-to-global news environment and encompassing new forms of online news as well as traditional news media organizations and outlets. The term encourages attention to the complexly structured, relationally positioned and defined and sometimes subtly differentiated forms of news that now compete and co-exist in the wider news field and which become reproduced in processes of news production. *See also* **ethnographic news studies**

news values   a set of journalistically recognized, but often unstated, criteria or attributes that can contribute to the newsworthiness of potential stories. 'Deviance', 'drama', 'violence', 'conflict', 'human interest' and good 'visuals', for example, are often regarded as universally operating news values. At best, however, they provide a partial, generalizing and often reductionist account of news selection processes and tend to underestimate practices of news shaping enacted by journalists.

overlapping communities of fate   *see* **civilizational community of fate**

parachute journalism   journalists who 'fly in' to a country and news story, often at short notice and with little background knowledge, file their story often based on a limited array of local sources and then fly home again. The inference embedded in the term is that this produces superficial and sometimes spurious news stories that can be manipulated by key sources. *See also* **hotel stand-ups**

political economy   a major theoretical approach that examines the ways in which markets, corporate competition and pursuit of sales, revenue and profits exert fundamental constraints and pressures on media businesses and the nature, forms and discourses of their output. The notion of determination as structural constraint shaping media operations is central to the political economy approach alongside considerations of media ownership and instrumental uses of media by elites. *See also* **cultural studies**

professional calculus of death   the professional enactment of journalist calculation and judgment about the newsworthiness of death and devastation in different parts of the world, its scale and significance, and leading to differential patterns and forms of news coverage. *See also* **forgotten disasters; hidden wars**

propaganda model   an influential position in the field of media research by Herman and Chomsky (1988) that argues that a confluence of five 'filters' effectively contain and control the nature of news output in the US (and by extension other western societies) and that these serve the purposes of elite propaganda and 'manufacture consent': (1) media ownership and control, (2) advertising pressure, (3) elite sources, (4) political criticism or 'flak' and (5) the prevailing political culture of US society (anti-communism or, more recently possibly, anti-Islam) all function according to the propaganda model to support US elite and corporate interests.

research paradigms   these broadly condition the kinds of questions asked, the conceptual and theoretical frameworks guiding research, the methodological approaches deployed, the epistemological assumptions about what constitutes 'knowledge' and the ontological views about the nature of 'reality'. A small number of paradigms only are likely to be ordering the research field and these will be in varying states of emergence, consolidation and challenge.

technological determinism   the view that the advent of new technologies determines or causes change. Research invariably demonstrates that technology cannot be isolated from its social, cultural, political and economic contexts and that technology at most facilitates change.

transnational media corporations   large corporations such as News Corporation or Disney that operate across national borders seeking to maximize revenues and profits through processes of economic concentration and centralization and involving the amalgamation of different market products and stages of production and distribution within the same holding company.

REFERENCES

Albrow, M. (1996) *The Global Age: State and Society Beyond Modernity*. Cambridge: Polity.

AlertNet (2005) AlertNet 'Top 10 "forgotten 'emergencies' " '. Available at: http:// www.alertnet.org/top10crises.htm.

Alexander, J. (2006) *The Civil Sphere*. Oxford: Oxford University Press.

Alexander, J. C. and Jacobs, R. N. (1998) 'Mass Communication, Ritual and Civil Society', in T. Liebes and J. Curran (Eds) *Media, Ritual and Identity*, London: Routledge.

Alexander, J., Giesen, B. and Mast, J. (2006) *Social Performance: Symbolic Action, Cultural Pragmatics and Ritual*. Cambridge: Cambridge University Press.

Allan, S. (2002) *Media, Risk and Science*. Buckingham: Open University Press.

Allan, S. (2004) 'The Culture of Distance: Online Reporting of the Iraq War', in S. Allan and B. Zelizer (Eds) *Reporting War*. London: Routledge.

Allan, S. (2006) *Online News: Journalism and the Internet*. Maidenhead: Open University Press.

Allan, S., Adam, B. and Carter, C. (Eds) (2000) *Environmental Risks and the Media*. London: Routledge.

Allan, S., Sonwalkar, P. and Carter, C. (2007) 'Bearing Witness: Citizen Journalism and Human Rights Issues', *Globalization, Societies and Education*, 5(3): 373–389.

Allan, S. and Zelizer, B. (Eds) (2004) *Reporting War: Journalism in Wartime*. London: Routledge.

Allen, C., Aziz, M., Bunglawala, I., Gluck, A., Hameed,T., Mair, H., et al. (2007) *The Search for Common Ground: Muslims, Non-Muslims and the UK Media*. London: Greater London Authority.

Allen, T. and Seaton, J. (Eds) (1999) *The Media of Conflict: War Reporting and Representations of Ethnic Violence*. London and New York: Zed Books.

Altheide, D. (2006) *Terrorism and the Politics of Fear*. New York: Altamira Press

Altheide, D. and Snow, R. (1979) *Media Logic*. Beverly Hills, CA: Sage.

Andersen, R. (2006) *A Century of Media, A Century of War*. New York: Peter Lang.

Anderson, A. (1993) 'Source-Media Relations: The Production of the Environmental Agenda' in A. Hansen (Ed.) (1993) *The Mass Media and Environmental Issues*. Leicester: Leicester University Press

Anderson, A. (1997) *Media, Culture and the Environment*. London: UCL Press.

Anderson, A. (2003) 'Environmental Activism and News Media', in S. Cottle (Ed.) *News, Public Relations and Power*. London: Sage.

Antilla, L. (2005) 'Climate of Scepticism: US Newspaper Coverage of the Science of Climate Change', *Global Environmental Change*, 15: 338–352.

Appadurai, A. (1996) *Modernity at Large: Cultural Dimensions of Globalization*. Minneapolis, MN: University of Minnesota Press.

Article 19 (2003) *What's the Story? Results from Research into Media Coverage of Refugees and Asylum Seekers in the UK*. London: Article 19. Available at www.article19.org.uk.

Azran, T. (2004) 'Resisting Peripheral Exports: Al Jazeera's War Images on US Television', *Media International Australia*, 113, 75–86.

Bacon, W. and Nash, C. (2002) *News/worthy: How the Australian Media Cover Humanitarian, Aid and Development Issues*. Canberra: AusAid.

Barthes, R. (1977) *Image, Music, Text*. London: Fontana.

Bauman, Z. (1998) *Globalization*. Cambridge: Polity.

Bauman, Z. (2007) *Liquid Times*. Cambridge: Polity.

Beattie, L., Miller, D., Miller, E. and Philo, G. (1999) 'The Media and Africa: Images of Disaster and Rebellion', in G. Philo (Ed.) *Message Received*. Harlow: Longman.

Beck, U. (1992) *Risk Society*. London: Sage.

Beck, U. (1999) *World Risk Society*. Cambridge: Polity.

Beck, U. (2000) 'Foreword', in S. Allan, B. Adam and C. Carter (Eds) *Environmental Risks and the Media*. London: Routledge.

Beck, U. (2005) *Power in the Global Age*. Cambridge: Polity.

Beck, U. (2006) *Cosmopolitan Vision*. Cambridge: Polity.

Beck, U., Giddens, A. and Lash, S. (1994) *Reflexive Modernization*. Cambridge: Polity.

Becker, H. (1967) 'Whose Side Are We On?', *Social Problems*, 14: 239–247.

Benhabib, S. (2002) *The Claims of Culture*. Princeton, NJ: Princeton University Press.

Benhabib, S. (2004) *The Rights of Others: Aliens, Residents and Citizens*. Cambridge: Cambridge University Press.

Bennett, L. (1990) Towards a theory of press-state relations in the United States, *Journal of Communication*, 40(2): 103–125.

Bennett, L. (2003) 'New Media Power: The Internet and Global Activism', in N. Couldry and J. Curran (Eds) (2003) *Contesting Media Power: Alternative Media in a Networked World*. Oxford: Rowan & Littlefield.

Bennett, L., Lawrence, R. and Livingston, S. (2007) *When the Press Fails: Political Power and the News Media from Iraq to Katrina*. Chicago, IL: University of Chicago Press.

Benthall, J. (1993) *Disasters, Relief and the Media*. London: I. B. Tauris.

Billig, M. (1995) *Banal Nationalism*. London: Sage.

Boltanski, L. (1999) *Distant Suffering: Politics, Morality, Media*. Cambridge: Cambridge University Press.

Boorstin, D. (1961) *The Image*. Harmondsworth: Penguin.

Bourdieu, P. (1993) *The Field of Cultural Production*. Cambridge: Polity.

Boyd-Barrett, O. (1998) 'Media Imperialism Reformulated', in D. K. Thussu (Ed.) *Electronic Empires: Global Media and Local Resistance*. London: Arnold.

Boyd-Barrett, O. (2004) 'Understanding: the Second Casualty', in S. Allan and B. Zelizer (Eds) *Reporting War*. London: Routledge.

Boyd-Barrett, O. (2005) 'A Different Scale of Difference', *Global Media and Communication*, 1(1): 15–19.

Boyd-Barrett, O. and Rantanen, T. (Eds) (1998) *The Globalization of News*. London: Sage.

Boykoff, M. and Boykoff, J. (2004) 'Balance as Bias: Global Warming and the US Prestige Press', *Global Environmental Change*, 14: 125–136.

Boykoff, M. and Boykoff, J. (2007) 'Climate Change and Journalistic Norms: A Case Study of US Mass-Media Coverage', *Geoforum*, 38: 1190–1204.

Bromley M. (2004) 'The Battlefield is the Media: War Reporting and the Formation of National Identity in Australia – From Belmont to Baghdad', in S. Allan and B. Zelizer (Eds) *Reporting War*. London: Routledge.

Brown, J. (2007) 'African Migrants Adrift for Three Days Rescued After Call to Coastguard', *The Independent*, 30.8.07.

Buckingham, D. (2000) *The Making of Citizens: Young People, News, Politics*. London: Routledge.

Bullert, B. (2000) 'Progressive Public Relations, Sweatshops, and the Net', *Political Communication*, 17(4): 403–407.

Butler, D. (1995) *The Trouble with Reporting Northern Ireland*. Aldershot: Avebury.

Butterworth, E. (1967) 'The 1962 Smallpox Outbreak and the British Press', *Race*, 7(4): 347–364.

Carey, J. (1989) *Communication as Culture: Essays on Media and Society*. London: Unwin Hyman.

Carey, J. (1998) 'Political Ritual on Television: Episodes in the History of Shame, Degradation and Excommunication' in T. Liebes, T. and J. Curran (Eds) *Media, Ritual and Identity*. London: Routledge.

Carma (2006) The Carma Report on Western Media Coverage of Humanitarian Disasters, Carma, European Office. Available at:http://www.carma.com/research/#research.

Carruthers, S. (2000) *The Media at War: Communication and Conflict in the 20th Century*. Basingstoke: Macmillan.

Carruthers, S. L. (2004) 'Tribalism and Tribulation: Media Constructions of "African Savagery" and "Western Humanitarianism" in the 1990s', in S. Allan and B. Zelizer (Eds) *Reporting War*. London: Routledge.

Carvalho, A. (2007) 'Ideological Cultures and Media Discourse on Scientific Knowledge: Re-reading News on Climate Change', *Public Understanding of Science*, 16: 223–243.

Castles, S. (2003) 'Towards a Sociology of Forced Migration and Social Transformation', *Sociology*, 37(1): 13–34.

Castles, S. and Miller, M. (2003) *The Age of Migration*, 3rd edn. Basingstoke: Palgrave.

Castells, M. (1996) *The Rise of the Network Society*. Oxford: Blackwell

Castells, M. (1997) *The Power of Identity*. Oxford: Blackwell.

Castells, M. (2001) *The Internet Galaxy*. Oxford: Oxford University Press.

Castells, M. (2007) 'Communication, Power and Counter-Power in the Network Society', *International Journal of Communication*, 1: 238–266.

Chalaby, J. (2002) 'Transnational Television in Europe: The Role of Pan-European Channels', *European Journal of Communication*, 17(2): 183–203.

Chapman, G., Keval, K., Fraser, C. and Gaber, I. (1997) *Environmentalism and the Mass Media: The North–South Divide*. New York: Routledge.

Chesters, G. and Welsh, I. (2006) *Complexity and Social Movements: Multitudes at the Edge of Chaos*. London: Routledge.

Chibnall, S. (1977) *Law-and-Order News*. London: Tavistock.

Chouliaraki, L. (2006) *The Spectatorship of Suffering*. London: Sage.

Clausen, L. (2003) *Global News Production*. Copenhagen: Copenhagen Business School Press.

Clayman, S. E. and Heritage, J. (2002) *The News Interview*. Cambridge: Cambridge University Press.

Cohen, A., Levy, M., Roeh, I. and Gurevitch, M. (1996) *Global Newsrooms, Local Audiences: A Study of the Eurovision News Exchange*. London: John Libby.

Cohen, S. (2001) *States of Denial: Knowing about Atrocities and Suffering*. Cambridge: Polity.

Corner, J. and Richardson, K. (1993) 'Environmental Communication and the Contingency of Meaning: A Research Note', in A. Hansen (Ed.) *The Mass Media and Environmental Issues*. Leicester: Leicester University Press.

Corner, J., Richardson, K. and Fenton, N. (1990) *Nuclear Reactions: Form and Response in Public Issue Television*. London: John Libby.

Cottle, S. (1998) 'Ulrich Beck, "Risk Society" and the Media: A Catastrophic View?', *European Journal of Communication*, 13(1): 5–32.

Cottle, S. (1999) From BBC Newsroom to BBC News Centre: On Changing Technology and Journalist Practices, *Convergence*, 5(3): 22–43.

Cottle, S. (2000a) 'TV News, Lay Voices and the Visualization of Environmental Risks', in S. Allan, B. Adam and C. Carter (Eds) *Environmental Risks and the Media*. London: Routledge.

Cottle, S. (2000b) 'Media Research and Ethnic Minorities: Mapping the Field', in S. Cottle (Ed.) *Ethnic Minorities and the Media: Changing Cultural Boundaries*. Buckingham: Open University Press.

Cottle, S. (Ed.) (2003a) *Media Organization and Production*. London: Sage.

Cottle, S. (Ed.) (2003b) *News, Public Relations and Power*. London: Sage.

Cottle, S. (2004) *The Racist Murder of Stephen Lawrence: Media Performance and Public Transformation*. London: Praeger.

Cottle, S. (2005) 'In Defence of "Thick" Journalism', in S. Allan (Ed.) *Journalism: Critical Issues*. Maidenhead: Open University Press.

Cottle, S. (2006a) *Mediatized Conflict: Developments in Media and Conflict Studies*. Maidenhead: Open University Press.

Cottle, S. (2006b) 'Mediatized Rituals: Beyond Manufacturing Consent', *Media, Culture and Society*, 28(3): 411–432.

Cottle, S. (2007) 'Ethnography and Journalism: New(s) Departures in the Field', *Sociology Compass*, 1(1): 1–16. Available at www.sociology-compass.com.

Cottle, S. (2008) 'Reporting Demonstrations: The Changing Media Politics of Dissent', *Media, Culture and Society*, 30(6): 853–872.

Cottle, S. and Nolan. D. (2007) 'Global Humanitarianism and the Changing Aid Field: "Everyone was Dying for Footage." ', *Journalism Studies*, 8(6): 862–878.

Cottle, S. and Rai, M. (2006) 'Between Display and Deliberation: Analyzing TV News as Communicative Architecture', *Media, Culture and Society*, 28(2): 163–189.

Cottle, S. and Rai, M. (2007) 'Australian TV News Revisited: News Ecology and Communicative Frames', *Media International Australia*, 122: 43–58.

Cottle, S. and Rai, M. (2008) 'Television News in India: Mediating Democracy and Difference', *International Communication Gazette*, 70(1): 76–96.

Cox. R. (2006) *Environmental Communication and the Public Sphere*. London: Sage.

Davis, A. (2003) 'Public Relations and News Sources', in S. Cottle (Ed.) *News, Public Relations and Power*. London: Sage.

Dayan, D. and Katz, E. (1992) *Media Events: The Live Broadcasting of History*. Cambridge: Harvard University Press.

DeChaine, D. R. (2005) *Global Humanitarianism: NGOs and the Crafting of Community*. New York: Lexington Books.

DeLuca, K. M. (1999) *Image Politics: The New Rhetoric of Environmental Activism*. London: Guilford Press.

Department for International Development (2000) *View the World: A Study of British Television Coverage of Developing Countries*. London: DFID.

Deuze, M. (2003) 'The Web and its Journalisms: Considering the Consequences of Different Types of News Media Online', *New Media and Society*, 5(2): 203–226.

Dobson, A. (2007) *Green Political Thought*, 4th edn. London: Routledge.

van de Donk, W., Loader, B., Nixon, P. and Dieter, D. (Eds) *Cyberprotest*. London: Routledge.

Dover, C. and Barnett, S. (2004) *The World on the Box: International Issues in News and Factual Programmes on UK Television 1975–2003*. London: Third World and Environmental Broadcasting Project.

Dryzek, J. (2000) *Deliberative Democracy and Beyond*. Oxford: Oxford University Press.

Dryzek, J. (2006) *Deliberative Global Politics*. Cambridge: Polity.

Economist (2007) 'Flood, Famine and Mobile Phones', *The Economist*, 26.7.07. Available at http://www.economist.com/world/international/.

Eder, K. (1996) *Social Constructions of Nature*. London: Sage.

Elliott, P. (1977) 'Reporting Northern Ireland: A Study of News in Great Britain, Northern Ireland and the Republic of Ireland', in UNESCO (Eds) *Ethnicity and the Media*. Paris: UNESCO.

El-Nawawy, M. and Iskander, A. (2003) *Al-Jazeera*. Cambridge MA. Westview Press.

Energy Watch Group (2007) *Oil Report*. Available at http://www.energywatchgroup.org.

Entman, R. E. (1993) 'Framing: Toward Clarification of a Fractured Paradigm', *Journal of Communication*, 43(4): 51–58.

Entman, R. E. (2004) *Projections of Power: Framing News, Public Opinion and U.S. Foreign Policy*. Chicago, IL: Chicago University Press.

Etkin, D. and Ho, E. (2007) 'Climate Change: Perceptions and Discourses of Risk', *Journal of Risk Research*, 10(5): 623–641.

Fan, D. and Ostini, J. (1999) 'Human Rights Media Coverage in Chinese East Asia', *Annals of the American Academy of Political and Social Science*, 566: 93–107.

Frazer, N. (2005) 'Transnationalizing the Public Sphere'. Available at http://www.republicart.net (12.4.08).

Freire, P. (1985) *Pedagogy of the Oppressed*. Harmondsworth: Penguin.

Gaber, I. and Willson, A. (2005) 'Dying for Diamonds, The Mainstream Media and NGOs: A Case Study of ActionAid', in W. de Jong, M. Shaw and N. Stammers (Eds) *Global Activism, Global Media*. London: Pluto Press.

Galtung, J. and Ruge, M. (1965) 'The Structure of Foreign News: The Presentation of the Congo,

Cuba and Cyprus Crises in Four Newspapers, *Journal of International Peace Research*, 1: 64–90.

Galtung, J. and Ruge, M. (1981) 'The Structure of Foreign News', in S. Cohen and J. Young (Eds) (1981)*The Manufacture of News: Deviance, Social Problems and the Mass Media*. London: Constable.

Gamson, W. A. and Modigliani, A. (1989) 'Media Discourse and Public Opinion on Nuclear Power: A Constructionist Approach', *American Journal of Sociology*, 95: 1–37.

Gandy, O. H. (1980) *Beyond Agenda Setting: Information Subsidies and Public Policy*. Norwood, NJ: Ablex.

Geertz, C. (1973) *The Interpretation of Cultures*. New York: Basic Books.

Giddens, A. (1976) *New Rules of Sociological Method*. London: Hutchinson.

Giddens, A. (1990) *The Consequences of Modernity*. Cambridge: Polity.

Giddens, A. (1994) *Beyond Left and Right*. Cambridge: Polity.

Giddens, A. (2002) *Runaway World*. London: Profile Books.

Giddens, A. (2005) 'Giddens and the "G" Word: An Interview with Anthony Giddens', *Global Media and Communication*, 1(1): 63–78.

Gilboa, E. (2005) The CNN Effect: The Search for a Communication Theory of International Relations, *Political Communication*, 22: 27–44.

Glasgow University Media Group (1985) *War and Peace News*. Maidenhead: Open University Press.

Glasser, M. (2006) 'Your Guide to Soldier Videos from Iraq', *Media Shift*, 1 August. Available at http://www.pbs.org/mediashift/2006/08.

Glenn, J. and Gordon, J. (2007) *State of the Future*. New York: World Federation of UN Associates.

Goodhart, M. (2005) *Democracy as Human Rights: Freedom and Equality in the Age of Globalization*. London: Routledge.

Greenberg, J. and Hier, S. (2001) 'Crisis, Mobilization and Collective Problematization: ' "Illegal" Chinese Migrants and the Canadian News Media', *Journalism Studies*, 2(4): 563–583.

Greenberg, J. and Knight, G. (2004) 'Framing Sweatshops: Nike, Global Production, and the American News Media', *Communication and Critical/Cultural Studies*, 1(2): 151–175.

Habermas, J. (1989) *The Structural Transformation of the Public Sphere*. Cambridge: MIT Press.

Habermas, J. (1997) *Between Facts and Norms*. Cambridge: Polity.

Hachten, W. and Scotton, J. (2007) *The World News Prism: Global Information in a Satellite Age*. Oxford: Blackwell.

Hall, S. (1981) 'A World at One with Itself', in S. Cohen and J. Young (Eds) (1981) *The Manufacture of News: Deviance, Social Problems and the Mass Media*. London: Constable.

Hall, S., Critcher, C., Jefferson, T., Clarke, J. and Roberts, B. (1978) *Policing the Crisis: Mugging the State and Law and Order*. London: Macmillan (reprinted 1986).

Hallin, D. (1986) *The 'Uncensored War?': The Media and Vietnam*. New York: Oxford University Press.

Hallin, D. (1994) *We Keep America on Top of the World*. London: Routledge.

Hallin, D. (1997) 'The Media and War', in J. Corner, P. Schlesinger and R. Silverstone (Eds) *International Media Research*. London: Routledge,

Halloran, J., Elliott, P. and Murdock, G. (1970) *Demonstrations and Communication: A Case Study*. Harmondsworth: Penguin.

Hamilton, J. M. and Jenner, E. (2004) 'Redefining Foreign Correspondence', *Journalism*, 5(3): 301–321.

Hammond, P. (2007) *Media, War and Postmodernity*. London: Routledge.

Hannerz, U. (2004) *Foreign News: Exploring the World of Foreign Correspondents* Chicago, IL, and London: University of Chicago Press.

Hannigan, A. (1995) *Environmental Sociology*. London: Routledge.

Hansen, A. (1991) 'The Media and the Social Construction of the Environment', *Media, Culture and Society*, 13(4): 443–458.

Hansen, A. (Ed.) (1993) *The Mass Media and Environmental Issues*. Leicester: Leicester University Press.

Hansen, A. (2000) 'Claims-making and Framing in the British Newspaper Coverage of the Brent Spar Controversy', in S. Allan, B. Adam and C. Carter (Eds) *Environmental Risks and the Media*. London: Routledge.

Harcup, T. and O'Neill, D. (2001) 'What is News? Galtung and Ruge Revisited', *Journalism Studies*, 2(2): 261–280.

Hargreaves, I., Lewis, J. and Speers, T. (2002) *Toward a Better Map: Science, the Public and the Media*. London: ESRC.

Harris, R. (1994) *The Media Trilogy*. London: Faber & Faber.

Harrison, P. and Palmer, R. (1986) *News out of Africa: Biafra to Band Aid*. London and Wolfboro, NH: Shipman.

Hartmann, P. and Husband, C. (1974) *Racism and the Mass Media*. London: Davis Poynter.

Harvey, D. (1989) *The Condition of Postmodernity*. Oxford: Blackwell.

Hawkins, V. (2002) 'The Other Side of the CNN Factor: The Media and Conflict', *Journalism Studies*, 3(2): 225–240.

Held, D. (2004a) *The Global Covenant*. Cambridge: Polity.

Held, D. (Ed.) (2004b) *A Globalizing World?* London: Routledge.

Held, D. and McGrew, A. (2003) 'The Great Globalization Debate: An Introduction', in D. Held and A. McGrew (Eds) *The Global Transformations Reader*. Cambridge: Polity.

Herman, E. and Chomsky, N. (1988) *Manufacturing Consent: The Political Economy of the Mass Media*. London: Vintage.

Herman, E. and McChesney, R. (1997) *The Global Media: The New Missionaries of Corporate Capitalism*. London: Cassell.

Hickman, L. (2007) 'Cry Wolf, But Gently', *The Guardian*, 10.11.07: 3.

Hilgartner, S. and Bosk, C. L. (1988) 'The Rise and Fall of Social Problems: A Public Arenas Model', *American Journal of Sociology*, 94(1): 53–78.

Höijer, B. (2004) 'The Discourse of Global Compassion: The Audience and Media Reporting of Human Suffering', *Media, Culture and Society*, 26(4): 513–531.

Holmes, J. and Niskala, M. (2007) 'Reducing the Humanitarian Consequences of Climate Change', International Federation of Red Cross and Red Crescent Societies. Available at http://www.ifrc.org/Docs/News/opinion07/07101001/index.asp.

Hoskins, A. (2004) *Televising War: From Vietnam to Iraq*. London: Continuum.

Hoskins, A. and O'Loughlin, B. (2007) *Television and Terror: Conflicting Times and the Crisis of News Discourse*. Basingstoke: Palgrave.

Ignatieff, M. (1998) *The Warrior's Honor: Ethnic War and the Modern Conscience*. London: Chatto & Windus.

Ignatieff, M. (2001) *Virtual War: Kosovo and Beyond*. London: Chatto & Windus.

International Council on Human Rights Policy (ICHRP) (2002) *Journalism, Media and the Challenge of Human Rights Reporting*. Geneva: ICHRP.

International Federation of Red Cross and Red Crescent Societies (2005) *World Disasters Report 2005*. IFRCRCS. Available at http://www.ifrc.org/publicat/wdr2005.

International Institute of Strategic Studies (IISS) (2007) *Strategic Survey 2007: The Annual Review of World Affairs*. London: IISS.

International Panel on Climate Change (IPCC) (2007) *Climate Change 2007: The Physical Science Basis. Summary for Policy Makers*. Geneva: IPCC Secretariat. Available at http://www.ipcc.ch/sp.

Iskander, A. and El-Nawawy, M. (2004) 'Al-Jazeera and War Coverage in Iraq: The Media's Quest for Contextual Objectivity', in S. Allan and B. Zelizer (Eds) *Reporting War*. London: Routledge.

Jacobsen, P. V. (2000) 'Focus on the CNN Effect misses the Point: The Real Media Impact on Conflict Management is Invisible and Indirect', *Journal of Peace Research*, 37(5): 547–562.

Jensen, K. (Ed.) (2000) *News of the World: World Cultures Look at Television News*. London: Routledge.

Jong, W., Stammers, N. and Shaw, M. (Eds) (2005) *Global Activism, Global Media*. London: Pluto Press.

Kaldor, M. (2001) *New and Old Wars: Organized Violence in A Global Era*. Cambridge: Polity.

Kaldor, M. (2003) *Global Civil Society*. Cambridge: Polity.

Katz, E. and Liebes, T. (2007) ' "No More Peace!": How Disasters, Terror and War have upstaged Media Events', *International Journal of Communication* 1(1): 157–166.

Keane, J. (2003) *Global Civil Society?* Cambridge: Cambridge University Press.

Kitzinger, J. (2004) *Framing Abuse: Media Influence and Public Understanding of Sexual Violence against Children*. London: Pluto Press.

Klein, N. (2007) *The Shock Doctrine: The Rise of Disaster Capitalism*. London: Allen Lane.

Klocker, N. and Dunn, K. (2003) 'Who's Driving the Asylum Debate? Newspaper and Government Representations of Asylum Seekers', *Media International Australia*, 109: 71–92.

Knightley, P. (2003) *The First Casualty*. London: André Deutsch.

Lash, S., Szerszynski, B. and Wynne, B. (Eds) (1996) *Risk, Environment and Modernity*. London: Sage.

Leith, D. (2004) *Bearing Witness: The Lives of War Correspondents and Photojournalists*. Milsons Point, NSW: Random House Australia.

Lester, L. (2006) 'Lost in the Wilderness? Celebrity, Protest and the News', *Journalism Studies*, 7(6): 907–921.

Lester, L. (2007) *Giving Ground: Media and Environmental Conflict in Tasmania*. Hobart, Tasmania: Quintus Publishing.

Lewis, J., Brookes, R., Mosdell, N. and Threadgold, T. (2006) *Shoot First Ask Questions Later: Media Coverage of the 2003 Iraq War*. New York: Peter Lang.

Lewis, J. Cusion, S. and Thomas, J. (2005) 'Immediacy, Convenience or Engagement? An Analysis of 24-hour News Channels in the UK', *Journalism Studies*, 6(4): 461–477.

Liebes, T. (1998) 'Television's Disaster Marathons: A Danger for Democratic Processes?', in T. Liebes and J. Curran (Eds) *Media, Ritual and Identity*. London: Routledge.

Linné, O. and Hansen, A. (1990) *News Coverage of the Environment: A Comparative Study of Journalistic Practices and Television Presentation in Denmark's Radio and the BBC.* Copenhagen: Forskningsrapport No. 1B/90.

Livingston, S. and Van Belle, D. (2005) 'The Effects of Satellite Technology on Newsgathering from Remote Locations', *Political Communication*, 22: 45–62.

Lorenzoni, I., Leiserowitz, A., Doria, M., Portinga, W. and Pidgeon, N. (2006) 'Cross-National Comparisons of Image Associations with "Global Warming" and "Climate Change" among Lay People in the United States of America and Great Britain', *Journal of Risk Research*, 9(3): 265–281.

Lowe, P. and Morrison, D. (1984) 'Bad News or Good News: Environmental Politics and the Mass Media', *Sociological Review*, 32(1): 75–90.

Lowe, T., Brown, K., Dessai, S., de Franca, M., Haynes, D. and Vincent, K. (2006) 'Does Tomorrow Ever Come? Disaster Narrative and Public Perceptions of Climate Change', *Public Understanding of Science*, 15: 435–457.

Lull, J. (2007) *Culture-On-Demand: Communication in a Crisis World*. London: BFI Publishing.

Lull, J. and Hinerman, S. (Eds) (1997) *Media Scandals: Morality and Desire in the Popular Market Place*. Cambridge: Polity.

MacBride, S. (1980) *Many Voices, One World*. Oxford: Rowman & Littlefield.

MacGregor, B. (1997) *Live, Direct and Biased? Making Television news in the Satellite Age*. London: Arnold.

Mackay, H. (2004) 'The Globalization of Culture?', in D. Held (Ed.) *A Globalizing World?* London: Routledge.

Macnaghten, D. and Urry, J. (1998) *Contested Natures*. London: Sage.

Make Poverty History (2006) 'Measuring the Reach of the Make Poverty History Media Campaign'. Available at http://www.makepovertyhistory.org/docs/measuringreachofmph.pdf.

Make Poverty History (2007) '2005: The Year of Make Poverty History'. Available at http://www.makepovertyhistory.org/media/index.html.

Marjoribanks, T. (2000) *News Corporation, Technology and the Workplace*. Cambridge: Cambridge University Press.

Marks, S. and Clapham. A. (2005) *International Human Rights Lexicon*. Oxford: Oxford University Press.

Marr, D. and Wilkinson, M. (2004) *Dark Victory*. Crows Nest, NSW: Allen & Unwin.

McChesney, R. (1999) *Rich Media, Poor Democracy: Communication Politics in Dubious Times*. Chicago, IL: University of Illinois Press.

McCoombs, M. and Shaw, D. (1972) 'The Agenda-Setting Function of the Mass Media', *Public Opinion Quarterly*, 35: 176–187.

McLuhan, M. (1964) *Understanding Media: The Extensions of Man*. New York: McGraw-Hill.

McNair, B. (2006) *Cultural Chaos: Journalism, News and Power in a Globalised World*. London: Routledge.

Médecins sans Frontières (2006) 'The Most Underreported Humanitarian Stories'. Available at http://www.doctorswithoutborders.org/publications/reports/2006top10_2005.ht$ml.

Media Tenor Journal (2006) 'Disasters Compared Across Media', *Media Tenor Journal*, 1: 26–28.

Michalski, M. and Gow, J. (2007) *War, Image and Legitimacy: Viewing Contemporary Conflict*. London: Routledge.

Miller, D. (2004) *Tell Me Lies: Propaganda and Media Distortion in the Attack on Iraq*. London: Pluto Press.

Miller, M. and Riechert, B. (2000) 'Interest Group Strategies and Journalistic Norms: News Media Framing of Environmental Issues', in S. Allan, B. Adam and C. Carter (Eds) *Environmental Risks and the Media*. London: Routledge.

Minear, L., Scott, C. and Weiss, T. (1996) *The News Media, Civil Wars and Humanitarian Action*. Boulder, CO: Lynne Rienner.

Moeller, S. (1999) *Compassion Fatigue: How the Media Sell Disease, Famine, War and Death*. London: Routledge.

Monbiot, G. (2007a) *Heat: How to Stop the Planet from Burning*. Cambridge, MA: South End Press.

Monbiot, G. (2007b) 'The Road Well Travelled', *The Guardian*, 30.10.07. Available at http://www.Monbiot.com/archives/2007/10/30.

Morrison, D. E. (1994) 'Journalists and the Social Construction of War', *Contemporary Record*, 8(2): 305–320.

Morrison, D. and Tumber, H. (1988) *Journalists at War: The Dynamics of News Reporting during the Falklands Conflict*. London: Sage.

Mouffe, C. (1996) 'Democracy, Power and the "Political" ', in S. Benhabib (Ed.) *Democracy and Difference*. Princeton, NJ: Princeton University Press.

Murata, K. (2007) 'Pro- and Anti-whaling Discourses in British and Japanese Newspaper Reports in Comparison: A Cross-Cultural Perspective', *Discourse and Society*, 18(6): 741–764.

Murdock, G. (1990) 'Redrawing the Map of the Communication Industries: Concentration and Ownership in the Era of Privatization', in M. Ferguson (Ed.) *Public Communication: The New Imperatives*. London: Sage.

Murray, C., Parry, K., Robinson, P. and Goddard, P. (2008) 'Reporting Dissent in Wartime: British Press, the Anti-War Movement and the 2003 Iraq War', *European Journal of Communication*, 23(7): 7–27.

Mythen, G. (2004) *Ulrich Beck: A Critical Introduction to the Risk Society*. London: Pluto Press.

Nash, D. (2007) 'Murdoch Spells Out News Response to Climate Change', *The Australian*, 10 May: 3.

Nash, K. (2008) 'Global Citizenship as Show Business: The Cultural Politics of Make Poverty History', *Media, Culture and Society*, 30(2): 167–181.

Nicholls, B. (1991) *Representing Reality: Issues and Concepts in Documentary*. Bloomington, IN: Indiana University Press.

Nordenstreng, K. and Varis, T. (1974) *Television Traffic: A One-way Street?* Paris: UNESCO.

Norris, P. (2002) *Democratic Phoenix: Reinventing Political Activism*. Cambridge: Cambridge University Press.

Opel, A. and Pompper, D. (Eds) (2003) *Representing Resistance: Media, Civil Disobedience and the Global Justice Movement*. Westport, CT: Praeger.

Ovsiovitch, J. (1993) 'News Coverage of Human Rights', *Political Research Quarterly*, 46: 671–689.

Oxfam (2007) *From Weather Alert to Climate Change*. Oxfam Briefing Paper 108.

Pallister, D. (2007) 'Junta Tries to Shut Down Internet and Phone Lines', *The Guardian*, 27 September: 5.

Pantti, M. and Wahl-Jorgensen, K. (2007) 'On the Political Possibilities of Therapy News: Media Responsibility and the Limits of Objectivity in Disaster Coverage', *Estudos em Communiçao*, 1: 3–25.

Paterson, C. and Sreberny, A. (Eds) (2004) *International News in the Twenty-First Century*. London: John Libby.

Pedelty, M. (1995) *War Stories*. London: Routledge.

Peters, H. P. (1995) 'The Interaction of Journalists and Scientific Experts: Co-operation and Conflict Between Two Professional Cultures', *Media, Culture and Society*, 17(1): 31–48.

Pew Research Centre for the People and the Press (2002) *Public News Habits Little Changed by September 11: Americans Lack Background to follow International News*. Washington, DC: Pew.

Philo, G. (1993) 'From Buerk to Band Aid', in J. Eldridge (Ed.) *Getting the Message: News Truth and Power*. London: Routledge.

Philo, G. (2007) 'Can Discourse Analysis Successfully Explain the Content of Media and Journalistic Practice?', *Journalism Studies*, 8(6): 175–196.

Ploughshares (2007) *Armed Conflict Report 2007 Summary*. Ontario: Project Ploughshares.

Pollard, N. (2005) 'Diary of a Disaster', *British Journalism Review*, 16(1): 7–12.

Poole, E. and Richardson, J. E. (Eds) (2006) *Muslims and the News Media*. London: I. B. Tauris.

Rai, M. and Cottle, S. (2007) 'Global Mediations: On the Changing Ecology of Satellite Television News', *Global Media and Communication*, 3(1): 51–78.

Reese, S. (2003) 'Framing Public Life: A Bridging Model for Media Research', in S. Reeese, O. Gandy and A. Grand (Eds) (2003) *Framing Public Life*. Mahwah, NJ: Lawrence Erlbaum Associates, Inc.

Reese, S., Rutigliano, L., Hyun, K. and Jeong, J. (2007) 'Mapping the Blogosphere: Professional and Citizen-based Media in the Global News Arena', *Journalism*, 8(3): 235–261.

Riegert, K. and Olsson, E. (2007) 'The Importance of Ritual in Crisis Journalism', *Journalism Practice*, 1(2): 143–158.

Ritzer, G. (Ed.) (2007) *The Blackwell Companion to Globalization*. Oxford: Blackwell.

Robertson. R. (1992) 'Mapping the Global Condition: Globalization as the Central Concept', in M. Featherstone (Ed.) *Global Culture*. London: Sage.

Robinson, P. (2002) *The CNN Effect: The Myth of News, Foreign Policy and Intervention*. London: Routledge.

Robinson, P. (2005) 'The CNN Effect Revisited', *Critical Studies in Media Communication*, 22(4): 344–349.

Rojecki, A. (2002) 'Modernism, State Sovereignty and Dissent: Media and the New Post-Cold War Movements', *Critical Studies in Media and Communication*, 19(2): 152–171.

Ross, S. (2004) *Toward New Understandings: Journalists and Humanitarian Relief Coverage*. New York: Columbia University Press.

Rotberg, R. I. and Weiss, T. (Eds) (1996) *From Massacres to Genocide: The Media, Public Policy and Humanitarian Crises*. Washington, DC: The Brookings Institute.

Saxton, A. (2003) 'I Certainly Don't Want People Like That Here': The Discursive Construction of "Asylum Seekers" ', *Media International Australia*, 109: 109–120.

Schiller, H. (2005) 'Not yet the Post-imperialist Era', in M. Durham and D. Kellner (Eds) *Media and Cultural Studies: Key Works*. Oxford: Blackwell.

Schlesinger, P. (1990) 'Rethinking the Sociology of Journalism: Source Strategies and the Limits of Media Centrism', in M. Ferguson (Ed.) *Public Communication*. London: Sage.

Seaton, J. (2005a) *Carnage and the Media: The Making and Breaking of News about Violence*. London: Penguin.

Seaton, J. (2005b) 'The Numbers Game: Death, Media, and the Public'. Available at http://www.opendemocracy.net/articles/.

Seib, P. (2004) *Beyond the Front Lines*. Basingstoke: Macmillan.

Seitz, J. (2008) *Global Issues: An Introduction*, 3rd edn. Oxford: Blackwell.

Serra, S. (2000) 'The Killings of Brazilian Street Children and the Rise of the International Public Sphere', in J. Curran (Ed.) *Media, Organization and Society*. London: Arnold.

Shaw, M. (1996) *Civil Society and Media in Global Crises*. London: St Martin's Press.

Shaw, M. (1999) 'Global Voices: Civil Society and Media in Global Crises'. Available at http://www.sussex.ac.uk/Users/hafa3/voices.htm.

Shaw, M. (2003) *War and Genocide*. Cambridge: Polity.

Shaw, M. (2005) *The New Western Way of War: Risk – Transfer War and its Crisis in Iraq*. Cambridge: Polity.

Shaw, M. (2007) *What is Genocide?* Cambridge: Polity.

Silverstone, R. (2007) *Media and Morality: On the Rise of the Mediapolis*, Cambridge: Polity.

Sinclair, J., Jacka, E. and Cunningham, S. (2002) 'Peripheral Vision', in J. Sinclair, E. Jacka and S. Cunningham (Eds) *New Patterns in Global Television: Peripheral Vision*. Oxford: Oxford University Press.

Sireau, N. and Davis, A. (2007) 'Interest Groups and Mediated Mobilization: Communication in the Make Poverty History Campaign', in A. Davis, *The Mediation of Power: A Critical Introduction*. London: Routledge.

Slattery, K. (2003) 'Drowning not Waving: The ' "Children Overboard" Event and Australia's Fear of the "Other" ', *Media International Australia*, 109: 93–108.

Sontag, S. (2003) *Regarding the Pain of Others*. New York: Farrar, Straus & Giroux.

Sonwalkar, P. (2001) 'India: Makings of Little Cultural/Media Imperialism?', *Gazette*, 63(6): 505–519.

Sonwalkar, P. (2004a) 'News Imperialism: Contra View from the South', in C. Paterson and A. Sreberny (Eds) *International News in the Twenty-first Century*. Eastleigh: John Libby.

Sonwalkar, P. (2004b) 'Out of Sight, Out of Mind?: The Non-Reporting of Small Wars an Insurgencies', in S. Allan and B. Zelizer (Eds) *Reporting War: Journalism in Wartime*. London: Routledge.

Sreberny, A. (2000) 'The Global and the Local in International Communications', in J. Curran and M. Gurevitch (Eds) *Mass Media and Society*. London: Edward Arnold.

Stern, N. (2007) Stern Review: The Economics of Climate Change. Executive Summary. Available at http://www.hm-treasury.gov.uk/independent_reviews/stern_review.

Stevenson, N. (1999) *The Transformation of the Media: Globalization, Morality, Ethics*. London: Longman.

Stockholm Institute for Peace Research (SIPRI) (2004) *SIPRI Yearbook 2004: Armaments, Disarmament and International Security*. Oxford: Oxford University Press.

Stoddard, A. (2003) 'Humanitarian NGOs: Challenges and Trends', *Humanitarian Policy Group Briefing*, No. 12, July. London: Overseas Development Institute.

Stone, J. (2000) *Losing Perspective: Global Affairs on British Terrestrial Television 1989–1999*. London: Third World and Environmental Broadcasting Project.

Szerszynski, B. and Toogood, M. (2000) 'Global Citizenship, the Environment and the Media' in S. Allan, B. Adams and C. Carter (Eds) (2000) *Environmental Risks and the Media*. London: Routledge.

Taylor, P. (1992) *War and the Media – Propaganda and Persuasion in the Gulf War*. Manchester: Manchester University Press.

Taylor, P. (2003) 'Journalism under Fire: the Reporting of War and International Crisis', in S. Cottle (Ed.) *News, Public Relations and Power*. London: Sage.

Tester, K. (1994) *Media, Culture and Morality* London: Routledge.

Thompson, J. (1995) *The Media and Modernity*. Cambridge: Polity.

Thompson, J. (2000) *Political Scandal: Power and Visibility in the Media Age*. Cambridge: Polity.

Thussu, D. K. (2003) 'Live TV and Bloodless Deaths: War, Infotainment and 24/7 News', in D. K. Thussu and D. Freedman (Eds) *War and the Media: Reporting Conflict 24/7*. London: Sage.

Thussu, D. (2007) *News as Entertainment: The Rise of Global Infotainment*. London: Sage.

Thussu, D. and Freedman, D. (Eds) (2003) *War and the Media: Reporting Conflict 24/7*. London: Sage.

Tierney, K., Bevc, C. and Kuligowski, E. (2006) 'Metaphors Matter: Disaster Myths, Media Frames and Their Consequences in Hurricane Katrina', *The Annals of the American Academy*, 604: 57–81.

Tomlinson, J. (1991) *Cultural Imperialism*. London: Pinter Press.

Tomlinson, J. (1999) *Globalization and Culture*. Chicago, IL: University of Chicago Press.

Tumber, H. (Ed.) (1999) *News: A Reader*. Oxford: Blackwell.

Tumber, H. and Palmer, J. (2004) *Media at War: The Iraq Crisis*. London: Sage.

Tumber, H. and Webster, F. (2006) *Journalists under Fire: Information War and Journalistic Practices*. London: Sage.

Turner, G. (2004) *Understanding Celebrity*. London: Sage.

Turner. V. (1982) *From Ritual to Theatre*. New York: PAJ Publications.

Ungar, S. (1998) 'Hot Crisis and Media Reassurance: A Comparison of Emerging Diseases and Ebola Zaire', *British Journal of Sociology*, 49(1): 36–56.

United Nations (2006) 'Stories the World Should Hear More About'. Available at http://www.un.org/events/tenstories/.

United Nations (2007a) *The Millennium Development Goals Report 2007*. New York: United Nations.

United Nations (2007b) *Africa and the Millennium Development Goals 2007 Update*. New York: United Nations.

United Nations Environmental Program (UNEP) (2001) 'What Are Natural Hazards and how they can become Natural Disasters: Awareness and Preparedness for Emergencies on a Local Level (APELL)'. Available at http://www.unep.fr/pc/apell/disasters.

United Nations Environmental Program (UNEP) (2007) 'Vulnerable in a World of Plenty', *Global Environment Outlook 4*, Fact Sheet 14. Available at www.unep.org/geo/geo4/.

United Nations Foundation (2007) 'Rapid Response Emergency Telecommunication'. Available at http://www.unfoundation.org/vodaphone/rapid_response_emergency_tele.asap.

United Nations High Commission for Refugees (UNCHR) (2007) 'World Refugee Day: Displacement in the 21st Century. A New Paradigm'. Available at http://www.unhcr.org/cgi-bin/texis/vtx/events?id=3e7f46e04.

Urry, J. (1999) 'Globalization and Citizenship', *Journal of World-Systems Research*, 2: 311–324. Available at http://jwsr.ucr.edu/.

Urry, J. (2002) *The Tourist Gaze*. London: Sage.

Urry, J. (2003) *Global Complexity*. Cambridge: Polity.

Utley, G. (1997) 'The Shrinking of Foreign News: From Broadcast to Narrowcast, *Foreign Affairs*, 76(2): 1–6.

van der Veer, P. and Munshi, S. (Eds) (2004) *Media, War and Terrorism*. London: Routledge.

Vidal, J. (2007) 'Climate Change to Force Mass Migration', *The Guardian*, 14.5.07. Available at http://www.guardian.co.uk/environment/2007/may14/.

Volkmer, I. (1999) *News in the Global Sphere: A Study of CNN and its Impact on Global Communication*. Luton: University of Luton Press.

Volkmer, I. (2002) 'Journalism and Political Crises in the Global Network Society', in B. Zelizer and S. Allan (Eds) *Journalism after September 11*. London: Routledge.

Volkmer, I. (2003) 'The Global Network Society and the Global Public Sphere', *Development*, 46(1): 9–16.

Waters, M. (2001) *Globalization*, 2nd edn. London: Routledge.

Weingart, P., Engels, A. and Pansegrau, P. (2000) 'Risks of Communication on Climate Change in Science, Politics and the Mass Media', *Public Understanding of Science*, 9: 261–283.

Wilcox, D. (2005) *Propaganda, the Press and Conflict: The Gulf War and Kosovo*. London: Routledge.

Wilkins, L. (2005) 'Plagues, Pestilence and Pathogens: The Ethical Implications of News Reporting of a World Health Crisis', *Asian Journal of Communication*, 15(3): 247–254.

Wilson, K. (2000) 'Communicating Climate Change through the Media: Predictions, Politics and Perceptions of Risks', in S. Allan, B. Adam and C. Carter (Eds) *Environmental Risks and the Media*. London: Routledge.

Wolfsfeld, G. (1997) *Media and Political Conflict: News from the Middle East*. Cambridge: Cambridge University Press.

Wolfsfeld, G. (2004) *Media and the Path to Peace*. Cambridge: Cambridge University Press.

World Health Organization (WHO) (2007) *A Safer Future: Global Public Health Security*. Geneva: WHO. Available at http://www.who.int/whr/2007/en.

Wykes, M. (2000) 'The Burrowers: News about Bodies, Tunnels and Green Guerillas', in S. Allan, B. Adam and C. Carter (Eds) *Environmental Risks and the Media*. London: Routledge.

Wynne, B. (1996) 'May the Sheep Safely Graze? A Reflexive View of the Expert-Lay Knowledge Divide', in S.Lash, B. Szerszynski and B. Wynne (Eds) *Risk, Environment and Modernity*. London: Sage.

Zelizer, B. and Allan, S. (Eds) (2002) *Journalism after September 11*. London: Routledge.

INDEX

Related books from Open University Press

Purchase from www.openup.co.uk or order through your local bookseller

MEDIA TECHNOLOGY
CRITICAL PERSPECTIVES

Joost van Loon

- What are media?
- Why are more and more objects being turned into media?
- How do people interconnect with the media in structuring their everyday lives?

In *Media Technology: Critical Perspectives*, Joost van Loon illustrates how throughout the course of society, different forms of media have helped to shape our perceptions, expectations and interpretations of reality.

Drawing on the work of media scholars such as Marshall McLuhan, Walter Benjamin, Roland Barthes and Raymond Williams, the author provides a theoretical analysis of the complexity of media processes. He urges the reader to challenge mainstream assumptions of media merely as instruments of communication, and shows how the matter, form, use and purpose of media technologies can affect content.

The book uses practical examples from both old and new media to help readers think through complex issues about the place of media. This helps to create a more innovative toolkit for understanding what media actually are and the basis for trying to make sense of what media actually do. It uses case studies and examples from television, radio, print, computer games and domestic appliances.

Media Technology is essential reading for undergraduate and postgraduate students on media, social theory and critical theory-related courses.

Contents

Acknowledgements – Introduction – A critical history of media technology – Alternative trajectories: Technology as culture – 'Media as extensions of wo/man': Feminist perspectives on mediation and technological embodiment – New media and networked (dis)embodiment – Conclusion: Theorizing media technology – Glossary – References – Index.

2007 192pp
978–0–335–21446–4 (Paperback)   978–0–335–21447–1 (Hardback)

UNDERSTANDING ALTERNATIVE MEDIA

Olga Guedes Bailey, Bart Cammaerts and Nico Carpentier

- What are alternative media?
- What roles do alternative media play in pluralistic, democratic societies?
- What are the similarities and differences between alternative media, community media, civil society media and rhizomatic media?
- How do alternative media work in practice?

This clear and concise text offers a one-stop guide through the complex political, social and economic debates that surround alternative media and provides a fresh and insightful look at the renewed importance of this form of communication.

Combing diverse case studies from countries including the UK, North America and Brazil, the authors propose an original theoretical framework to help understand the subject. Looking at both 'old' and 'new' media, the book argues for the importance of an alternative media and suggests a political agenda as a way of broadening its scope.

Understanding Alternative Media is valuable reading for students in media, journalism and communications studies, researchers, academics, and journalists.

Contents

Acknowledgements – Foreword – Introduction – Part I Theorizing Alternative Media – Four approaches to alternative media – An introductory case study Radio Favela: Representing alternative media – Part II Case Studies – Serving the community – Community approaches in western radio policies – Diasporas and alternative media practices – An alternative to the mainstream – Blogs in the second Iraqi war: Alternative media challenging the mainstream? – Ethnic-religious groups and alternative journalism – Linking alternative media to the civil society – Online participation and the public sphere: Civil society mailing lists and forums – The Brazilian landless rural workers' movement: Identity, action, and communication – Alternative media as rhizome – Translocalization, glocalization and the internet: The radioswap project – Jamming the political: Reverse-engineering, hacking the dominant codes – Conclusion – Glossary – Acronyms – Further reading – References – Index.

2007 216pp
978–0–335–22210–0 (Paperback)   978–0–335–22211–7 (Hardback)

MEDIATIZED CONFLICT

Simon Cottle

We live in times that generate diverse conflicts; we also live in times when conflicts are increasingly played out and performed in the media. *Mediatized Conflict* explores the powered dynamics, contested representations and consequences of media conflict reporting. It examines how the media today do not simply report or represent diverse situations of conflict, but actively 'enact' and 'perform' them.

This important book brings together the latest research findings and theoretical discussions to develop an encompassing, multidimensional and sophisticated understanding of the social complexities, political dynamics and cultural forms of mediatized conflicts in the world today. Case studies include:

- Anti-war protests and anti-globalization demonstrations
- Mediatized public crises centering on issues of 'race' and racism
- War journalism and peace journalism
- Risk society and the environment
- The politics of outrage and terror spectacle post 9/11
- Identity politics and cultural recognition

This is essential reading for Media Studies students and all those interested in understanding how, why, and with what impacts media report on diverse conflicts in the world today.

Contents

Series editor's foreword – Acknowledgements – Mediatized conflict in the world today – Getting a fix on mediatised conflict: Paradigms and perspectives – Reporting Demonstrations and protest: Public Sphere(s), public screens – From moral panics to mediatised public crises: Moving stories of 'race' and racism – War journalism: Disembodied and embedded – Peace journalism and other alternatives: On hopes and prayers – Media, 'risk society' and the environment: A different story? – From 'terrorism' to the 'global war on terror': The media politics of outrage – Identity politics and cultural difference: On mediatised recognition – Mediatized conflict: Conclusions – References – Index.

2006   232pp
978–0–335–21452–5 (Paperback)   978–0–335–21453–2 (Hardback)